LIBRARY SCIENCE TEXT SERIES

Developing Library Collections. By G. Edward Evans.

The Humanities: A Selective Guide to Information Sources. 2nd ed. By A. Robert Rogers.

Immroth's Guide to the Library of Congress Classification. 3rd ed. By Lois Mai Chan.

Introduction to AV for Technical Assistants. By Albert J. Casciero and Raymond G. Roney.

Introduction to Cataloging and Classification. 6th ed. By Bohdan S. Wynar, with the assistance of Arlene Taylor Dowell and Jeanne Osborn.

An Introduction to Classification and Number Building in Dewey. By Marty Bloomberg and Hans Weber.

Introduction to Library Science: Basic Elements of Library Service. By Jesse H. Shera.

Introduction to Library Services for Library Technicians. By Barbara E. Chernik.

Introduction to Public Services for Library Technicians. 3rd ed. By Marty Bloomberg.

Introduction to Technical Services for Library Technicians. 4th ed. By Marty Bloomberg and G. Edward Evans.

Introduction to United States Public Documents. 2nd ed. By Joe Morehead.

Library Management. 2nd ed. By Robert D. Stueart and John Taylor Eastlick.

Map Librarianship: An Introduction. By Mary Larsgaard.

Micrographics. By William Saffady.

Problems in Library Management. By A. J. Anderson.

The School Librarian as Educator. By Lillian Biermann Wehmeyer.

The School Library Media Center. 3rd ed. By Emanuel T. Prostano and Joyce S. Prostano.

Science and Engineering Literature: A Guide to Reference Sources. 3rd ed. By H. Robert Malinowsky and Jeanne M. Richardson.

The Vertical File and Its Satellites: A Handbook of Acquisition, Processing, and Organization. 2nd ed. By Shirley Miller.

The Collection Program
in
Elementary and Middle Schools

THE COLLECTION PROGRAM
IN
ELEMENTARY AND MIDDLE SCHOOLS
Concepts, Practices, and Information Sources

PHYLLIS J. VAN ORDEN

Illustrations by
William R. Harper

LIBRARIES UNLIMITED, Inc.   **Littleton, Colorado**
1982

584814

LIBRARIES UNLIMITED, INC.
P.O. Box 263
Littleton, Colorado 80160

Library of Congress Cataloging in Publication Data

Van Orden, Phyllis.
    The collection program in elementary and middle schools.

    (Library science text series)
    Includes bibliographies and index.
    1. School libraries--United States.
2. Instructional materials centers--United States.
3. Collection development (Libraries). I. Title.
II. Series.
Z675.S3V33   025.2'1878   82-15325
ISBN 0-87287-335-8   AACR2

Z
675
.S3
V33
1982

TABLE OF CONTENTS

LIST OF ILLUSTRATIONS

INTRODUCTION

Collection development can be an exciting and demanding challenge requiring special knowledge, skills, and attitudes. While the general principles and techniques of collection development can be applied to most settings, the unique factors of each media program result in new and changing demands requiring flexibility and creativity. To assist media personnel in facing these challenges, this work:

1. Describes the environment within which media center collections exist.

2. Presents principles, techniques, and common practices of collection development.

3. Raises issues that affect all collections but which must be resolved in accordance with the goals and needs of a particular collection.

4. Identifies sources of help, e.g., documents, agencies, and associations.

5. Suggests approaches to handling a wide range of situations and demands upon the collection.

The purpose of this introductory text is to provide an overview of the processes and procedures associated with developing, maintaining, and evaluating a collection at the building level. To achieve this goal, the processes and procedures practiced in elementary and middle schools have been discussed in relation to educational theory and principles of collection development.

This book reflects the opinion that the collection is the key element of the media program and that it provides the means for meeting informational and instructional needs of the school. To serve these needs, the collection must be considered as a physical entity, composed not only of its internal resources but also of the informational and instructional resources available from external information sources and education agencies. This work attempts to fill a void in the literature by bringing together concepts from curriculum theory, children's literature, audiovisual education, and library science. The work reflects the concept that collection program activities interact in a cyclical pattern, and proposes that the principles of collection development, selection, and acquisition be addressed together in a school's policy statement.

The book is divided into three parts: I. The Setting, II. Selection of Materials, and III. Administrative Concerns.

Part I, The Setting, examines the media collection in its relationship to the educational setting and discusses general principles of collection development. This portion of the book establishes the environmental framework: the external ties to educational and informational systems and the internal relationship of the collection to the media program. Chapter 1, The Media Program and Its Environment, presents an overview of the external and internal relationships of the media program. Chapter 2, The Collection, examines six perspectives of the concept of collection on which the process of collection development is based. Chapter 3, The Collection Program, identifies the activities involved in building and maintaining a collection. The principles presented serve as an introduction to fuller discussions of each activity in the remaining chapters. Chapter 4, Issues about Collection, is designed to provide readers with an opportunity to examine their personal feelings and opinions on issues which affect all collections. Chapter 5, The Collection's External Environment, describes the environments that shape the collection and to which it must respond. In chapter 6, policies and procedures are discussed in light of the previously mentioned relationships and framework. Chapter 7 suggests steps toward developing policy statements and identifies sources of assistance.

Part II, Selection of Materials, moves from the theoretical aspects of Part I into the practical considerations of materials selection. Chapter 8, Selection Procedures, identifies selection tools and suggests ways to involve teachers and students in making selection decisions. Chapter 9, General Selection Criteria, takes a broad approach, focusing on criteria that apply to all materials. Chapters 10, Criteria by Format: Visual Materials, and 11, Criteria by Format: Multisensory Materials, discuss the advantages, disadvantages, and criteria for individual formats. The remaining chapters of this part address criteria to be considered when selecting materials to meet specific school and user needs: Chapter 12, Meeting Curricular and Instructional Needs; Chapter 13, Meeting the Typical Needs of Individuals; and Chapter 14, Meeting the Special Needs of Individuals.

Part III, Administrative Concerns, describes the operations involved in developing and managing a collection: Chapter 15, Acquisition Procedures; Chapter 16, Maintaining the Collection; and Chapter 17, Evaluating the Collection. The book closes with a brief chapter, Creating an Initial Collection and Closing a Collection.

Although the principles and, frequently, the practices of collection development apply to both elementary and secondary schools, this book focuses on the collection program in the elementary and middle school settings. Although these collections are often a part of a system or district media program, detailed attention will not be given to the operation of media programs at the district level.

Due to the introductory nature of this text, there are many processes and techniques that can only be briefly discussed. For example, children's rights and intellectual freedom are topics basic to the functions of the media program and worthy of far greater coverage than is given in this work. The sources of information identified in the recommended readings for chapter 4 have been chosen to provide a more indepth treatment of these areas.

This book is addressed to individuals preparing to work, or presently working, in elementary and middle school media centers. While the examples offered in this book are from public school library media programs, the principles, practices, techniques, and materials discussed are also applicable to parochial and independent schools. The information presented also addresses the needs of individuals working in Canada.

There are many standard works that cover various aspects of school media programs. The current work is not intended to duplicate such efforts. Rather, an attempt has been made to focus on the media program collection — the point where earlier works intersect. Many of these standard works are referred to in the text or are listed in appendices.

Appendix 1 identifies agencies and associations that offer services and/or publications of interest to media specialists. Appendix 2 identifies bibliographic and selection tools, including articles that discuss various types of materials or needs in greater detail than addressed in the text.

AUTHOR'S COMMENTS

Writing a book can be either a solitary or a collective experience. This book has been both. A recurring theme in this work is that one must know one's self. The solitary moments of writing have given me that opportunity. I hope the ideas presented here will also provide that opportunity for the readers. So, in part, this work is dedicated to those who will carry out the ideas expressed here.

Fortunately, a book, like life, can also be a collective experience. Students, teachers, administrators, and colleagues have played a role in the creation of this book. Some may recognize themselves, although their names have been changed. Many individuals, both from the past and present, have participated in dialogues about ideas expressed here and participated in the necessary detail work. I appreciate the interest, support, and effort that each person contributed. May our dialogue continue as we add new participants.

Phyllis Van Orden

September 1981

PART I

The Setting

Miss, what kind of butterfly is this? What do hamsters eat? Where can I find a picture of Saturn? Do you have a story that will make me cry? Don't we have any new horse stories? I've read all of these. Why don't we have any good comic books? How can I copy this map? Questions such as these bombard the media specialist as students seek information. Teachers' voices enter the fray to make requests. *I need a bulletin board idea! Do you remember the poem I used on Flag Day last year? Why doesn't this recorder work? Where's the filmstrip I always use to start my unit on Greece? One of my friends mentioned their school used a new film on bicycle safety; can we get it for our students? What can I do to get Rebecca to read something besides dog stories? Would you help Amy and Matt make a transparency for their report?*

How can a collection satisfy all of these requests? Collections that are responsive to users' needs are the result of the planning and care of dedicated media specialists: individuals who have thought about why collections exist, what they should be, and how they relate to the school and the users. An effective collection cannot simply appear and endure unaltered; it must evolve, respond to changing demands. The following chapters describe "The Setting" of the collection within the media program and suggest ways collections can meet these changing needs.

1
THE MEDIA PROGRAM AND ITS ENVIRONMENT

An opening-day scene: You arrive in late August for the teacher-preparation days before students arrive for the new school year. As the new media specialist on the school's faculty, you are eager to learn about Jefferson Elementary School — its curriculum, its faculty, and its students — and to prepare the media program for the coming year. As you familiarize yourself with the collection, teachers arrive in the media center.

First to arrive is Donna, a fifth-grade teacher, who, obviously, has been planning for classes. She wants to arrange for a series of meetings with you to discuss the resources and media instruction she needs for her first two units. Donna alternates the science and social studies units so students can concentrate on one at a time. She will start with the science unit on light and wants the subject to capture the pupils' curiosity. After presenting general information to them, she will divide the class into teams based on the children's interests and questions. To stimulate curiosity, Donna plans to have a science corner in her classroom and to display a variety of lenses, prisms, and other materials whose characteristics the children can explore before any formal teaching begins.

Donna researched the characteristics of her class and knows the science corner needs books that can be read by children whose reading levels range from the second to the seventh grade. Recognizing all children do not prefer reading, she wants other materials that also present the basic information, perhaps study prints and filmstrips. As you talk with Donna, you realize she knows the needs and abilities of her students and that she tries to provide a wide range of experiences for them, using various media and teaching strategies.

Maggie, a kindergarten teacher, looks for a picture set on schools to help the children feel at home in their new surroundings. She's also interested in having some stories to read aloud at those moments when children become overly excited. Maggie asks for your assistance in locating sound recordings for musical activities.

A second-grade teacher, Irene, arrives as you start to help Maggie. Irene uses an individualized approach to teach reading and needs beginning-to-read materials for children whose vocabulary levels range from the primer level to third grade. Irene asks for your assistance in locating materials she can use to test children's reading skills, along with materials children can use to work independently on basic reading skills.

Marie, an experienced fourth-grade teacher, arrives with Chuck, a first-year teacher. Chuck's preparation was in secondary education, but he has been assigned a sixth-grade class. Marie tries to ease some of Chuck's anxieties and seeks your advice about materials that appeal specifically to sixth-graders. In her own class, Marie likes to start the year by observing each child's interests. You watch her gather a variety of items: 8mm film loops on baseball, pamphlets on the care of pets, a few plays, some science fiction and mystery stories, a rock specimen display, and a kit on making puppets. She explains to Chuck that she places these materials around the classroom to attract children into groups with common interests.

The principal comes dashing into the room to ask about materials on mainstreaming. He has to present a program for the Rotary Club and wants a film or videotape to use as a discussion-starter.

These activities, occurring in the first hour of opening day, reflect only a few of a school staff's needs. They illustrate, however, the kinds of requests that media specialists encounter. They also show, as resources move out to classrooms and the Rotary Club, that the media program is not limited to what happens within the media center itself. The media program supports all media needs throughout the school.

The American Association of School Librarians (American Library Association) and the Association for Educational Communications and Technology in the 1975 joint guidelines, *Media Programs: District and School*,[1] describe the media program as "a combination of resources that includes people, materials, machines, facilities, and environments, as well as purposes and processes."[2] This definition implies that the media program is a result of the interaction of its *components*: users, materials, facilities, environment, and media professionals. The integration of these components is achieved through the *functions* of the program: design, consultation, information, and administration.[3] The media program, through the integration of its components and functions, provides services that are "designed to assist learners to grow in their ability to find, generate, evaluate, and apply information."[4] The media professional is responsible for carrying out the functions in the most effective and efficient manner.

Media Program's Environment

The media program is composed of a collection and other interacting components as shown in figure 1. The internal environment of the media program consists of the collection, the major resource of the internal environment, interacting with the other components of the program.

Neither the collection nor the media program is an end in itself; both are means to achieve the educational goals of the school. The media

Figure 1. The Collection and Its Environment

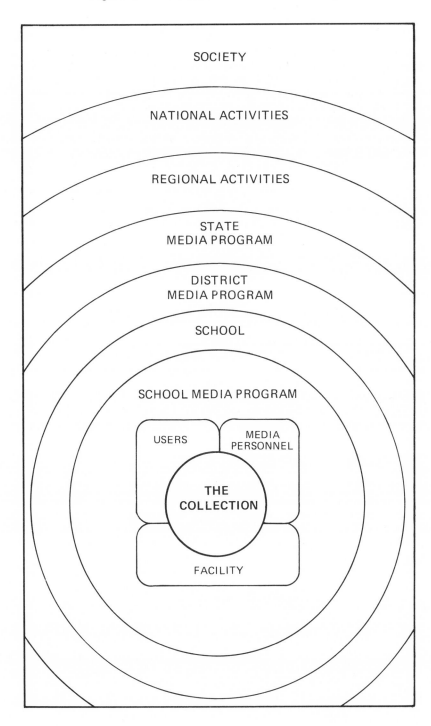

program must also function as an integral part of other systems that form its external environment as shown in figure 1. The relationship of the media program to other systems, whether formally or informally established, affects the program and its collection. First, the media program is a part of the school in which it functions. Second, the media program frequently is part of its district or system media program. Third, the program is part of media programs within the state. Fourth, the program may be part of regional activities; for example, a member of a formal network connecting several school districts or types of libraries. Fifth, the media program is part of activities and agencies at the national level. Sixth, the individual media program is influenced by society's view of information and education. These relationships, functioning as the external environment, affect the quality of the individual media program.

The quality of a particular media program also depends on the level of its integration with the total school program. Is the media program an essential part of the total school program? This question is a crucial one to consider when planning, implementing, or evaluating a media program. Many sources suggest ways to operate and evaluate media programs, but such recommendations must be considered from the perspective of the school in which the media program functions.

Criteria for an Effective Media Program

To meet the school's media needs effectively, the media program must:

1. Be an essential part of the total school program.

2. Be responsive to the curricular and instructional needs of the school.

3. Be responsive to the needs and interests of students, teachers, and administrators.

4. Exemplify the total media concept, providing access to varied materials, necessary equipment, trained personnel, and resources housed outside the media center.

5. Have a staff who adequately plans and carries out the selection, maintenance, and evaluation of materials.

Media Specialist's Role

The responsible media specialist must apply these criteria to the philosophy, goals, and objectives of the school within which he/she functions. *Media Programs: District and School* emphasizes this point, noting "the guidelines are stated with recognition of alternative choices that may better serve individual program requirements."[5] This set of guidelines rightly places the responsibility for planning an individual media program upon those involved with the program. The media specialist is the individual who understands the potential value of the media program to the school, but the media specialist cannot effectively integrate the program alone. Everyone involved with the school is responsible for the media program.

The media specialist's education, skill, ability, and human relations sensitivity are called upon in efforts to involve others in the program. The media specialist should look to the administrator for help in interpreting the philosophy, goals, and objectives of the school as they relate to the media program. But the role of administrators as leaders of the school implies an involvement far greater than this example. Martin and Carson stress this point in their observation:

> Principals are the key persons in the development of exemplary school library media programs.... Without the principal's support and leadership, the strong media specialist falters and the weak one is lost. In both situations the school program and the children for whom it was designed suffer. School principals who both understand the philosophy and support the implementation are needed to develop school media programs which are a basic driving force for excellence.[6]

The media specialist faces a major challenge as he or she attempts to involve administrators, teachers, and students in planning and implementing the media program. Responsibilities for the collection, however, provide opportunities for interaction with everyone. First, the media specialist should identify the needs of the users. Second, steps should be taken to involve administrators and teachers in the development of policies. Third, an effort should be made to invite students, teachers, and administrators to participate in the selection of materials for the collection. Other examples of this interaction will be identified as the collection program activities are examined. It is the responsibility of a media specialist to ensure that opportunities for interaction occur.

Summary

The media program is an entity with interacting components: users, materials, facilities, and environment. An effective media program is an essential part of the total school program. The integration of the media program with the total school program is achieved through the functions of design, consultation, information, and administration. The media program's external environments include the school it serves and its district or system media program, media programs within the state, regional activities, national agencies and activities, and society.

The media specialist is responsible for carrying out the functions of the media program and involving administrators, teachers, and students in the program. The collection activities provide opportunities to involve others.

These internal and external relationships influencing the media program and their implications for the collection provide the focus for this book. This chapter has identified and described the setting of the media program, a place in which the media specialist plays an important role. Chapter 2 explores the collection as a concept. Chapter 3 introduces collection program activities that will be discussed in greater depth in following chapters.

Notes to Chapter 1

[1]American Association of School Librarians, American Library Association and Association for Educational Communications and Technology, *Media Programs: District and School* (Chicago, IL: American Library Association; Washington, DC: Association for Educational Communications and Technology, 1975), p. 128.

[2]Ibid., p. 4.

[3]Ibid., pp. 5-6.

[4]Ibid., p. 4.

[5]Ibid., p. 1.

[6]Betty Martin and Ben Carson, *The Principal's Handbook on the School Library Media Center* (Syracuse, NY: Gaylord Professional Publications, 1978), p. 9.

Chapter 1 Bibliography

Adams, Anne H., and Hurlbut, Allan S. "School Libraries That Are Not Book Prisons." *National Elementary Principal* 52 (1972): 52-54.

Adams, Charles W. "The School Media Program: A Position Statement." *School Media Quarterly* 2 (1974): 127-43.

American Association of School Librarians, American Library Association, and Association for Educational Communications and Technology. *Media Programs: District and School.* Chicago, IL: American Library Association; Washington, DC: Association for Educational Communications and Technology, 1975.

Colby, Edmund K. "Elementary School Library Media Services: How Children View Them." *Catholic Library World* 5 (1978): 158-60.

Cox, Carl T. "A Total System View of the School Library." *School Media Quarterly* 1 (1972): 36-40.

Hannigan, Jane A. "The Promise of Media Programs: District and School." *School Media Quarterly* 2 (1973): 9-14.

Hug, William A. "Thoughts on Media Programs: District and School." *School Media Quarterly* 3 (1975): 109-14.

Kingsbury, Mary. "Priorities for Rounding Out a Century." *Wilson Library Bulletin* 50 (1976): 395-98.

Martin, Betty and Carson, Ben. *The Principal's Handbook on the School Library Media Center.* Syracuse, NY: Gaylord Professional Publications, 1978.

Wehmeyer, Lillian W. "The Student-Centered Media Center." *California School Libraries* 45 (1974): 19-24.

2
THE COLLECTION

Traditionally, the term "collection" has been used to describe the resources, mainly print items, housed in a single room of a school. This room, the "library," contained some books, a few magazines, and perhaps a newspaper rack. A student or teacher searching for information went to this library — a collection confined to the printed matter within its walls. If Mike, a fifth-grade student, entered such a traditional school library with a bird's nest, he would have looked for information about the nest in the encyclopedias and books about birds. If he could not find a picture of this particular nest, he would have probably left the library disappointed, unable to find out what kind of nest he had found. In today's media center, Mike could have compared his nest with those in the realia collection or located an illustration of it on charts or in filmstrips. If he wished to know more, the media specialist could contact a local natural history museum or borrow materials from another media center. Today's child need not be limited in his search by mere walls.

If a collection is indeed the key element in the media program, a broader concept of "collection" is needed than that defined by four walls. To think of a collection as merely the holdings of an individual facility creates a limited view of what a collection can be. A more comprehensive definition of a collection is revealed by an analysis of several somewhat overlapping perspectives. This chapter discusses these perspectives, showing that a collection:

1. Is a "physical entity."

2. Is composed of materials in printed, visual, auditory, and tactile formats with associated equipment, and includes textbooks and related instructional materials and systems.[1]

3. Fulfills purposes:
   a. meets the needs of the school goals and programs;
   b. meets the informational, instructional, and personal · needs of users.

4. Provides access to human and materials resources in the community.

5. Provides access to information and materials from other library/information systems.
6. Is an element within the media program.

The overlapping quality of these perspectives is an indication of their many-faceted external and internal relationships (see figure 2). The concept of the "collection" influences how effectively materials are made available.

Figure 2.   Overlapping Perspectives of Collection

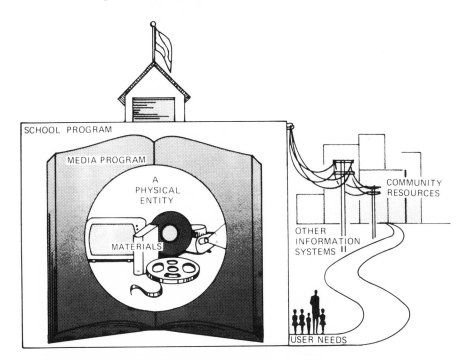

Accessibility and availability are also key concepts in the definition of "collection." When an item is accessible, that means it exists and can be located. Today, Mike, our budding ornithologist mentioned above, may go to the card catalog in the media center and find that the collection not only has books but also has actual nests. Mike now knows the items he needs are in the collection; at this point, the information is accessible. Availability implies that the items can be in hand at the moment they are needed. When Mike goes to the shelf and finds an illustration of his nest or finds another nest like his, the information is available. If he is referred to the local science museum where he can obtain the information, it is accessible; when he goes to the museum and uses the information, it is available.

The interval between accessibility and availability can be crucial for the child with a limited attention span. This is also true for the classroom teacher whose students need information "right now" but who are studying a new subject by the time the information is available. How a collection is approached, both in concept and in practice, can directly affect whether accessibility and availability, or both, are provided.

Physical Entity

The collection is a physical entity; the individual items collectively create a whole. The worth of a single item must be viewed in relation to other items in the collection as shown in figure 3. When deciding whether to add or withdraw a specific item, it should be evaluated as an entity and in relation to the collection by asking:

Is the same information in the collection, even if in a different format?

Figure 3.   Material Evaluation

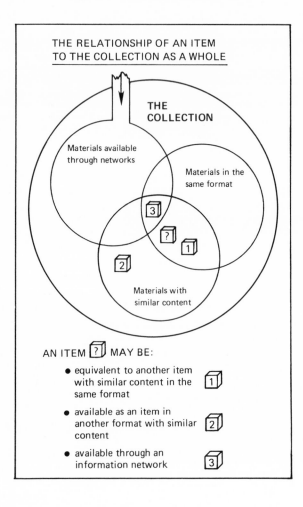

If so, do you need this information in this format?

Is the same or a similar item quickly available through a network?

Is there a need that this particular item uniquely fills?

Questions like these help identify the relationship of one item to the others in the collection.

Schools that intershelve materials on the same subject regardless of format are physically demonstrating the relatedness of the individual items. If inadequate physical space or other limitations do not allow this integration, the user must rely upon the catalog and other bibliographic tools to reveal all potential information sources.

If the collection comprises all the materials throughout the school, the depth and coverage of the collection can be expanded. Centralized bibliographic control provides the expansion by informing people where materials are located. This approach to collection is particularly important in open schools, or ones with team teaching, where resources are permanently housed in the areas of highest use. Even in schools with self-contained classrooms, centralized bibliographic control provides access to materials permanently housed together or spread throughout a building; all materials should be considered as information resources for the entire school and should be made accessible to all potential users.[2]

Materials can also include information that is not stored in the traditional sense, but that is made accessible through bibliographic control or through computer terminals. Human resources, field trips, and computer programs are made accessible to the users through these means.

As other definitions of "collection" and the processes involved in building a collection are examined, the reader will find that the concept of the collection as a physical entity is basic and serves as the focal point for all functions of the media program.

Materials

The second definition of a collection emphasizes format and recognizes that information is gained through use of the senses. Children who have developed efficient reading skills may find print materials most useful; children who have developed aural or visual literacy may find audiovisual materials easiest to use. Certain learning processes require participation by several individuals, so games or models might be preferred. For teaching drills, programmed texts or computer programs may be the most effective format.

A wide range of learning experiences can be offered through a collection that includes the materials identified in figure 4 (page 30). To use these materials, the collection must also contain appropriate equipment. This list provides a starting point for identifying materials commonly found in schools, but does not include all the materials that schools have found useful. Collections may also include postcards;

Figure 4. Formats Commonly Found in Collections

PRINTED FORMATS	VISUAL FORMATS	TACTILE FORMATS
• Books	Still Images:	• Games
• Periodicals	• Filmstrips (silent	• Toys
• Newspapers	and sound)	• Models
• Pamphlets	• Slides	• Sculpture
• Microforms	• Transparencies	• Specimen
	• Graphics (posters,	
AUDITORY FORMATS	art prints, study	INSTRUCTIONAL
• Reel-to-reel tapes	prints, maps, globes)	FORMATS
• Cassette tapes	Moving Images:	• Textbooks
• Phonodiscs	• 16mm films (silent	• Multimedia
• Audiocards	and sound)	packages
	• Super 8mm films	
	(silent and sound)	
	• Videotapes	

pets; materials that support creative activity: carpentry tools, easels, paints, printing presses, puppets; braille materials; dial access information systems; talking typewriters, calculators, and microcomputers. The list is virtually endless, for children gather information in a wide variety of ways and from many sources.

The term "integrated" describes a collection that includes materials in a variety of formats (both print and nonprint), selected to meet the information-seeking habits of its users. By providing the same content in more than one format, the collection can accommodate the learning styles of different students and teaching patterns that include small group, large group, and individualized instruction.

To integrate a collection effectively, one must be familiar with the characteristics of the various formats, their advantages and disadvantages, their compatibility with other formats, their equipment needs, their purposes and potential uses. It is necessary to evaluate the technical and physical characteristics of each item in the collection as well as the quality of its content, its potential for use, and its relationship to other items within the collection.

Purposes

A third way to define "collection" is to identify its purposes. First, the collection should meet the needs of the school's goals and programs. Second, the collection must meet the informational, instructional, and personal needs of the users. These purposes often overlap, but each has specific implications for collection activities.

School Goals and Program Needs

To make the media program an integral part of the school, the media specialist must learn about the school's programs and goals. The specialist will need to learn about the philosophy behind the school's goals, objectives, and programs (curricular and noncurricular); its people (administrators, teachers, students, staff, parents); and its facility. Each of the elements has implications for planning, building, and evaluating the collection. Curriculum plans and teaching strategies will need to be studied and discussed. Does the school have programs for gifted children? Programs of speech therapy, remedial reading, and career guidance? Short-term school projects, such as "Energy Day," or public relations projects? Does the school sponsor a student council, safety patrol, drama club, or other group?

The goals and programs can be analyzed by asking questions such as:

Are formats needed that are suitable for large groups?

Is information to be subject-oriented or skill-oriented?

Is there an emphasis on individualized study?

Informational, Instructional, and Personal Needs

A collection comprises communication media that can meet the informational, instructional, or personal needs of users. Bretz distinguishes a difference of purpose between informational and instructional media:

The purpose of the instructional system is achieving learning in a *learner*; the purpose of the information system is informing an information *user.* An information system may indeed be part of an instructional system, but can play only a limited role in the instructional process. Merely informing someone does not necessarily affect his file of knowledge....

The information user generally has a task at hand which he is interested in resolving; he acquires information, uses it in his task, and may forget it quickly—if he ever retains it at all. Information systems are designed for *use* and for the convenience of the user. Instructional systems are designed to achieve *learning*—to affect the knowledge of the learner.[3]

Groups of people have been described in looking at the programs of a school. Each group has needs that should be identified and considered in relation to the collection. Administrators need materials for in-service programs, publicity, and speeches. Teachers need ideas about new teaching methods and other information to aid them professionally. The nonteaching personnel and parents can find information in the professional collection to aid them in their work with children.

The student population exhibits a wide range of needs, abilities, and interests. Children's ages, sexes, personalities, physical characteristics, interests, experiences, and backgrounds affect their use of materials. It should also be remembered that each individual develops at a different rate. The media specialist needs to know the abilities and interests of each student. Some children will be just beginning to develop reading, listening, and viewing skills, while others will be sophisticated users of all types of media. Children from homes where tapes, records, stereo systems, movie projectors, and minicomputers are commonplace, may have been exposed to technology unfamiliar to their teachers.

Within one class, students' abilities in all skills may vary by as many levels as the number of the grade. For example, a sixth-grade class may include children reading from the second-grade through the eighth-grade level.

Physically disabled children also require special materials, such as large print materials for the partially sighted.

If the collection, a physical entity, is to fulfill its purposes (see figure 4, page 30), materials must be evaluated to ascertain if the needs of the school and users are being met. For example, if materials on particular subjects are normally requested for immediate use, they should be readily available. If the needs are infrequent, or not anticipated, other sources may be tapped.

Access to Resources of the Community

A fourth way to define the collection requires that it provide access to the human and material resources of the community. Access can be provided through listings in the card catalog, notebooks, or information packets distributed to teachers. The listings need to identify the participating institution or agency, suggest a person to contact, list the resources and services offered, and identify the intended audience. Museums, businesses, industries, and local government agencies often encourage students to visit on field trips, provide personnel to visit schools, or develop programs for children. For example, a natural foods store distributing cookies made from kelp can be an effective learning experience about the resources of the sea. The range of resources is only limited by imagination and the size of the community where the collection is located.

People are also valuable information sources. Human resources can provide career information, share travel slides, demonstrate hobbies or crafts, and relate local history. Government officials, business people, and other members of the community are often available for student interviews.

The integration of these sources of information expands the collection by bringing the school and the community closer together. The media specialist should evaluate the ability of these information sources to fulfill the needs of the school and the users.

Access to Resources from Other Library/Information Systems

The fifth perspective of the collection—providing access to information and materials from other library/information systems—recognizes the sharing of resources to provide access to materials belonging to other institutions.

Within the District Media Program

Many building-level media programs, programs that meet the needs of a single school, are units of school district or system media programs that have goals and objectives for all programs within their system. The district-level media program's personnel and resources often provide a wide range of services and guidance to the individual school program. The system may provide centralized purchasing and processing of materials and union lists of the holdings of the school system, giving accessibility to resources outside the walls of the school. Film libraries, professional libraries, or other special collections may be used by all schools within the district. A description of the operations and services of a district media program are beyond the scope of this work; however, attention will be given to those aspects directly relating to the building-level media program's collection.

Within the State

In the United States, education is the responsibility of the state. Each state has a philosophy, goals, and objectives for its educational programs, including the media program. Media consultants affiliated with either the State Department of Education or the State Library can often provide valuable assistance in sponsoring in-service education programs, providing examination centers, distributing information, and offering guidance through on-site visits to individual schools. For media specialists operating without the advantage of a district or system media program, the state media consultant is a key contact—someone the school media specialist will want to know.

Other state agencies can provide information about the state and often have personnel who will visit schools to talk to students about the environmental or economic concerns of the state. State agencies and associations often publish lists of resources available within a state.

Within the Region

The media program and the media specialist have formal or informal relationships with groups and agencies within the county or in regions of a state. County-level professional associations can often provide programs and contacts useful to the media specialist. Some states have regional examination centers where the specialist can personally evaluate materials and attend in-service programs.

Networks comprised of a variety of types of libraries and information centers provide access to the information and materials found in the participating agencies. Networks are not limited to regions — they can be found within a school system, on a community-wide basis, or at the county, state, national, and international levels.

Within the Nation

Both the school and the media program have national affiliations that provide guidance and serve as information sources. The two professional associations most directly involved with media programs are the American Association of School Librarians and the Association for Educational Communications and Technology. They jointly wrote the current guidelines, *Media Programs: District and School.* Each association provides other sources of information and assistance. Throughout this book, references will be provided to some of the specific documents or services that they and other associations provide (see Appendix 1).

Within Society

The school and the media program are units of the educational and informational systems of our society. Society's concerns about education and information influence the building-level media program. Two examples illustrate this relationship.

Society's concern about its physically disabled members has led to legislation and funding that affects school and media programs. In the late 1970s, many media specialists evaluated how well their collections served the needs of physically disabled children.

Nationally based groups and agencies, such as NCLIS (National Commission on Libraries and Information Science), are addressing the question of how this society will meet its informational needs. Media specialists are participating in these discussions. NCLIS' *The Role of the School Library Media Programs in Networking*[4] describes how school media programs can contribute to networks and enumerates the benefits and problems that exist.

Benefits of These Relationships

A collection at the building level can benefit from these formal and informal relationships with education and information agencies. As the media specialist learns about the possibilities, he or she should ask how access to this information and materials will benefit the collection.

Element within the Media Program

Finally, the collection can be viewed as an element within the school's media program. An analysis of the program's functions (information, consultation, design, and administration) shows that they interact with the collection.

The "information function" results in "resources and services appropriate to user needs and devises delivery systems of materials, tools, and human resources to provide for maximum access to information in all its formats."[5] Thus, the collection must be seen as an information source for its users.

The consultation function occurs as media professionals work with teachers to plan learning situations and as they "work with teachers and students in the evaluation, selection and production of materials."[6] Through this function, the collection meets the needs of users and the goals of the school programs.

The design function, a planning activity, includes establishing goals, priorities, and policies; developing materials for self-instruction; and establishing criteria for selection. This function shapes the collection as an entity and establishes criteria for selection of materials based on the characteristics of formats, the preferences of users, and the availability of materials through networks.

The administration function is "concerned with the ways and means by which program goals and priorities are achieved."[7] This function includes day-to-day supervision of collection development and maintenance activities, and the operation of delivery systems.

These functions operate in a cyclical pattern as shown in figure 5. The consultation and information functions are primarily user-oriented, resulting from direct interaction with the user of the materials. The design and administration functions are primarily collection-oriented, involving the development and control of materials.

Figure 5. The Relation of Program Functions

FUNCTIONS OF THE MEDIA PROGRAM

User-Oriented Functions   *Collection-Oriented Functions*

CONSULTATION
  • assessing user needs and opinions

DESIGN
  • developing the collection

INFORMATION
  • providing access to materials

ADMINISTRATION
  • managing ongoing processes

The collection must be designed to meet the needs identified in the consultation function. The resulting collection must be administered to provide for the informational needs of the users. To continue the process, users provide feedback through consultation, thus identifying new needs that must be met by further design and administrative activity. The interaction of the four functions of the media program should result in a collection that more and more effectively meets the needs of the school and users.

Summary

The concept of a collection affects how effectively the media program will function within the total school program. If the view of the collection is limited to the materials contained within one area of the school, resources available to students and teachers are also limited. If the definition is extended to include resources available through the building, or even through networks within other libraries, the accessibility of materials is increased.

If it is agreed that a collection should support the school's program and meet the needs of users, then there is a responsibility to know the program and the users to ensure that their needs are met. Policies and procedures should be designed to facilitate these purposes.

At the same time, there is the reality that a collection in one building cannot physically hold, nor financially afford, all the materials that are requested. This is the point where the knowledge and discretion of the media professional come into play.

Notes to Chapter 2

[1]American Association of School Librarians, American Library Association and Association for Educational Communications and Technology, *Media Programs: District and School* (Chicago, IL: American Library Association; Washington, DC: Association for Educational Communications and Technology, 1975), p. 63.

[2]In schools in the process of moving from classroom collections to centralized collections, a commitment to this concept is critical.

[3]Rudy Bretz, *A Taxonomy of Communication Media* (Englewood Cliffs, NJ: Educational Technology Publications, 1971), p. 11.

[4]Task Force on the Role of the School Library Media Program in the National Program, *The Role of the School Library Media Program in Networking* (Washington, DC: National Commission on Libraries and Information Science, 1978).

[5]American Association of School Librarians, *Media Programs*, p. 8.

[6]Ibid., p. 7.

[7]Ibid., p. 9.

Chapter 2 Bibliography

American Association of School Librarians, American Library Association, and Association for Educational Communications and

Technology. *Media Programs: District and School.* Chicago, IL: American Library Association; Washington, DC: Association for Educational Communications and Technology, 1975.

Anderson, Ronald H. *Selecting and Developing Media for Instruction.* New York, NY: Van Nostrand Reinhold, 1976.

Bretz, Rudy. *A Taxonomy of Communication Media.* Englewood Cliffs, NJ: Educational Technology Publications, 1971.

Quinlan, Iola. "Developing Effective Library Media Centers—Now." *Illinois Libraries* 55 (1973): 479-85.

Shadick, Robert G. "The Library: Powerhouse for Instructional Improvement." *National Elementary Principal* 40 (1961): 22-24.

Task Force on the Role of the School Library Media Program in the National Program. *The Role of the School Library Media Program in Networking.* Washington, DC: National Commission on Libraries and Information Science, 1978.

3
THE COLLECTION PROGRAM

The term "collection program" in this book denotes the processes necessary to develop and maintain a collection. The media specialist carries out the collection program by:

1. Knowing an existing collection or creating one.

2. Knowing the community (external environment).

3. Assessing needs of the school's programs and the users.

4. Establishing collection development policies and procedures (the overall plan).

5. Creating the basis for selection (policies and procedures to guide selection decisions).

6. Identifying criteria (the basis for evaluating materials).

7. Planning for and implementing the selection process: identifying and obtaining tools, arranging for personal examination of materials, involving others in decision-making.

8. Establishing acquisition policies and procedures (guides to obtaining materials).

9. Setting up a maintenance program.

10. Evaluating the collection.

These 10 activities draw on the information presented in the previous chapters and establish the framework for the remaining chapters of the book. The purpose of this chapter is to present an overview of the relationships among the processes involved in the collection program as illustrated in figure 6. The media specialist, however, does not have control over all the factors influencing collection activities. The second portion of this chapter describes possible sources of constraint.

Figure 6. Processes of the Collection Program

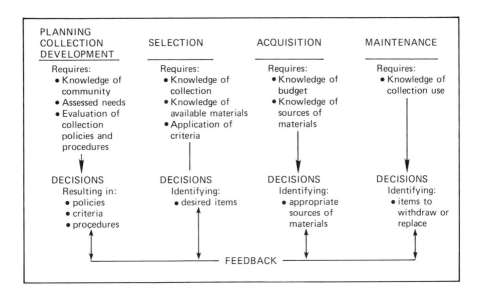

Collection Program Activities

This book approaches the collection program based on the knowledge of the concepts of "collection" discussed in chapter 2. The manner in which the media specialist carries out the collection activities will determine how successfully the collection reflects the principles addressed in those definitions. Knowledge, skill, and sensitivity is required to systematically plan and carry out collection activities.

Knowing an Existing Collection or Creating a New One

If a collection is to serve as a communication and information base, the media specialist must know the users' needs and the resources of the collection. Browsing is an easy way to learn about a collection. When walking through the collection, do you recognize titles or equipment? Are materials housed in unusual areas? Will students overlook them? Are recordings housed behind unmarked cabinets or drawers? Put yourself in the position of a student. Would you find those materials? Would the card catalog help you? Test a few entries.

As you wander through the collection, pause and examine items that are new to you. A quick glance at tables of contents or book jackets can provide you with a general sense of the books in the collection. Scan the album jackets to see what recordings are in the collection. Examine the teacher's guides to audiovisual materials to see what subjects are covered and what formats are included in the collection. Make notes about materials that are new to you or areas that need a sign, or some other aid, to make materials more accessible. Equipment should be housed in an area convenient to the materials that require it. Is there a ready reference area? Are these materials duplicated in the circulating collection? The collection is not limited to materials in the "media center." Check the teacher's lounge or work areas to see if professional journals or other materials are housed there.

As you gather these first impressions, you will want to check the media center's procedure manual to see if unusual situations are explained. Ten copies of a particular 8mm film loop may seem unusual, but the manual may state a good reason for having them. Suppose on opening day you find sets of encyclopedias on rolling carts. This is often a clue that the media staff is responsible for distributing encyclopedia sets to classrooms. You may find a note from a thoughtful predecessor that prevents you from listening to a teacher say, "Oh, I had that set last year. I told her I want a different one this year." As the school year gains momentum and you begin working with teachers and students, you will soon find that you feel very familiar with the collection.

If your job requires that you create a new collection, guidelines will help you know where to begin. This challenging and exciting opportunity will be discussed in chapter 18. Whether you use guidelines, outside consultants, or both, all advice must be adjusted to the needs of the community, the school, and the users.

Knowing the Community

A basic consideration of collection developers is the relation of the media program to the school, to other educational/informational institutions and agencies, and to its external environment as shown in figure 1 (page 21). The community, its geographical, political, economic, cultural, and social characteristics — all influence the collection. School objectives requiring specialized materials, libraries or information agencies in the community environment that duplicate materials in the school collection, and attitudes about education held by citizens — all are examples of possible influences from these environments.

Assessing Needs

Because it is a major purpose of the collection to fulfill the informational and instructional needs of its users, then the media specialist must identify what these needs are. Who does the collection serve? What are their informational needs? What are the teachers' instructional needs? The specialist can begin to answer these questions by researching the characteristics of the users, learning which teaching methods are used, and how children are grouped for their learning experiences. Knowledge of the existing collection, the school, the community, and the needs that have been assessed must all be integrated into the plans and policies that dictate how a collection will develop.

Establishing Collection Development Policies and Procedures

The plans and policies of a collection development policy should reflect the short- and long-term goals of the library. Factors such as audience demand, need, and expectation; the information world; fiscal plans; and the history of the collection must be integrated into the policies and plans.[1]

Collection development policies refer to information resources available within the community or accessible through information systems and specify that these materials need not be purchased. If the public library shares its community history collection with the school, the collection policy statement may confine acquisitions of these materials to student projects, such as taped interviews of local residents or slide presentations about historical landmarks.

Creating the Basis for Selection

The selection policy is only one of the elements that make up the collection program policy; however, it may be the only formally established policy. Even if the school lacks a long-range development policy, a selection policy is needed to guide the media specialist's day-to-day choice of new materials. Selection policies establish principles of selection that guide the collection toward the library's goals outlined in the collection development policy. Selection procedures are the specific processes that implement selection policies.

Identifying Criteria

Criteria, the standards by which items will be evaluated, are a major part of the selection policy. Criteria that assess the item itself and its relation to the collection development policy must be established. Generally accepted criteria include: literary quality, currency, accuracy of information, appeal and value to children, application within the curriculum, and quality and format of presentation. Criteria need to be established for specific formats or for materials to be used by specific types of users.

Planning for and Implementing the Selection Process

One must examine the item or consult evaluative information about the item in order to make a selection decision. Sources that provide this type of information include selection tools, reviewing journals, and bibliographic essays. These are valuable references to consult during the process and should be readily accessible. It is the media specialist's responsibility when planning for the selection process to make these tools available, to preview and examine materials, and to arrange for the participation of students, teachers, and administrators in the selection process. To plan for the selection process, the media specialist should obtain bibliographic and selection tools that will facilitate actual decision-making. These tools provide information as to whether an item is available for purchase, rent, or loan. Materials should be secured for reviewing, previewing, and other means of personal evaluation; and planning should be done about how to involve teachers, administrators, and students in this decision-making.

"Selection" has been described as a decision that an item is worth adding to the collection. At this point in the process, individual items have been assessed against established criteria and policies. The criteria, policies, and procedures noted earlier are not the only factors that influence a media specialist's decisions. Hartz adds that there are "the more subtle influences: the selector's skills and prejudices, his opinions and values."[2] Media specialists should put aside personal biases and remain objective in order to make successful selection decisions.

Establishing Acquisition Policies and Procedures

Acquisition, the process of obtaining materials, is a direct result of the collection development policies and the selection policies and procedures. Acquisition policies and procedures implement selection decisons. It is these processes that actually get the material into the library.[3] Acquisition policies determine who will supply materials; acquisition procedures establish the process for obtaining these materials. Acquisition policies establish ways to determine the appropriate source for material; that is, the source that is the quickest and most economical. Acquisition policies are the principles that help the media specialist decide whether to purchase materials from a jobber, a company that handles titles from several publishers, or to purchase them directly from the publisher or a local store. The media specialist will decide which magazine agency to use and when to use distributors of audiovisual materials, rather than going directly to the publisher/producer. Acquisition procedures establish the processes by which the media specialist orders, receives, and pays for the materials.

Setting Up a Maintenance Program

One of the most important and often neglected functions of the collection program is collection maintenance. Decisions must be made to replace, remove, mend, or rebind materials and how long to keep materials such as magazines. Equipment must be kept in working condition. If the media center has super 8mm films, are there appropriate projectors? Are there sufficient supplies of consumable items such as projector bulbs and slide mounts so they can be readily replaced? How will heavily used items be replaced? Will you wait until the item is no longer usable before you reorder? How many times can an item be mended or spliced before it is no longer useful? If you wait, will the item still be available? The media specialist will obviously need to establish policies and procedures for these activities.

Inventory time provides an excellent opportunity to systematically check the condition of all items, but the collection may not be inventoried frequently enough to spot the deterioration of some items. Planning for the systematic maintenance of all materials is an important step toward keeping the collection ready for use.

Establishing Plans for Evaluation

Both the collection and the policies and procedures that govern its growth must be evaluated. Many questions need to be raised. In what ways does the collection have value? Value can be assessed quantitatively, that is, the number of items in the collection, and qualitatively, for example, how well the needs of users are met. A collection is an evolving entity that must respond to its environment; evaluation is the way media professionals assess a collection to determine if its response is effective.

Ideally, evaluation is an ongoing process; however, everyday demands often interfere. Evaluation of a collection is also a complex process. Plans need to be made for an evaluation system that is both manageable and comprehensive so that media specialists can effectively respond to changes in the collection or its environment.

Interaction of the Activities

One can view these activities as a continuum (figure 7, page 44) in which one activity leads to and influences the next. These activities are not isolated; they interact in a cyclical arrangement. Thus, a change in one activity often causes changes in others.

The collection development policy establishes priorities that directly affect both selection and acquisition activities. Fermi Middle School is adopting a new approach to teaching science in which students are to learn through observation, experimentation, and individual or group investigation, rather than through the use of a textbook. The collection development policy must thus be changed. If, due to budgetary constraints, the collection cannot meet all the demands of the new program and fulfill the other informational and instructional needs of the school, then the revised collection policy may read: "Priority will be given to the purchase of materials that support the concepts and skills presented in the science curriculum." As a result, the acquisition policy would have to be revised to read: "Science books will be purchased regardless of binding (hardback, library binding, or paperback). Books on other subjects will be purchased only in library binding."

The media specialist should establish policies that provide guidance with flexibility so that anticipated changes can be accommodated. As new formats are developed in the future, new selection criteria will need to be established.

The preceding discussion identified the interrelated processes that comprise the collection program. None of the processes is isolated; each evolves as external constraints and influences act on the collection program.

Figure 7.   The Interaction of Collection Program Activities

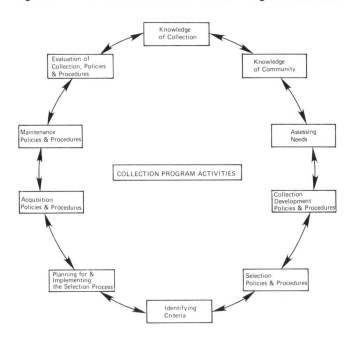

Factors That Govern Collection Activities

The media specialist is responsible for the development and implementation of the collection program. However, the media specialist cannot control all the factors that influence collection activities. The media program must operate within policies adopted by the board of education. The goals of the district and the school must also be met. The districts established by the school board may change yearly and affect the composition of the student body/potential users of the collection. Legislation at the state or federal level may dictate that children with physical or other disabilities are mainstreamed into the regular classrooms. Shifts in student population bring new demands on the collection and must be accommodated in the collection program.

System/District Media Programs

When the building-level media program is part of a system or district media program, there are many advantages, especially for the beginning media specialist. The system's media program coordinator or director is often someone to turn to for guidance. The district-level guidelines for media programs and the selection policy adopted by the governing body can also aid the media specialist in her/his work. There may be opportunities to examine new materials and take teachers to exhibits and demonstrations at district meetings. System media programs offer many services to help establish and maintain the collection program.

Constraints can also be imposed by the system. An "approved buying list" generated by a district-wide committee may limit the range of titles that can be purchased. If you face this situation, ask how orders can be placed for items not on the list. In some systems, titles on specific subjects must be ordered at specified times. Typically, science materials are ordered in December, replacements in March, etc. While this practice is efficient for the processing operation, it imposes constraints upon the collection program. The school that was implementing the science curriculum changes would have had a difficult, if not impossible, job trying to fulfill the curriculum needs under such regulations.

Financial Support and Control

The institution's funding policies, including its policies regulating use of outside funding sources, impose constraints on the collection program. Media specialists are compelled to operate within the limits set by budget allocations. The type of budgeting can also affect collection activities. A traditional line-item budget establishes a flat amount for media program materials. Further restrictions are imposed when line-item budgets are divided by format. This type of funding can conflict with demands that the collection meet needs of school programs and individual users.

Collection development, as described in this chapter, is more successful with a form of program budgeting that allows priorities to be based on program objectives and needs.

The collection is affected by the school's position on the use of outside funding. Some school districts do not participate in federally sponsored programs, such as the Elementary and Secondary Education Act. Many agencies or groups have regulations that control what can be purchased with the funds they provide and have limitations on the type of use or user for whom materials may be purchased. For example, funding may not apply to storage facilities and personnel.

Sometime in your career as a media specialist, a school official will inform you that you have a large sum of money to be spent on materials for specific users within a week or 10 days. This situation does not encourage thoughtful planning or selection, but is typical of outside funding announcements. Try to be alert to possible sources of outside funding, to learn what they will fund and when the funding will occur. Your record of anticipated needs and desiderata file will be essential when this situation arises.

Budget control and authorization of purchases are potential trouble spots for the media specialist. In some cases, the principal will control the budget. A salesperson may visit the principal and promote a package deal with a price that sounds like a bargain. If the media specialist is not consulted, the principal may learn after the purchase that 1) the collection already contains these materials; 2) the materials do not meet any needs of the collection; or 3) the materials require equipment not available in the school. Work with principals and purchasing agents to avoid problems such as these.

School Facilities

The limitations of the physical facilities and/or the physical plant can create constraints on the collection. Film viewing areas require adjustable lighting, especially if students take notes on the information presented in the film. Use of media is frequently limited by the availability of safe electrical outlets. If the media center serves a several-story building, viewing equipment should be available on each level.

Many items in the collection (such as picture books, large study prints, or art prints) will require specialized storage units. When evaluating materials, consider how and where they will be stored and used.

Collections in Networks and Multitype Libraries

Networks, created by libraries sharing resources, can provide information services outside the capabilities of your collection. If your school participates in a network, what are your responsibilities? What materials, services, and financial obligations are included in the agreement? Networks today offer cooperative purchasing programs, cataloging and processing, computerized data bases, delivery systems, production services, examination centers, serials cooperatives, and sharing of resources.[4]

You may be working in a library that serves both school and public. Serving the needs of patrons that range from preschoolers to adults creates advantages and disadvantages for the collection. While you have the advantage of knowing the community readers, you face a possible conflict of demands within the collection. Should the collection be directed to the curricular and instructional needs of the students or toward general informational and recreational needs of the public? Is there a separate budget for each purpose? Are materials for adults housed with those for children? Questions such as these should be answered by the policies and procedures outlined in your collection program.

Summary

The goal of information accessibility can be reached by carrying out the collection program activities outlined in this chapter. At the most basic level, media specialists cannot make information accessible unless we know it exists. The importance of knowing the collection increases as you gain knowledge of the users and their needs. Poetry books, art works, and picture stories that deal with mathematical concepts may be overlooked if you and the mathematics teacher consider only the items classified in the 500 section.

To ensure that information is accessible, policies and procedures may need to be altered as needs change. However, media specialists must consider all the demands on the collection when initiating changes. The Fermi Middle School media center staff faced an awkward and demanding situation when the new science curriculum was implemented. Materials in the collection were inadequate to support both the new curriculum and the needs of individual users. As a result, circulation of science materials had to be limited to teachers; this was difficult to explain to the children, but necessary to support school priorities. Even the maintenance policy was affected. For a two-year period, priority was given to mending and repairing science-oriented materials. Also, titles dealing with science were removed from the collection only when the information in them was known to be inaccurate.

What effect did the Fermi situation have on requests from teachers for materials on other subjects? The language arts teachers had just embarked on a series of mini-courses dealing with the special interests of students, such as science fiction, mysteries, and sports heroes. Their instructional program required the availability of many titles written from the fourth- through ninth-grade reading level. These needs could not be adequately met.

Situations such as these illustrate how easy it is to overreact to an immediate problem at the expense of the collection as a whole. The collection can be responsive to all the demands made upon it, if it is remembered that a change in one collection program activity may necessitate a change in other activities. The discussions and examples found throughout the remaining chapters of this book address ways to carry out all the activities of the collection program effectively to, indeed, make materials accessible.

Notes to Chapter 3

[1]Hendrik Edelman, "Selection Methodology in Academic Libraries," *Library Resources and Technical Services* 23 (1977): 34.

[2]Frederic R. Hartz, "Selection of School/Media Materials," *Catholic Library World* 47 (1976): 425.

[3]Edelman, "Selection Methodology," p. 34.

[4]Samples of existing networks are briefly described in Task Force on the Role of the School Library Media Program in the National Program, *The Role of the School Library Media Program in Networking* (Washington, DC: National Commission on Libraries and Information Science, 1978), pp. 73-85.

Chapter 3 Bibliography

Edelman, Hendrik. "Selection Methodology in Academic Libraries." *Library Resources and Technical Services* 23 (1977): 33-44.

Hartz, Frederic R. "Selection of School/Media Materials." *Catholic Library World* 47 (1976): 425-29.

Shipman, Joseph C. "Collection Building." In *Encyclopedia of Library and Information Science*, edited by Allen Kent and Harold Lancour. Vol. 5, pp. 160-68. New York, NY: Marcel Dekker, 1971.

Task Force on the Role of the School Library Media Program in the National Program. *The Role of the School Library Media Program in Networking.* Washington, DC: National Commission on Libraries and Information Science, 1978.

4
ISSUES ABOUT COLLECTION

Media specialists continually rely on their decision-making abilities while implementing the processes of the collection program. The decisions the specialist makes will reflect on his/her perception of the characteristics of collections, views about the responsibility of a selector, and philosophical positions on many issues. To act in a professional manner also calls for the specialist to know himself or herself—strengths, weaknesses, and biases.

To help the media specialist explore individual perceptions about the characteristics of collection and views of selection responsibility, this chapter addresses the following questions:

Is there a minimum quantitative requirement for a collection (a "base collection")? What is meant by "core collection"?

What is a balanced collection? Is it a legitimate goal? Does a collection need equal numbers of print and nonprint materials? Should both sides of issues be represented in collections? Should priority be given to materials that are popular over materials that have greater literary value?

The media specialist's approach to collection program activities also reflects his or her philosophical positions on many issues. For example, the materials selected attest to the specialist's perception of the terms "intellectual freedom" and "children's rights," and stances taken on these and many other issues will consciously or unconsciously influence decisions about the collection. To help the media specialist explore his/her positions, this chapter examines the questions:

What is meant by intellectual freedom for children?

Do children have rights to read, view, and listen?

The chapter closes with a brief discussion of "selector's bias."

This chapter offers different viewpoints for consideration. No answers are given. The media specialist, as an individual, needs to reflect on the opinions expressed in this chapter and by the writers of the recommended readings. You, the media specialist, must know yourself. Where do you stand on the issues? What is your philosophical position?

How the issues on collection development will be resolved is up to society and our profession. The issues are not new. The opinions held by society and members of our profession are constantly under review. This chapter can only highlight the issues and help you examine your own views.

Base and Core Collections

Common questions about collections include: Are there minimum quantitative requirements (a base) for a collection? Is a core collection needed for a media program to function? The first question can be answered quantitatively, while the second can be answered by examining subject coverage, item quantities, formats, or specific titles.

Opinions vary considerably about the actual number of items that must be in a collection at any one time. Guidelines for media programs issued by state boards of education or professional associations offer recommendations and generally endorse the concept that decisions must be based on the needs of the individual school. The national guidelines, *Media Programs: District and School*, endorse this position in several passages relating to the base, or minimal-level, collection needed to carry out a media program. For example,

> A single model for the collection of materials and equipment is not presented ... since decisions concerning amounts of materials, their formats and quantities of supporting equipment are made on the basis of program and user needs.[1]

This statement emphasizes that the collection fulfills the purpose of meeting program and user needs whether they are instructional, informational, or personal in nature. Users' interests and preferences must be considered when choosing between materials of different content, level of coverage presentation, or type of formats. To meet these needs, interests, and preferences, the guidelines recommend that a *base* collection in

> a school with 500 or fewer students [should] have a minimum collection of 20,000 items or 40 per student.... It is possible that the collection in larger schools may provide the needed range of content, levels, forms of expression, and formats at a ratio of less than 40 items per student.[2]

Some media specialists and administrators think that the minimum quantitative numbers recommended in figure 8 are too high. However, the quantities are reasonable when one considers the resources necessary to integrate a media program into a school's overall program.

When studying "guidelines" or other standards statements, consider the following questions: Do you and your school share the philosophical basis on which the document is written? Do you perceive the role of the media program to be that expressed in the document? Do you agree with the assumptions on which the recommendations are

Figure 8. Recommended Base Collection

BASE COLLECTION FOR A SCHOOL OF 500 OR FEWER STUDENTS	
QUANTITY RECOMMENDATIONS	
FORMAT	RECOMMENDATION
Books	8,000 to 12,000 volumes
Periodicals and newspapers	50 to 175 titles
Microform reader and printer	2 readers: 1 portable and 1 reader/printer
Filmstrips: sound and silent	500 to 2,000 items
Filmstrip projectors	10 projectors and 30 viewers
Slides and transparencies	2,000 to 6,000 items
Slide and transparency equipment	6 slide projectors, 10 slide viewers, 10 overhead projectors
Graphics: posters, art and study prints, maps and globes	800 to 1,200 items
16mm and super 8mm sound and silent films, and videotapes	Access to 3,000 sound items, 6 sound projectors, 500 to 1,000 silent super 8mm films, 20 cartridge-loaded or open-reel projectors
Audio recordings	1,500 to 2,000 items, 30 audio reproduction units with earphones
Educational broadcast radio	5 AM/FM receivers
Games and toys	400 to 750 items
Models and sculpture	200 to 500 items
Specimens	200 to 400 items

Source: American Association of School Librarians, American Library Association and Association for Educational Communications and Technology, *Media Programs:District and School,*(Chicago: American Library Association; Washington, D.C.: Association for Educational Communications and Technology, 1975), pp.70-81.

Note: this listing does not include the items recommended under miscellaneous equipment or local production.

based? Are the recommendations stated in terms applicable to your situation?

The term "base" collection is used in *Media Programs: District and School* to denote the minimal-level collection needed to carry out a media program.

Many selection tools use the term "basic collection" and "core collection" when recommending specific titles. *Core Media Collections for Elementary Schools*, which recommends nonprint titles, uses this terminology. *Elementary School Library Collection*, uses the designation "Phase 1" to denote print and nonprint items recommended for the "opening day" collection. Full bibliographic information about these and other tools is provided in Appendix 2.

The selection tools and guidelines, such as *Media Programs: District and School*, are good resources for material selection and budget planning. Their broad-based approach is designed to be useful to many schools. When the media specialist uses these resources, however, the needs of the individual school must be considered. Taylor observes that the authors of these resources are external to individual school situations.[3] Information about the individual school's programs and users is necessary if these tools are to meet particular needs. The following questions will help the media specialist determine which recommendations apply to particular situations.

If it met the quantitative recommendations, would the collection fulfill its purposes? Would the recommended items provide the content coverage needed?

Do the users in your school prefer the types of formats recommended?

The following examples further illustrate the importance of considering individual school situations before implementing the recommendations. If your program serves children in kindergarten through third grade, does the collection need the 50 to 175 periodical and magazine titles recommended in *Media Program: District and School*? Unless you purchase many duplicate titles, you will not find enough individual magazine titles appropriate for the interests and abilities of children in those grades.

If you are in a middle school, do you need toys in the collection? If teachers work primarily with individuals or small groups, do you need transparencies or other materials suitable to large group presentations? Are titles recommended in the selection tools needed for the school curriculum, or are they of personal interest to the students, or both?

Balanced Collections

Another term that appears frequently in discussions about collections is the word "balanced." The term may refer to 1) the number of print items versus the number of nonprint items within a collection; 2) the quantity of items on various subjects; 3) the representations of both sides of issues addressed within the collection; or 4) the issue of demand selection (purchasing what is popular) versus quality selection (purchasing items of literary value).

Quantitative Balancing

In the 1950s and 1960s, guidelines recommended that collections have a percentage of materials on specific subjects or that collections include a minimum number of items in specified formats. This quantitative approach to collection development often overlooked the purposes of fulfilling the needs of the school and the users. These early attempts to create a "well-rounded" or "balanced" collection of materials in varied formats unfortunately led media specialists to make purchases on the basis of format, according to Vandergrift.[4] Erickson agrees, noting it may be better to have adequate coverage in 10 formats than inadequacy in 20.[5]

The subject-proportion approach often leads to the acquisition of rarely used items that could be obtained through networks. Zealous application of quantitative approaches to collection development, while convenient and easily accounted for, is ultimately ineffective. It is easier to say, "Oh, we have the standard number of items in this format or on that subject" than to demonstrate that the materials in the collection are meeting the needs of the school and the users.

The writers of *Media Programs: District and School*, aware of the problem and its consequences, write:

> Final decisions about the mix of materials including actual quantities in each category, [should be] made in the individual school. The development of the media collection [should be] based on program goals and characteristics of the school and reflect needs, prior action and resources.[6]

This advice should not be lost in a quick reading or application of the recommendations found in *Media Programs: District and School.*

Both Sides of an Issue Represented in the Collection

The term "balanced collection" can also be interpreted as a collection whose materials represent both sides of issues. The advocates of this position express the belief that children should learn to gather and evaluate information, viewing this skill as necessary for the preservation of democracy. Others argue that children need direction and guidance, or that truly objective presentations are unavailable in children's materials.

Careful examination of information at the child's level reveals some limitations. Frequently, a work presents only one viewpoint on a controversial topic. Pringle writes:

Bias is usually inevitable and, to an extent, well-informed bias is desirable. An oft-quoted standard for children's books about controversies is that they should be "objective and balanced." This is an extraordinary goal, considering that everyone involved in the controversies, including Nobel laureate scientists, is being subjective and biased.[7]

When you, the media specialist, examine materials about controversial subjects (such as drugs) consider the following questions: Are commonly used drugs (such as aspirin) mentioned? Is the fact that some illegal drugs have medicinal uses included? The exclusion of relevant facts is only one way to bias information. The choice of words, use of visuals, vocal inflection, or filming techniques may also be used to elicit emotional rather than rational responses. Frightening situations or scenes of adolescent rebellion are often used in films about alcohol, driving, or sex to create an emotional response.

Objective information does exist. Some presenters carefully indicate when information is based on fact or opinion. Sometimes, opposing views may be presented in the same work. One example of a book that clearly distinguishes fact and opinion is Jack Denton Scott's *Discovering the Mysterious Egret* (Harcourt, 1978). Tracing the migration of the egret to the United States, the author uses the following phrases: "no one seems to know," "some naturalists formerly believed," "actually, very little is known," "one fact is certain." This type of treatment does not "talk down" to the reader and it raises curiosity.

Demands for objectivity within one work may put constraints on the writer. Pringle observes:

It seems unreasonable to expect complete objectivity from a writer who is well-informed about an issue and cares about the outcome. More realistic goals for a controversial book are that the writer be as objective as possible, and present differing views. Objectivity, or something close to it, comes easily when a writer has little or nothing at stake in the outcome of a controversy.[8]

If all the works of a collection create a body of information, how can a balanced viewpoint be achieved? If individual works do not include opposing views, do separate works create the balance? Is balance important to you, the media specialist, and the users? Pamphlets, newspaper clippings, and magazine articles are often used to create this balance.

Demand Selection versus Quality Selection

A third approach to balance within the collection examines the conflict between literary value and popular appeal. Should the collection include items that are popular but lack literary merit? Should the collection have quality materials that may not be demanded? Is quality more important than appeal? What role do libraries have in preserving and providing quality materials? Do libraries exist to meet only the demands of the majority?

Proponents of both sides of the issue of quality versus demand argue vehemently, generating lively debate in conversations and in print.[9]

The issue of demand selection versus literary selection is complex, having many facets and implications that cut across the boundaries of content, format, and reading level. For example, should the media specialist purchase something that is popular when others have pointed out that it has racial, ethnic, or sexual stereotypes? Do you buy heavily in visual materials because someone says that no one reads anymore? Do you buy only quality materials to ensure that children will have an opportunity to know such works?

Some people argue that if children do not find a desired item in the media center, they will go away with a negative attitude about libraries for their entire lives. Others argue that it is a professional responsibility to motivate children by exposing them to materials that will help them develop literary and aesthetic tastes.

An ongoing debate centers on the inclusion in the collection of series titles from "fiction factories" where writers are hired to complete a prepared character and plot outline (formula writing).[10] The debate, carried on since the 1920s over the Nancy Drew and Hardy Boys series, is a prime example of the demand versus quality issue. Children ask for these titles.

There are a number of questions that should be considered. Do you recognize that children have recreational needs? Are you aware of the nationwide promotion activities, the television series, and the wide distribution of these series in many stores across the country? How do you weigh that information against other demands on the collection? How do you interpret the goal of motivating children to read? Is the "type of literature" a concern in your answer? Are you concerned about helping the child develop an appreciation of literature?

On one side of the debate are writers such as Broderick[11] who take the position that the popular series draw students to the collection so that other works can be suggested when the child is ready. Her position is supported by Nagle,[12] who views the series as a means of motivating reading. Those who disagree include Israel,[13] who states that having these series in the collection implies that they are "good" and thus we, as media specialists, are dishonest to the child about the materials by including them in the collection. Are there other works that have the same appeal and offer "more lasting quality and literary merit?"[14] "Yes," according to the compilers (Birtha, Carson, Corlies, Swarr, Goodgon) of two bibliographies.[15]

The questions raised about series books can be raised about other materials. Comics, materials from the pop culture, and books or filmstrips based on popular television programs are a few examples. Do you think comics should be in the collection? On what basis would you include them? Do you perceive any differences in value in *Peanuts, Mad Magazine, Batman*, and *Wonder Woman*? Do you consider these materials different from information presented in comic-book form? One library uses the "Code of the Comics Magazine Association of

America"[16] in its selection policy to determine if the violence portrayed in a comic book is unacceptable.

Balance as a Goal

An initial question in this chapter was: "Is a balanced collection a legitimate goal?" The discussions on interpretation of the term "balance" point out some of the complexities of the question. Quantitative practices may ensure variety, but do not ensure that program and user needs will be met. Objectivity in children's materials, while desirable, may be hard to find. Popular selection over literary selection may provide materials of appeal, but limit the experiences of students. Other issues raised in this discussion are directly related to how intellectual freedom and the rights of children are interpreted.

Intellectual Freedom for Children

How you, the media specialist, perceive intellectual freedom as it applies to children and how you define children's rights will influence what information you make available and accessible to children. These issues are complex and can be viewed within "political, social, economic, psychological, religious, ethical, and ethnic contexts as well as the pornographic."[17]

"Intellectual freedom," as defined in the *Intellectual Freedom Manual* means the right of any person to believe whatever he wants on any subject, and to express his beliefs or ideas in whatever way he thinks appropriate. The freedom to express one's beliefs or ideas, through any mode of communication, becomes virtually meaningless, however, when accessibility to such expressions is denied to other persons. For this reason, the definition of intellectual freedom has a second, integral part; namely, the right of unrestricted access to all information and ideas regardless of the medium of communication used. Intellectual freedom implies a circle, and that circle is broken if either freedom of expression or access to the ideas expressed is stifled.[18]

If only that part of the circle dealing with freedom of access is considered, the principle of intellectual freedom, which also protects the rights of those who wish to protest, may easily be overlooked.

Are selection and censorship really the same? Asheim makes a distinction between them when he states:

selection begins with presumption in favor of liberty of thought, whereas censorship begins with a presumption in favor of thought control.[19]

He perceives selection as democratic, censorship as authoritarian, and reminds us:

> it is the librarian's responsibility as a representative of the public in a democratic society, to be a selector and to resist censorship.[20]

If, as media professionals, we accept this responsibility, what are the implications? Krug describes the dilemma:

> At least in theory, I believe that all librarians, including school librarians, should be able to choose materials from the full range of those available. Of course, the implications of this position, particularly for school librarians, means trouble with a capital T. Nevertheless, librarians must be prepared for some controversy if they adhere to their professional ethics and stand squarely on the principles of intellectual freedom, applying them to all patrons, including children.[21]

For librarians working with children, the dilemma is not easy to resolve for Asheim draws our attention to a barrier against intellectual freedom:

> Parents still have the right, of course, to control their own child's reading, but they are no longer equally free to interfere with the right of other people's children to read what they will. And the librarian has been delegated to be the mediator who will treat fairly both of those rights.[22]

While parents do have legal rights regarding their children, the courts have begun to assert that children, too, have constitutional rights that must be safeguarded. Opinions differ regarding the influence of court decisions on society's attitude about the child. Recent court cases of interest have been summarized in figure 9 (page 58). In writing about the child's right to read, Procuniar states:

> After the Supreme Court decisions in *Tinker [c. Des Moines]* and other cases, Judith Krug of the American Library Association's Office of Intellectual Freedom wrote that "the U.S. Supreme Court has laid to rest the concept of *in loco parentis* as it relates to the mind. The Constitution and Bill of Rights apply to all citizens regardless of age." There is now, she believes, free choice, regardless of age, in the matters of the mind. I think Krug has clearly overestimated the influence of the court, but I am inclined to suggest that we should behave as if matters were settled, while organizing to fight the many attempts to abridge these rights.[23]

Are the adults who work with children ready to ensure those rights? Procuniar cautions that "the intellectual rights of children, despite court decisions, are still in the hands of adults reluctant to permit children any

Figure 9. Recent Court Decisions on Intellectual Freedom

1. *Minarcini v. Strongville City School District*, 541 F.2d 577 (6th Cir. 1976), in which Circuit Court Judge Edwards states:

   > A library is a storehouse of knowledge. When created for a public school it is an important privilege created by the state for the benefit of the students in the school. That privilege is not subject to being withdrawn by succeeding school boards, whose members might desire to "winnow" the library for books the content of which occasioned their displeasure or disapproval.

   Quoted from page 25 of the report, "The Strongsville Decision," *School Library Journal* 23 (November 1976): 23-26; discussed in "Who's in Charge of School Libraries? A Commentary" by Lillian N. Gerhardt, pages 27-28.

2. *President's Council, District 25 v. Community School Board No. 25*, 457 F.2d 289 (2d Cir. 1974), in which the court upheld the right of the school board to ban materials is cited by O'Neil as "the one instance where a federal appellate court has discussed library circulation policies and access to controversial materials; the presence of a substantial first amendment issue was all but overlooked." Robert M. O'Neill, "Libraries, Librarians, and First Amendment Freedoms," *Human Rights* 4 (Summer 1975): 295-96.

3. *Davis v. Page*, 385 F.Supp. 395 (1974). A case in which parents of elementary school students on the basis of their religious beliefs objected to their children not being excused from the classroom while audiovisual equipment was being used. The court's concern for the educational future of the children is stated as:

   > Audiovisual equipment is used in the teaching of nearly every school subject from arithmetic to zoology. I take judicial notice that audiovisual techniques are favored by educators and that they are an integral part of the educational process. As presented in this case, they are nonsectarian in purpose and manner.

   Davis v. Page at 400.

degree of freedom."[24] How does the media specialist weigh that observation against Farson's statement that:

> A child's ignorance is a strong political ally of adult society, and adults have learned to rely heavily on it. Even the institutions that are designed to educate and inform children serve double duty by also keeping them ignorant and dependent.[25]

He identifies the library as a prime example of an institution "designed to provide information to children [and yet where] we find the most serious prohibitions against them."[26]

Agreement is found in Jenkinson's reply to his own question, "Who Attempts to Censor Materials in the Schools?"

> Note how that question is phrased. The word *attempts* is significant since only a person in authority can actually censor materials. But anyone can bring sufficient pressure to bear on a person in authority so that books will be censored.[27]

Jenkinson classifies people and organizations who make this attempt as being 1) students; 2) parents; 3) teachers; 4) school librarians; 5) school administrators; 6) school board members; 7) clergy; and 8) organizations that precipitate censorship incidents.[28] Included in this latter group are Mel and Norma Gablers' Educational Research Analysts, Inc.[29] and

> other organizations that supply reviews for concerned parents [such as] America's Future in New Rochelle, New York, the John Birch Society, PONYU (Parents of New York-United), and the many concerned citizens groups that are springing up across the country. Organizations actively involved in attempting to remove books that are racist or sexist are the National Organization of Women (NOW) and the Council on Interracial Books for Children.[30]

We live in a world of adult-generated "-isms": racism, sexism, ageism, pluralism, and pacifism—influences that are felt daily. Gerhardt describes our dilemma:

> The illogic of it all is what makes library collection development for children as fascinating as it is frustrating. It is a totally unreasonable situation that public and school librarians face in their selection practices today. On the one hand, we have the full weight of the American Library Association coming down on the side of representation of all points of view and full access to all sorts of information as the only worthwhile approach to collection building. On the other, we have a general agreement by the public and by many librarians that children require guidance in the development of personal taste and personal values. We have both within and without library service angry groups calling for the eradication in children's library collections of all negative stereotypes of the races, the sexes or the national or ethnic groups residing in this country. These same groups generally support the idea of a free press.[31]

The responsibility to ensure that the child has a right to accurate information is thus not an easy one. Does the media specialist weigh each item individually or look at the collection as a whole? It must be recognized that a child forms attitudes about his environment by age five. If materials that offend some individuals are removed, there is a danger that all such requests might have to be accommodated. If efforts are made to present both sides of all issues, how can it truly be ensured that a child will always be exposed to both sides of an issue?

The base has been laid by others, and their efforts can be built on. For if we believe in the values of democracy and in children, then those seeking to work with children must share Procuniar's observation that:

> To give democracy a chance of success, we need to develop adults who are capable of choice and decision making. The more we protect and shelter our children, the less they will be able to participate meaningfully in the democratic process. Democracy also involves the right of people to make bad choices and to have succeeding generations decide that the people's earlier choice was in error.[32]

Jenkinson, after studying censorship for several years, expresses these concerns:

> I fear that students might lose the right to learn, the right to read, the right to explore ideas. Whenever I see petitions and guidelines like those mentioned in this article [guidelines for removal of materials], I shudder.[33]

Jenkinson is not alone in his thinking; his concerns are shared by many people and groups.

Positions on People's Rights

A number of professional groups have attempted to express their views through statements on people's rights. This section presents nationally endorsed statements supporting intellectual freedom and the child's right to information. Such statements are frequently endorsed by boards of education in their district policies on materials.

The first statement is the American Library Association's "Library Bill of Rights," which was adopted in 1948 and amended in 1961, 1967, and 1980. The history of this statement and the supporting and interpretative statement can be found in *Intellectual Freedom Manual*.[34]

Library Bill of Rights*

The American Library Association affirms that all libraries are forums for information and ideas, and that the following basic policies should guide their services.

1. Books and other library resources should be provided for the interest, information, and enlightenment of all people of the community the library serves. Materials should not be excluded because of the origin, background, or views of those contributing to their creation.

---

*Reprinted by permission of the American Library Association.

2. Libraries should provide materials and information presenting all points of view on current and historical issues. Materials should not be proscribed or removed because of partisan or doctrinal disapproval.

3. Libraries should challenge censorship in the fulfillment of their responsibility to provide information and enlightenment.

4. Libraries should cooperate with all persons and groups concerned with resisting abridgment of free expression and free access to ideas.

5. A person's right to use a library should not be denied or abridged because of origin, age, background, or views.

6. Libraries which make exhibit spaces and meeting rooms available to the public they serve should make such facilities available on an equitable basis, regardless of the beliefs or affiliations of individuals or groups requesting their use.

Adopted June 18, 1948
Amended February 2, 1961, June 27, 1967, and January 23, 1980, by the ALA Council

The American Association of School Librarians endorsed the 1967 version in 1976.[35] This division of the American Library Association had a separate statement in the early 1970s that still appears in many school policies and in the literature.

The second statement is the Association for Educational Communications and Technology's "Statement on Intellectual Freedom," directed to filling a void for a statement on "evaluation and selection of educational media as a vital part of student learning in elementary and secondary classrooms."[36]

Statement on Intellectual Freedom *

The Association for Educational Communications and Technology

The First Amendment to the Constitution of the United States is a cornerstone of our liberty, supporting our rights and responsibilities regarding free speech both written and oral.

The Association for Educational Communications and Technology believes this same protection applies also to the use of sound and image in our society.

Therefore, we affirm that:
Freedom of inquiry and access to information — regardless of the format or viewpoints of the presentation — are fundamental to the development of our society. These rights must not be denied or abridged because of age, sex, race, religion, national origin, or social or political views.

---

*Reprinted by permission of the Association for Educational Communications and Technology.

Children have the right to freedom of inquiry and access to information; responsibility for abridgement of that right is solely between an individual child and the parent(s) of that child.

The need for information and the interests, growth, and enlightenment of the user should govern the selection and development of educational media, not the age, sex, race, nationality, politics, or religious doctrine of the author, producer, or publisher.

Attempts to restrict or deprive a learner's access to information representing a variety of viewpoints must be resisted as a threat to learning in a free and democratic society. Recognizing that within a pluralistic society efforts to censor may exist, such challenges should be met calmly with proper respect for the beliefs of the challengers. Further, since attempts to censor sound and image material frequently arise out of misunderstanding of the rationale for using these formats, we shall attempt to help both user and censor to recognize the purpose and dynamics of communication in modern times regardless of the format.

The Association for Educational Communications and Technology is ready to cooperate with other persons or groups committed to resisting censorship or abridgement of free expression and free access to ideas and information.

Adopted by:

AECT Board of Directors
Kansas City
April 21, 1978[37]

The handbook in which this statement is found identifies the "basic assumptions for interpreting the statement" as including:

With every freedom or right comes a responsibility. Responsible, intelligent study must be based on a wide range of ideas and opinions to be examined and developed through reading, listening, viewing, experiencing, and discussing.

. . . .

Selectors of educational media must recognize that no material is value free, but rather, reflects the values of the culture of the time and place when and where created.[38]

The handbook provides information and guidelines to assist in developing policies or dealing with challenges of materials in the collection.

The third statement is the Educational Film Library Association's "Freedom to View." This statement is a corollary to "The Freedom to Read"[39] statement of the American Library Association.

Freedom to View*

The FREEDOM TO VIEW, along with the freedom to speak, to hear, and to read, is protected by the First Amendment to the Constitution of the United States. In a free society, there is no place for censorship of any medium of expression. Therefore, we affirm these principles:

1. It is in the public interest to provide the broadest possible access to films and other audiovisual materials because they have proven to be among the most effective means for the communication of ideas. Liberty of circulation is essential to insure the constitutional guarantee of freedom of expression.

2. It is in the public interest to provide for our audiences, films and other audiovisual materials which represent a diversity of views and expression. Selection of a work does not constitute or imply agreement with or approval of the content.

3. It is our professional responsibility to resist the constraint of labeling or prejudging a film on the basis of the moral, religious or political beliefs of the producer or filmmaker or on the basis of controversial content.

4. It is our professional responsibility to contest vigorously, by all lawful means, every encroachment upon the public's freedom to view.

This statement was originally drafted by the Educational Film Library Association's Freedom to View Committee, and was adopted by the EFLA Board of Directors in February, 1979. Additional copies may be obtained for 20¢ (to cover postage and handling) from: Educational Film Library Association, 43 West 61 Street, New York, New York 10023.

THIS STATEMENT WAS ADOPTED BY THE BOARD OF DIRECTORS
OF THE ASSOCIATION FOR EDUCATIONAL COMMUNICATIONS
AND TECHNOLOGY ON DECEMBER 1, 1979
Association for Educational Communications & Technology
1126 16th Street, N.W., Washington, D.C. 20036

This statement was originally drafted by the Educational Film Library Association's Freedom to View Committee, and was adopted by the EFLA Board of Directors in February, 1979. It was endorsed by the American Library Association's Intellectual Freedom Committee and ALA Council in June, 1979, and by the AECT (Association for Educational Communications & Technology) Board of Directors in December, 1979.

When examining the statements, consider the rationale for, and the meanings and interpretations of, the words used. Do you share the belief expressed in these statements? Are they ones you would recommend for adoption by your school board?

Selector's Bias

The media specialist should be aware of his/her own biases and preferences so that personal prejudices do not inadvertently affect

---

*Reprinted by permission of the Educational Film Library Association.

his/her selection decisions. Knowing one's self is an important pre-requisite for handling the professional responsibilities relating to the collection program.

Personal views can unconsciously influence actions. For example, if you are an advocate of the women's liberation movement, will your sensitivity to the treatment of women dominate your evaluation of materials? Will you be equally sensitive to the treatment of racial or ethnic groups? Are you an active conservationist or supporter of the antinuclear energy movement? Will your position on such issues cloud your evaluation of materials presenting different views? A purpose of the collection is to fulfill the needs of all individuals in the school. If you sense that your personal views are outweighing your professional judgment, seek other people's opinions.

A different type of selector's bias occurs when a media specialist orders a disproportionate number of materials in support of a program of personal interest. A media specialist who has a strong storytelling program may be tempted to purchase materials for the adult storyteller rather than for the child user. Another media specialist, an advocate of puppets as a major aid in helping children develop communication skills, may spend an unusually large amount of money on materials related to puppetry. Storytelling and puppets can be worthwhile components of the media program; however, the media specialist's chief programs and interests are not the only activities that the collection supports.

Next time you visit a media center, examine the collection. Can you detect any bias on the selector's part?

Summary

How a media specialist perceives the collection in terms of the concepts of core, base, balance, and objectivity will influence the decisions that will be made. Selection decisions reflect the media specialist's position on the issue of demand selection versus quality selection. Media specialists must recognize that their personal views on issues, such as intellectual freedom and children's rights, affect their professional activity. Keeping oneself informed about developments in the areas of intellectual freedom, the children's rights movement, and legal decisions will be a professional responsibility throughout a media specialist's career.

Above all, the media specialist should respect people (this includes children and parents), listen to them, and know himself or herself.

Notes to Chapter 4

[1]American Association of School Librarians, American Library Association, and Association for Educational Communications and Technology, *Media Programs: District and School* (Chicago, IL: American Library Association; Washington, DC: Association for Educational Communications and Technology, 1975), p. 68.

[2]Ibid.

[3]Kenneth I. Taylor, "Media in the Context of Instruction," *School Media Quarterly* 4 (1976): 238.

[4]Kay E. Vandergrift, "Selection: Reexamination and Reassessment," *School Media Quarterly* 6 (1978): 104.

[5]Carlton W. H. Erickson, *Administering Instructional Media Programs* (New York, NY: Macmillan, 1968), p. 63.

[6]American Association of School Librarians, *Media Programs*, p. 69.

[7]Laurence Pringle, "Balance and Bias in Controversial Books," *Appraisal* 12 (1979): 2.

[8]Ibid., p. 3.

[9]Two examples of articles and rebuttals are 1) Lillian L. Shapiro, "Quality or Popularity? Selection Criteria for YAs," *School Library Journal* 24 (1978): 23-27; Reactions: Jack Forman, "YA Selection Criteria—A Second Opinion," *School Library Journal* 25 (1978): 51, and "SLJ/Letter," *School Library Journal* 25 (1978): 2; and 2) Linda Silver, "Judging Books *Is* Our Business," *School Library Journal* 25 (1979): 35; Reactions: "SLJ Letters," *School Library Journal* 25 (March): 74; 25 (April): 3; 25 (May): 5; 26 (October): 66.

[10]Staff writers of *Fortune Magazine*, " 'For It Was Indeed He,' " in *Only Connect: Readings on Children's Literature*, edited by Shelia Egoff, G. T. Stubbs, and F. L. Ashley (Toronto: Oxford University Press, 1969), p. 51.

[11]Dorothy M. Broderick, *Library Work with Children* (New York, NY: H. W. Wilson, 1977), pp. 24-25.

[12]Terry Lynn Nagle, "The Case of the Offensive Nancy Drew," *Catholic Library World* 50 (1978): 79; "Comments": 80-81.

[13]Callie Israel, "Intellectual Freedom and Children," *Ontario Library Review* 56 (1972): 74.

[14]Jessie Birtha, et al., "A Bibliography: What to Do When They Ask for Nancy Drew," *Catholic Library World* 51 (1979): 69.

[15]Ibid., 69-75; Goodgion, Laurel F., "Who Done It (Besides Nancy Drew)?" *School Library Journal* 24 (1978): 34-35.

[16]Evelyn Minick and Judy Kurman, " ... And My Branch," *Unabashed Librarian* 18 (1976): 3.

[17]Lester Asheim, "The Public Library Meets the Censor," *Texas Library Journal* 18 (1979): 44.

[18]Office for Intellectual Freedom of the American Library Association, comp., *Intellectual Freedom Manual* (Chicago, IL: American Library Association, 1974), p. vii.

[19]Asheim, "The Public Library," p. 46.

[20]Ibid., pp. 46-47.

[21]Judith F. Krug, "Censorship—The Malady Lingers On: A Librarian Speaks," *Today's Education* 65 (1976): 48.

[22]Asheim, "The Public Library," p. 48.

[23]Pamela Ellen Procuniar, "The Intellectual Rights of Children," *Wilson Library Bulletin* 51 (1976): 163.

[24]Ibid., p. 164.

[25]Richard Evans Farson, *Birthrights* (New York, NY: Macmillan, 1974), p. 83.

[26]Ibid., p. 84.

[27]Edward B. Jenkinson, "Dirty Dictionaries, Obscene Nursery Rhymes, and Burned Books," in *Dealing with Censorship*, edited by James E. Davis (Urbana, IL: National Council of Teachers of English, 1979), p. 6.

[28]Ibid., pp. 6-7.

[29]Jenkinson presents a fuller description of their activities in "How the Mel Gablers Have Put Textbooks on Trial," in *Dealing with Censorship*, pp. 108-16. Other groups are described in J. Charles Park, "Clouds on the Right: A Review of Pending Pressures against Education," in *Dealing with Censorship*, pp. 96-107.

[30]Jenkinson, "Dirty Dictionaries," p. 7. A more extensive discussion of organizations precipitating censorship incidents is provided in Edward B. Jenkinson, *Censors in the Classroom: The Mind Benders* (Carbondale, IL: Southern Illinois University Press, 1979).

[31]Lillian N. Gerhardt, "Bias, Prejudice, and the Growing '-Ism Schism," in *Excellence in School Media Programs*, edited by Thomas J. Galvin, Margaret Mary Kimmel, and Brenda H. White (Chicago, IL: American Library Association, 1980), pp. 26-27.

[32]Procuniar, "Intellectual Rights," pp. 166-67.

[33]Jenkinson, "Dirty Dictionaries," p. 12.

[34]Office for Intellectual Freedom, *Intellectual Freedom Manual* (Chicago, IL: American Library Association, 1974).

[35]This endorsement replaced "The School Library Bill of Rights for School Media Center Programs" adopted by AALS in 1969.

[36]Intellectual Freedom Committee, Association for Educational Communications and Technology, *Media, the Learner, and Intellectual Freedom: A Handbook* (Washington, DC: Association for Educational Communications and Technology, 1979), p. 10.

[37]Ibid., pp. 12-13.

[38]Ibid., p. 14.

[39]Office for Intellectual Freedom, *Intellectual Freedom Manual*, Part 2, pp. 14-19.

Chapter 4 – Recommended Readings

Balance

Fast, Betty. "Looking at the 'Balanced' Collection." *Wilson Library Bulletin* 50 (1976): 370-71. Also in *Excellence in School Media Programs*, edited by Thomas J. Galvin, Margaret Mary Kimmel, and Brenda H. White, pp. 61-63. Chicago, IL: American Library Association, 1980.

Pringle, Laurence. "Balance and Bias in Controversial Books," *Appraisal* 12 (1979): 1-5.

Vandergrift, Kay E. "Are We Selecting for a Generation of Skeptics?" *School Library Journal* 23 (1977): 41-43.

Children's Rights

Bronars, Joanne R. "Children's Rights and Intellectual Freedom." *Educational Forum* 43 (1979): 290-98.

"Children's Rights: Education and Legal Issues, a Symposium." *Interchange: A Journal of Educational Studies Published Quarterly by the Ontario Institute for Studies in Education* 8 (1977-1978): 1-209.

Clark, Geraldine. "Bureaucracy or Commitment?" *School Library Journal* 16 (1970): 25-26.

Donelson, Kenneth L. *The Students' Right to Read.* Urbana, IL: National Council of Teachers of English, 1972.

Edelman, Marian Wright. "What Society Does to and for Its Children." *School Library Journal* 26 (1979): 25-30.

Farson, Richard Evans. *Birthrights.* New York, NY: Macmillan, 1974.

Finley, Patricia. "Advocating Children's Rights." *Top of the News* 31 (1975): 305-307.

Kimmel, Margaret Mary. "Children's Rights, Parents' Rights – A Librarian's Dilemma." *School Library Journal* 27 (1980): 112-14. Reprinted from *Excellence in School Media Programs*, edited by Thomas J. Galvin, Margaret Mary Kimmel, and Brenda H. White. Chicago, IL: American Library Association, 1980.

Levine, Alan, and Carey, Eve. *The Rights of Students.* Rev. ed. New York, NY: Discus, Avon Books, 1977.

Michael, James J. "Children's Freedom and the Public Library: An Interview." *Journal of Clinical Child Psychology* 1 (1971-1972): 12-15.

Minudri, Regina U. "Irresistible Forces and Immovable Objects." *School Library Journal* 26 (1979): 39-41.

Procuniar, Pamela Ellen. "The Intellectual Rights of Children." *Wilson Library Bulletin* 51 (1976): 163-67.

Rodham, Hillary, ed. *The Rights of Children.* Reprint Series No. 9. Cambridge, MA: Harvard Educational Review, 1974.

Sussman, Alan N. *The Rights of Young People: The Basic ACLU Guide to a Young Person's Rights.* New York, NY: Discus, Avon Books, 1977.

Comics

Arlin, Marshall, and Roth, Garry. "Pupils' Use of Time While Reading Comics and Books." *American Educational Research Journal* 15 (1978): 201-16.

"Code of the Comics Magazine Association of America, Inc." *Unabashed Librarian* No. 18 (1976): 4-6.

Dorrell, Larry, and Carroll, eds. "Spider-Man at the Library." *School Library Journal* 27 (1981): 17-19.

Eisner, Will. "Comic Books in the Library." *School Library Journal* 21 (1974): 75-79.

Goodgion, Laurel. " 'Holy Bookshelves!' Comics in the Children's Room." *School Library Journal* 23 (1977): 37-39. Also in *Young Adult Literature in the 1970s*, edited by Jana Varlejs, pp. 345-49. Metuchen, NJ: Scarecrow Press, 1978.

Mazer, Norma Fox. "Comics, Cokes, and Censorship." *Top of the News* 32 (1976): 167-70. Also in *Young Adult Literature of the 70's*, edited by Jana Varlejs, pp. 211-14. Metuchen, NJ: Scarecrow Press, 1978.

Demand versus Quality Selection

Asheim, Lester. "The Professional Decision." In *2 Library Lectures.* Kansas State Teachers College, 1959. Also in *Background Readings in Building Library Collections*, edited by Phyllis Van Orden and Edith B. Phillips, pp. 9-18. 2nd ed. Metuchen, NJ: Scarecrow Press, 1979.

Birtha, Jessie; Carson, Sheila; Corlies, Frances; and Swarr, Patricia. "What to Do When They Ask for Nancy Drew." *Catholic Library World* 51 (1979): 69-75.

Broderick, Dorothy M. *Library Work with Children.* New York, NY: H. W. Wilson, 1977.

Goodgion, Laurel. "Who Done It (Besides Nancy Drew)?" *School Library Journal* 24 (1978): 34-35.

Israel, Callie. "Intellectual Freedom and Children." *Ontario Library Review* 56 (June 1972): 73-74.

Nagle, Terry Lynn. "The Case of the Offensive Nancy Drew." *Catholic Library World* 50 (1978): 79.

Shapiro, Lillian L. "Quality or Popularity? Selection Criteria for YAs." *School Library Journal* 24 (1978): 23-27; Reactions: Jack Forman, "YA Selection Criteria—a Second Opinion." *School Library Journal* 25 (1978): 51; "SLJ/Letters." *School Library Journal* 25 (1978): 2.

Sheviak, Margaret T. "Which Treats of the Importance of Worthwhile Children's Literature." *Hoosier School Libraries* 14 (1974): 12-15.

Silver, Linda. "Judging Books *Is* Our Business." *School Library Journal* 25 (1979): 35. "SLJ Letters." *School Library Journal* 25 March: 74; 25 April: 3; 25 May: 5; 26 October: 66.

Soderbergh, Peter A. "The Stratemeyer Strain: Educators and the Juvenile Series Book, 1900-1980." In *Only Connect*, edited by Shelia Egoff, G. T. Stubbs, and L. F. Ashley, pp. 63-73. 2nd ed. New York, NY: Oxford University Press, 1980.

Staff Writers of *Fortune Magazine.* " 'For It Was Indeed He.' " In *Only Connect: Readings on Children's Literature*, edited by Shelia Egoff, G. T. Stubbs, and L. F. Ashley, pp. 41-61. Toronto: Oxford University Press, 1969.

Intellectual Freedom

Broderick, Dorothy M. "Intellectual Freedom and Young Adults." *Drexel Library Quarterly* 14 (1978): 65-77.

Broderick, Dorothy M. "Racism, Sexism, Intellectual Freedom, and Youth Librarians." *PLA Bulletin* 31 (1976): 122-25, 152.

Cormier, Robert. "The Cormier Novels: The Cheerful Side of Controversy." *Catholic Library World* 50 (1978): 6-7.

Coughlan, Margaret. "Guardians of the Young ... " *Top of the News* 33 (1977): 137-48.

Cox, C. Benjamin. *The Censorship Game and How to Play It.* Bulletin 50. Arlington, VA: National Council for the Social Studies, 1977.

Darling, Richard. "Access, Intellectual Freedom, and Libraries." *Library Trends* 27 (1978): 315-26.

Davis, James E. *Dealing with Censorship.* Urbana, IL: National Council of Teachers of English, 1979.

Donelson, Ken. "Ruminating and Rambling: The Censorship of Non-print Media Comes to the English Classroom." *English Journal* 62 (1973): 1226-27.

Eaglen, Audrey B. "The 'Warning Bookmark': Selection Aid or Censorship?" *Library Acquisitions: Practice and Theory* 3 (1979): 65-71.

Fraenek, Jack R., ed. "Critique and Commentary: Censorship and the Schools." *Social Education* 42 (1978): 118-22. Includes Ken Carlson, "Censorship Schould Be a Public Not a Professional Decision," and David T. Naylor, "Censorship in Our Schools: The Need for a Democratic Perspective."

Gerhardt, Lillian N. "Bias, Prejudice, and the Growing '-Ism' Schism." In *Excellence in School Media Programs*, edited by Thomas J. Galvin, Margaret Mary Kimmel, and Brenda H. White, pp. 23-31. Chicago, IL: American Library Association, 1980.

Gerhardt, Lillian N. "Who's in Charge of School Libraries? A Commentary." *School Library Journal* 23 (1976): 27-28.

Harvey, James A., ed. "Intellectual Freedom and School Libraries: An In-depth Case Study." Theme Issue. *School Media Quarterly* 1 (1973): 111-35.

Hentoff, Nat. *The First Freedom: The Tumultuous History of Free Speech in America.* New York, NY: Delacorte, 1980.

Intellectual Freedom Committee. *Media, the Learner, and Intellectual Freedom: A Handbook.* Washington, DC: Association for Educational Communications and Technology, 1979.

Jenkinson, Edward B. *Censors in the Classroom: The Mind Benders.* Carbondale, IL: Southern Illinois University Press, 1979.

Jenkinson, Edward B. "Organized Censors Rarely Rest: A Special Issue on Censorship." Theme Issue. *Indiana English* 1 (1977). Reprint available from the National Council of Teachers of English.

Kanawha County, West Virginia: A Textbook Study in Cultural Conflict. Washington, DC: National Education Association, 1975.

Krug, Judith F. "Censorship in School Libraries: National Overview." *Journal of Research and Development in Education* 9 (1976): 52-59.

Nelson, Eva. "Why We Hardly Have Any Picture Books in the Children's Department Any More: A Brief Fantasy." *Top of the News* 29 (1972): 54-56.

Office for Intellectual Freedom of the American Library Association. *Intellectual Freedom Manual.* Chicago, IL: American Library Association, 1974.

O'Neil, Robert M. "Libraries, Librarians, and First Amendment Freedoms." *Human Rights* 4 (1975): 295-312.

Scott, Gloria Steinberg. "Paperback Censorship: An Idea Whose Time Has Gone." *Media and Methods* 11 (1975): 14-15.

Silver, Linda R. "Standards and Free Access—Equal but Separate." *School Library Journal* 26 (1980): 26-28.

White, Mary Lou. "Censorship—Threat over Children's Books." *Elementary School Journal* 75 (1974): 2-10.

Woodworth, Mary L. "Intellectual Freedom and the Young Adult" in *Libraries and Young Adults: Media, Services, and Librarianship*, edited by JoAnn V. Rogers, pp. 50-61. Littleton, CO: Libraries Unlimited, 1979.

Woodworth, Mary L. *Intellectual Freedom, the Young Adult, and Schools: A Wisconsin Study.* Rev. ed. Madison, WI: Communication Programs, University of Wisconsin-Extension, 1976.

Chapter 4 Bibliography

American Association of School Librarians, American Library Association, and Association for Educational Communications and Technology. *Media Programs: District and School.* Chicago, IL: American Library Association; Washington, DC: Association for Educational Communications and Technology, 1975.

Asheim, Lester. "The Public Library Meets the Censor." *Texas Library Journal* 55 (1979): 44-48.

Birtha, Jessie; Carson, Shelia; Corlies, Frances; and Swarr, Patricia. "What to Do When They Ask for Nancy Drew." *Catholic Library World* 51 (1979): 69-75.

Broderick, Dorothy M. *Library Work with Children.* New York, NY: H. W. Wilson, 1977.

Davis, James E. *Dealing with Censorship.* Urbana, IL: National Council of Teachers of English, 1979.

Erickson, Carlton W. H. *Administering Instructional Media Programs.* New York, NY: Macmillan, 1968.

Farson, Richard Evans. *Birthrights.* New York, NY: Macmillan, 1974.

Galvin, Thomas J.; Kimmel, Margaret Mary; and White, Brenda H., eds. *Excellence in School Media Programs.* Chicago, IL: American Library Association, 1980.

Gauger, Luica. "How I Use Comic Books Good at My Branch." *Unabashed Librarian* No. 18 (1976): 3.

Goodgion, Laurel F. "Who Done It (Besides Nancy Drew)?" *School Library Journal* 24 (1978): 34-35.

Intellectual Freedom Committee. *Media, the Learner, and Intellectual Freedom: A Handbook.* Washington, DC: Association for Educational Communications and Technology, 1979.

Israel, Callie. "Intellectual Freedom and Children." *Ontario Library Review* 56 (1972): 73-74.

Jenkinson, Edward B. *Censors in the Classroom: The Mind Benders.* Carbondale, IL: Southern Illinois University Press, 1979.

Krug, Judith F. "Censorship — the Malady Lingers On: A Librarian Speaks." *Today's Education* 65 (1976): 48-49.

Minick, Evelyn, and Kurman, Judy. " ... And My Branch." *Unabashed Librarian* No. 18 (1976): 3.

Nagle, Terry Lynn. "The Case of the Offensive Nancy Drew." *Catholic Library World* 50 (1978): 79; "Comments": 80-81.

Office for Intellectual Freedom of the American Library Association. *Intellectual Freedom Manual.* Chicago, IL: American Library Association, 1974.

O'Neill, Robert M. "Libraries, Librarians, and First Amendment Freedoms." *Human Rights* 4 (1975): 295-312.

Procuniar, Pamela Ellen. "The Intellectual Rights of Children." *Wilson Library Bulletin* 51 (1976): 163-67.

Scott, Jack Denton. *Discovering the Mysterious Egret.* New York, NY: Harcourt Brace Jovanovich, 1978.

Sigler, Ronald F. "Using EFLA's Intellectual Freedom Statement." *Sightlines* 13 (1979): 3.

Staff Writers of *Fortune Magazine.* " 'For It Was Indeed He.' " In *Only Connect: Readings on Children's Literature*, edited by Shelia Egoff, G. T. Stubbs, and L. F. Ashley, pp. 41-61. Toronto, ON: Oxford University Press, 1969.

"The Strongsville Decision." *School Library Journal* 23 (1976): 23-26.

Taylor, Kenneth I. "Media in the Context of Instruction." *School Media Quarterly* 4 (1976): 224-28, 237-41.

Vandergrift, Kay E. "Selection: Reexamination and Reassessment." *School Media Quarterly* 6 (1978): 103-11.

5

THE COLLECTION'S EXTERNAL ENVIRONMENT

The collection is not an isolated entity. Instead, it is one component of the media program, a program within a school that is in a district and a state. The school is also part of the local community it serves. Relationships with these components of the environment influence the collection program. For instance, financial support for educational programs may reflect many things: community attitudes toward the value of having a variety of information sources available to children, public concern about expenditures in a slow economy, or society's attitudes about the quality of education. Earlier discussion on the issues of children's rights and intellectual freedom pointed out significant differences of opinion. A later chapter on "Meeting Curricular and Instructional Needs" describes different viewpoints on what education should be.

This chapter examines characteristics of the collection program environment: the community, the district, and the state, including:

1. Information about the environment pertinent to the media program.

2. Sources for that information.

3. Implications of the information for the collection program.

Value of Knowledge of the Environment

Why is the relationship of the collection program to the environment so important? The institutions and people who use the collection have needs that the collection should fulfill. In addition, bibliographic records can make users aware of other information sources, both in the community and in external agencies.

The people in these environments are often responsible for establishing the directions, limitations, and strategies under which the media specialist will be working. Their goals and attitudes about education and information will support or challenge the media specialist's views. Their actions will influence the financial support and selection policies of the collection program.

"Power, Survival, and Betty Fast," Sullivan's essay honoring a well-known and respected school librarian, addresses the value of community awareness:

> She [Betty Fast] believed in knowing her community, and she knew it. Not everyone sees that so clearly and not every librarian understands both how significant and how simple it is. Community surveys, questionnaires, and a dozen other trappings of getting to know the community do not take the place of being alert on shopping trips in the community, reading about it, asking intelligent questions at community organization meetings, which might be those of parent-teacher associations or local business groups. There are sensible ways, and ways accessible to almost all of us, to find where the power lies. It is important to work with the community in terms of its own goals, and to relate library needs and goals to them.[1]

If you do not know the people who make decisions and set strategies, how can you communicate with them, or make plans that meet their needs? Your daily contacts within the school and the local community offer opportunities to discover needs, receive requests, recognize attitudes, and offer services. How well do you know the people at the district and state levels who will establish policies that affect your budgets, programs, and operational activities? Use your initial visit to the district and school to observe these environmental structures and form your own impressions.

Local Community

Beyond the school grounds lies a group of businesses, offices, factories, and residences full of people who have a vested interest in the activities of the school program — the local community. The term "local community" has two meanings. The first meaning refers to the area that surrounds the physical site occupied by the school, including adjacent institutions, agencies, businesses, and residences. A second interpretation relates to the area where students live. This may be the same as the first setting, or students may be transported to the school from a broader area.

How do you learn about the community? Generally, the five best sources are the school district, the local chamber of commerce, news media, governmental agencies, and the public library. All of these sources can provide maps, surveys, brochures, community profiles, lists of local activities, and directions to other information sources, such as planning councils or historical societies. The public library may have surveyed already the community's information needs and can share the findings with you.

If you decide to design your own community survey, be prepared for a major project. You will need to plan strategies, develop materials, collect data, and analyze results. Costs will be incurred for materials, telephone, postage, travel, personnel salaries, and computer services. However, it is easier and less expensive to create a community profile using information from the sources identified earlier. An overview, taken from secondary sources, may not be as detailed as a custom-tailored survey, but it is a good base on which to start. This summary of characteristics should include the items identified in figure 10.

Figure 10.   Information about the Community

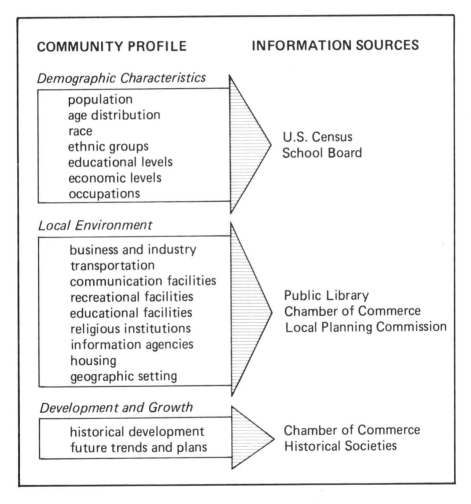

COMMUNITY PROFILE   INFORMATION SOURCES

Demographic Characteristics

   population
   age distribution
   race
   ethnic groups   U.S. Census
   educational levels   School Board
   economic levels
   occupations

Local Environment

   business and industry
   transportation
   communication facilities
   recreational facilities   Public Library
   educational facilities   Chamber of Commerce
   religious institutions   Local Planning Commission
   information agencies
   housing
   geographic setting

Development and Growth

   historical development   Chamber of Commerce
   future trends and plans   Historical Societies

How does this profile help the media specialist with the collection program? If you find that the community is composed of young families, they are more apt to support educational programs than a community made up predominantly of retirees. The educational level of the population may be a further clue to the willingness of the citizens to support schools financially.

Census data about racial, ethnic, and language backgrounds may indicate types of materials needed in the collection. If children come from Cuban homes, you will want to have Spanish-language materials. You may also want to incorporate Cuban folklore that parallels literature familiar to American children. In communities with refugees and immigrants, you will also need materials that will help the indigenous children and teachers understand the new members of their community.

Stability of the population also affects the collection. A community without an influx of young families may face the situation where declining student population leads to closing or consolidating schools. If you are in a school that serves migratory families, you may need to consider a change in formats. Children of inner-city factory workers or migrant workers may spend six weeks or less at your school. The family's decision to move may happen suddenly, outside of the child's control. In this situation, it may be better to select mostly paperback books and not fret about loss of hardback materials.

Even the child's home conditions affect their use of materials. Rosa, a third-grader, is responsible for seeing that her five-year-old brother and three-year-old sister are fed, clothed, and supervised. She is a good reader and likes to read aloud to her younger siblings, as well as to the children of another family who share the same apartment.

Rosa was only permitted to take out two books overnight. The media specialist felt that it was unfair to ask Rosa to keep track of books for a longer period of time: it placed an additional burden on this very responsible child. Rosa happily renewed her books or took out new ones each morning—giving her an opportunity to receive encouragement and personal attention from the media staff.

Contrast Rosa's experience with that of Liza, whose home has a live-in maid. Liza flatly demanded materials—then left them wherever she pleased when she was ready to move on to another activity. Until Liza's mother volunteered to work in the media center, she did not realize how conditioned her children were to having someone wait on them and pick up after them.

Other children may come from homes where religious convictions of the parents may affect the children's use of materials. The legal cases noted in chapter 4 highlighted a few examples of parental pressures on the schools—for instance, the case of the parents who opposed the use of audiovisual materials on religious grounds. In other examples, parents were opposed to specific titles. If these parents served on the committee to develop selection policies, their attitudes would conflict with individuals supporting the concept of intellectual freedom.

The community's geographical setting also influences the demand on the collection. To map a student's mobility, look at your community's transportation patterns. How easily can children get to the public library or other information agencies? Limiting factors may include the absence of mass transit, pedestrian walks, or bike trails. The children at Jefferson Elementary School had to cross two major highways to reach the public library. For the students dependent on bicycle transportation, their school's media center was their only source of materials for instructional or recreational needs.

The location of the community, its climate, and its recreational patterns also make demands on the collection. If students are active in 4-H clubs, Scout troops, or other activities, you will soon learn of these interests. Schools in areas where skiing, snowmobiling, or surfing are regular activities need appropriate materials in the collection.

Many communities support recreational and educational programs for citizens of all ages. Children may regularly attend functions in museums, zoological gardens, art institutes, and concert halls. These interests result in demands on the collection. The school may have a planetarium that is open to the students and the public. Certainly, this collection will need a stronger astronomy collection than a school without this facility.

Your most valuable ally may be the public library's children and young adult specialist. Questions you will want to raise are: What services do libraries and other information agencies offer to students? Is there a branch library near your school, or do the children use a bookmobile? Do school and public libraries offer cooperative programs or services? Can you borrow public library materials for classroom use? If so, for how long a period of time? Has the school established a procedure to alert the public library of forthcoming assignments? Do the two library systems share selection policies or plan collections jointly?

Principles of cooperation between media centers and public libraries can be derived from the attitudes and philosophy espoused in the following document, "The Ohio Children's Library Bill of Rights":[2]

The Ohio Children's Library
Bill of Rights*

With so much to learn in a time of tremendous pressure and with the great need in the future for social understanding, it is vital that children today have a wide choice of learning experiences, recreational pursuits, and meaningful adult relationships. To contribute to this choice, the services (some unique and some complementary) of both the school media center and the public library are necessary.

Therefore, it is declared that all children living in the State of Ohio should be guaranteed the following library rights from

SCHOOL MEDIA CENTERS

On the spot closely related current curriculum materials to satisfy curiosity generated by classroom activity (kindergarten through sixth grade) and to assist with research for assignments.

Print and non-print media, with appropriate equipment, to support and encourage the development of reading, listening and reviewing skills.

A production center to assist in the design and creation of new media and materials.

Professionally qualified media specialists, who organize, administer and interpret materials and services.

Personal guidance and individual understanding to increase skill in selection and evaluation of all media.

---

*Reprinted by permission of the Ohio Library Association.

Variety programming to provide learning enrichment and pleasure.

Individual and group instruction in the organization and use of the resources to develop increasing levels of independent selection.

The recognition of media center service as essential in the total education process to establish a foundation for effective use of high school, college and other libraries.

and
PUBLIC LIBRARIES

Access to books and other materials after school, Saturdays, and summer, with special *emphasis on voluntary use* for personal satisfaction.

The important *preschool experience* with books and storytelling to provide motivation for learning to read.

New titles and materials kept current and a collection widely diversified with *advanced adult materials readily available.*

Professionally qualified librarians to offer *reading guidance and friendly interest. Special service if exceptional in any way*—gifted, mentally or physically handicapped.

Variety programming to interpret materials and stimulate excitement for library use.

Leadership from library oriented adults (parents, teachers, university students, group leaders, church workers) who have expanded their knowledge of children's books *and from community agencies which have received programming assistance.*

The placement of children's literature with the mainstream of literature for all ages, and the opportunity to prepare for a lifetime of reading and learning in an ongoing institution.

Cooperation to strengthen the responsibility of each institution should be jointly explored through regularly scheduled communication concerning: book selection; sharing of materials and equipment; special programming; library orientation; workshops; book lists; publicity; teacher relationships; curriculum development; information exchange.

Annual evaluation of these library rights for children will promote a continuing effort for their establishment and maintenance.

Adopted by the Ohio Library Association Board of Directors
September 8, 1972

Local college and university libraries should also be visited. Their collections include reference works and other bibliographic tools that you cannot afford for your collection.

The Community as an Educational Experience

A useful guide to educational experiences in the community, *Yellow Pages of Learning Resources* (see Appendix 2), identifies a wide range of cooperative organizations and individuals. It explains how to contact citizens and representatives of institutions, suggests questions to ask and situations to observe, and describes the learning experiences to be gained. In alphabetical order, the directory covers accountants, airports, cemeteries, city halls, garbage men, junkyards, taxicab drivers, tree stumps ... all the way to zoos! Teachers can use this guide to plan field trips and invite guest speakers. As a media specialist, you will find guides like this a helpful reminder of the vast range of resources within the community.

A sample catalog card for a health food store might be organized similar to figure 11.

Figure 11. Bibliographic Record for Community Resource

```
Green Acres Nature Food Store / Ms. Eatright, owner. —
    Our Town (112 Liveoak Ave., 99999) : Phone 555-5555,
    9:00 a.m.—4:00 p.m.

    Audience level: 4th—7th grades.
    Ms. Eatright will visit classes to discuss natural foods.
Students, in groups of 12, can visit the store for an hour
tour that includes the sampling of food goods.  The store
can supply cookies made from kelp for the science units
on foods from the sea.
    Available everyday except Saturday and Sunday.


    1. Natural foods.  2. Seafoods.  3. Tours.  4. Science—
Community Resources—Stores.  I. Eatright, Ms.
```

Cataloging of community and human resources according to AACR2
by Doris H. Clack, professor of cataloging at Florida State University.

Additional information that teachers may find useful includes: preferred time and/or dates for field trips; resource people available at the site; time needed to travel to the location; types of experiences; charges; presence of eating facilities and restrooms; rules concerning the use of cameras and tape recorders; and the availability of preparation materials for use before the visit, such as films or slide shows.

The human resource listings can be arranged like community resource files. You may be looking for people with travel experiences, hobbies, collections, talents, or occupations. Some individuals can be identified through speakers' bureaus, extension agencies, and directories of local artists, authors, and illustrators. A sample catalog card might include items similar to those in figure 12 (page 80). Additional information you may want to list includes: cost, time needed to arrange for a program, and whether the individual can best be interviewed in the classroom or at his/her place of work.

So far, this book has covered the traditional uses of community and human resources: field trips, guest speakers, and interviews. Rosenstein, assessing the limitations of the traditional approach, suggests that students have a more in-depth experience by actually working with an individual. He claims that:

Figure 12.   Bibliographic Record for Human Resource

McPhail, Scotty.
    Coal mining experiences. — Contact through District
Media Center : Phone 444—4444, ext. 556, 9:00 a.m.—3:00 p.m.

    Audience level: 4th grade up.
    Mr. McPhail, who worked in the coal mines as a child, will
visit classes to describe his experiences and demonstrate the use
of a miner's cap. He will also bring and explain his model of a
coal mine.
    Available on Wednesdays and Fridays with a minimum of
2 days notice.

    1. Coal mines and mining—Human resources.

Only when teachers and administrators begin to perceive the
community as a learning resource for individuals rather than
entire classes will they really be able to exploit the local
community for meaningful educational experiences.[3]

To do this, he proposes that a child spend a day, a week, or even a month
in the kitchen of a local gourmet cook, the studio of a local artist, or the
construction site of a building.[4]
    Students may also use community and human resources to develop
an oral history of the community. Neuenschwander suggests that "a
chief use of oral history ... is to relate students' personal worlds to local
surroundings and society at large."[5] Students can interview senior
residents of a community and record their reminiscences of what school
was like many years ago. Things of interest to children provide a natural
starting place for such conversations. Just think of questions children
commonly ask, such as "What did you do for fun if you didn't have
television?" The tapes of such interviews can become valuable
resources for the historical section of the media collection.
    Children can also gather information about their community in
other ways. For example, Marie's third-grade class interviewed their
parents and grandparents as part of a statewide project of the State
Library on the founding of small towns. Using data sheets prepared by
the historical archives section of the State Library, the children queried
their parents as to how long they had lived in the community, why they
had moved there, and how far this was from their previous home. When
possible, children interviewed their grandparents, asking them the same
series of questions. Each child kept one copy of the report for his family
and the other was submitted to the archives collection and made
available to the citizens of the state.
    These examples identify only a few of the educational experiences
available in any given community. As you get to know local community

people, ask for their suggestions. Those at the school district and state level will doubtless have many ideas, but don't overlook the suggestions of your neighbors, students, parents, and everyone else you meet. The school custodian or cook may have valuable experiences to share.

The School District

A community's attitudes about, and expectations of, education are inevitably translated into policies of the school district. Awareness of the district's priorities can alert the media specialist to demands that may be placed on the collection. If the school board emphasizes basic education, be prepared to relate the media program to that approach; if the district emphasizes computer literacy, be prepared to meet that priority. If a curriculum area is to be reviewed, become involved. These kinds of decisions can be made by administrators, board members, teachers, or media personnel, but preferably by a combination of these.

By attending or listening to school board meetings, you will have an opportunity to see how the members interact and how they approach the issues. Find out the positions the board members have taken on matters concerning media programs. You will find that many school board policies directly or indirectly affect the media program. For example, the Montgomery County (Maryland) Public School has a policy that:

> Students must be actively involved in the learning process. Therefore, in each course and at each grade level, students shall be encouraged to participate in establishing course goals, suggesting interest areas, planning classroom activities, and in appraising the course. Student suggestions and recommendations concerning curricular offerings and opportunities shall be permitted at any time and shall be solicited by the professional staff.[6]

This Montgomery County policy is reflected in the following guidelines for the media program's use of the materials budget:

1. An advisory committee consisting of the head librarian, two other faculty members, and two students appointed by the student council will advise the principal and head librarian on student requests.

2. An allotment of 15 percent of these funds for new materials will be designated for student requested materials.[7]

The district's administrative hierarchy affects communication and decision-making. Determine what types of decisions are made at the district and regional levels, along with those made at the individual school level. Is the principal autonomous? Where do media personnel fit into the organization chart? Where do staff of special projects—perhaps those funded by state or federal programs — fit into the organization chart? Determine how you can participate in the decision-making process.

If you work in a large district with a central media supervisor, you may have little direct contact with other district personnel; however, in many schools this is not the case. Be assertive about establishing good lines of communication. When the central administrative staff visits your building to look into other matters, be sure to meet them. You may have to be the one to ask the curriculum coordinator for resources that would help teachers in your building.

The district teacher organization can also serve the media program. Are media specialists represented on the negotiating team? What media concerns are considered? Does the contract call for certain provisions on behalf of the media staff, collections, or production facilities? Does the contract address intellectual freedom or spell out who should be involved in material selections? Media specialists should not overlook the mutual concerns they share with teachers concerning working conditions and access to materials.

If your district has a public information office, it can help you track down information or publicize your needs to the community. The information staff has already developed contacts with people in the local mass media (newspapers, magazines, radio and television stations) and can guide you to those who can help. If you want to involve the general public in your development of policies, this staff can also help you.

The District Media Program

The district media program's history reveals important clues to the level and consistency of support for media personnel. Decisions at this level also determine the focus of both your services and the collection.

Before you are hired, you may be interviewed by the media supervisor or district media coordinator. When talking with other district staff members, a number of questions should be raised. How is the district media program administered? Is the district coordinator or supervisor part of the central administrative staff? What services are offered by the district media center? In a highly developed system, these services may include centralized ordering and processing, an examination collection, a district professional collection, special production facilities and equipment, repair services, delivery services, or a film library. Is there a district-wide manual or policy handbook? Are consultant services provided? What roles do the district media personnel play in determining budgets? Are in-service programs provided for media personnel? By learning answers to these questions, you can identify the magnitude of your responsibilities and identify the services you can expect from others.

Another group of questions relates to how materials are selected and made accessible to students and teachers. Are selection committees appointed on a district-level basis, rather than at the building level? How does one become a member of the district selection committee? If an "approved list" is used for purchasing, ask how you can purchase items not on that list. Are there delivery services between buildings and the district center? What interlibrary loan procedures have been established? The answers to this set of questions reveal the control you have over selection and the ease with which you can borrow materials from other collections. In examining these relationships, you can learn how much you and the collection can or must depend upon the district organization.

The State

Another crucial relationship is that between school and state. School goals and objectives reflect broad guidelines developed by the state. Frequently, legislators encourage certain educational goals. For example, the Wisconsin Legislature enacted in Chapter 121.02(j) that:

> as of July 1, 1975 all school districts shall "provide adequate instructional materials, texts and library services which reflect the cultural diversity and pluralistic nature of American society."[8]

This is implemented, as follows, through Wisconsin's Administrative Code for schools:

> All students shall be provided access to a current, balanced collection of books, basic reference materials, texts, periodicals, and audiovisual materials which depict in an accurate and unbiased way the cultural diversity and pluralistic nature of American society.[9]

An analysis of the administrative code reveals the identification of the general types of materials to be found in collections, a requirement that materials be recent and suggested criteria by which materials should be judged.

Similar legislation may exist within your state. Your district supervisor or the state-level school media supervisor/consultant can provide this information. The latter position may be in the State Department of Education (or Public Instruction) or in the State Library. Your state media association can also provide information about efforts to create legislative change.

When you contact the state consultant or media association, inquire about the publications they produce. Examples of the type of information you can obtain this way are illustrated by the following documents. The Pennsylvania School Librarians Association's publication, *The Pennsylvania Guide for School Library Media Specialists*, includes facts about school libraries in that state and offers helpful suggestions on a wide range of topics. The Florida Department of Education's *Media Handbook* includes state standards for school media centers, sample policies and forms, as well as advice about other aspects of the media program.

The state consultant and the association are two contact points for keeping up-to-date on services, programs, legislation, and standards. Your involvement in these activities is an essential part of your professional role.

Summary

The degree to which the media specialist can make information accessible to students will be dependent upon the environment in which he or she must operate. The community's attitude toward funding education will have a direct bearing on the number of dollars media specialists have to spend. The community's attitude toward education and perception of the appropriateness of information sources can influence the choice of materials and formats. One community may recognize that children learn through their senses and need materials in a variety of formats. Another community may think that such materials are frills and not needed for learning to take place.

The community's attitudes about education, children's rights, and intellectual freedom will be reflected in the policies of the board of education. The media collection, as a part of that school system, must operate within the guidelines of such policies. As you carry out your responsibilities as a media specialist, learn where decisions are made, by whom, and how you can participate.

You can participate! Your position should afford you opportunities to participate in many activities within your school district. Your memberships and participation in local, county, state, and national associations will provide further opportunities to participate in and to hear of changes that will affect your collection.

Notes to Chapter 5

[1]Peggy Sullivan, "Power, Survival and Betty Fast," in Thomas J. Galvin, Margaret Mary Kimmel, and Brenda H. White, eds., *Excellence in School Media Programs* (Chicago, IL: American Library Association, 1980), p. 223.

[2]*Cooperation: A Bibliography of School-Public Library Relations* (Columbus, OH: Ohio Library Association, n.d.), pp. 12-13.

[3]Irving Rosenstein, "Using Community Resources," *Educational Leadership* 30 (1972): 129.

[4]Ibid.

[5]John A. Neuenschwander, *Oral History as a Teaching Approach*, Developments in Classroom Instruction Series (Washington, DC: National Education Association, 1976), p. 37.

[6]Montgomery County Public School, *Evaluation and Selection of Instructional Materials and Equipment* (Rockville, MD: Department of

Educational Media and Technology—Evaluation and Selection, Summer 1974), p. 3.

[7]Ibid., p. 7.

[8]"Long-range Plan for School Library Media Program Development," *Wisconsin Library Bulletin* 72 (1976): 231.

[9]Ibid.

Chapter 5 Bibliography

Committee on Outreach Programs for Young Adults. Youth Services Division. American Library Association. *Look, Listen, Explain: Developing Community Library Services for Young Adults.* Chicago, IL: American Library Association, 1975.

Gerhardt, Lillian N. "Children's Access to Public Library Services: Prince George's County Memorial Public Library, Maryland, 1980." *Library Quarterly* 51 (1981): 20-37.

Gotsick, Priscilla. *Assessing Community Information and Service Needs.* Public Library Training Institutes, Library Service Guide 2. Morehead, KY: Appalachian Adult Education Center, Morehead State University, November 1974.

Kunz, Arthur H. "The Use of Data Gathering Instruments in Library Planning." *Library Trends* 24 (1976): 459-72.

Lyman, Helen Huguenor. *Literacy and the Nation's Libraries.* Chicago, IL: American Library Association, 1977.

Neuenschwander, John A. *Oral History as a Teaching Approach.* Developments in Classroom Instruction Series. Washington, DC: National Education Association, 1976.

Palmour, Vernon E.; Bellassai, Marcia C.; and DeWath, Nancy V. *A Planning Process for Public Libraries.* Chicago, IL: American Library Association, 1980.

Prostano, Emanuel T., and Prostano, Joyce S. *The School Library Media Center.* Littleton, CO: Libraries Unlimited, 1971.

Rosenstein, Irving. "Using Community Resources." *Educational Leadership* 30 (1972): 128-30.

Sullivan, Peggy. "Power, Survival, and Betty Fast." In *Excellence in School Media Programs*, edited by Thomas J. Galvin, Margaret Mary Kimmel, and Brenda H. White. Chicago, IL: American Library Association, 1980.

Wurman, Richard Saul, ed. *Yellow Pages of Learning Resources.* Cambridge, MA: MIT Press, 1972.

Young Women's Christian Association of the USA. Bureau of Research and Program Resources. *Look beneath the Surface of the Community.* New York, NY: National Board of the Young Women's Christian Association of the USA, 1968.

6
POLICIES AND PROCEDURES

How can media specialists ensure that the collection reflects the goals of the media program and the school? It is a major task to think through and articulate the answers to the "why, what, how, and by whom" questions involved in the creation and maintenance of a collection. By establishing policies and procedures, media specialists assign responsibility for selection, facilitate quality selection decisions, and help protect the teachers' and students' right of intellectual freedom.

This chapter:

1. Delineates the differences between policies and procedures.
2. Discusses the value of written policy and procedure statements.
3. Defines types of policies.
4. Identifies the elements of a collection program policy.

Chapter 7 will describe the steps involved in creating policy and procedure statements, present a model selection policy, and provide references to associations and agencies that can provide assistance to schools that are developing policy and procedure statements.

Differences between Policy Statements and Procedure Statements

Policy and procedure statements guide the activities of the collection program. Figure 13 illustrates the fundamental differences between policies and procedures. Policies explain "why" the collection exists, establishing the basis for all the collection program activities, and delineate "what" will be included in the collection, defining the scope of the collection. Procedure statements explain "how" policies will be implemented and identify "who" is responsible. Policies, therefore, need to be developed before procedure statements can be written.

Figure 13. How Policies and Procedures Differ

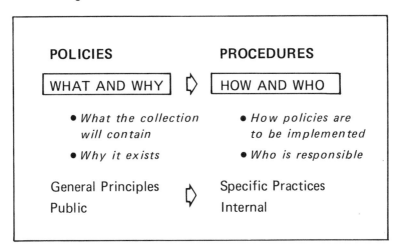

Policy statements should be issued separately from procedure statements. Many policy statements often include both policies and procedures without differentiating their functions.

Policy statements tend to be general in tone, moving toward the achievement of the "ideal" and allowing for flexibility and change. An example of the two types of statements can illustrate their different functions. A policy statement might read: "Materials reflect the pluralistic character and culture of American society." A procedure statement stemming from that policy may read: "Specialized selection tools, such as *Literature by and about the American Indian* and *Books on American Indians and Eskimos*, will be used and purchases made of items with two favorable reviews." This is very specific and should be revised on a regular basis so the selection tools provide current information about availability and cost of the items. The need to update procedures regularly is one argument for issuing the two types of statements separately.

You can examine documents entitled "collection policy," "selection policy," or "materials policy" to see if policies and procedures are properly distinguished. Questions you should ask include:

Does the statement address why the collection exists, or whom it is to serve? (a policy)

Does the statement explain how the collection will be created? (a procedure)

Does the statement explain in general terms what will be included? (a policy)

Does the statement explain how materials will be identified for consideration? (a procedure)

Your examination of existing statements will probably reveal that both policies and procedures are in the same document. The inclusion of both statements in a document entitled "policy" can be confusing and can necessitate more frequent updatings than is necessary when policies and procedures are in separate documents. Merritt elaborates:

> It is possible that two documents are needed: first, a general statement of policy for the information of the public and for use in controversy; and second, a more detailed internal document for the day-to-day guidance of the library staff. The two could be bound together for some purposes and used separately for others.[1]

Think of the policy statement as a public document. The policy states the library's goals, communicates the purpose of the collection, and establishes general principles for selection. The procedure statements are the library's internal document; they guide the day-to-day operations. Many authors who write about library policies frequently do not distinguish between the two statements; even sources quoted in this chapter refer to policy statements that contain both policies and procedures.

Value of Written Policy and Procedure Statements

Policy and procedure statements provide direction and guidance for the decisions made in carrying out the collection program activities. The assumption is made that unless the policy statement is written, it is an ineffective tool for directing media specialists' activities or for explaining our actions to others. This guidance is the chief internal reason for having a *written* policy statement and a *written* procedure statement. The *Intellectual Freedom Manual* addresses this point by stating:

> Why is written policy stressed? First, it encourages stability and continuity in the library's operations. Library staff members may come and go but the procedures manual, kept up-to-date, of course will help assure smooth transitions when organization or staff changes occur. Second, ambiguity and confusion are far less likely to result if a library's procedures are set down in writing.[2]

Did you notice how the above quotation combines policies and procedures at the same time that it describes their differences? The point to remember is that written policy and procedure statements can guide the internal operations of the library.

Another reason for having a written policy statement is to communicate with others the reason for inclusion of materials in the collection. In cases where materials in the collection are challenged as inappropriate, the presence of a policy that has been carefully developed and fully adopted by the proper body can serve as a defense of their inclusion. The *American School Board Journal* advised its readers:

> Don't put off writing policy until book banners swamp or wreak havoc with your broad meeting agenda. In the absence of a written policy, many of your district's books may be tried, not by lay and professional educators, but by headlines in your local press.[3]

Gerhardt reminds us:

> Experience can show very quickly that without a written agreement stating who is in charge of the library, the librarian's role in selection and collection management can be swept aside when a panicky principal responds to a parent's complaint, when any authoritarian superintendent of schools may, without discussion with principals or librarians, overreact to a single complaint, or when group pressure threatens to engage in title-by-title quarrels over library book acquisitions.[4]

A reason frequently given for the lack of a written policy is that developing policy statements is time-consuming. This reason is hardly valid when compared with the benefits of a written policy. Consider this expenditure of time against the advantages:

1. Promotion of the development of the collection on principles that reflect institutional goals and user needs, e.g., outlining the scope and coverage of the collection.
2. Establishment of general principles for selection decision, e.g., guidance for consistency in material selection.
3. Justification for inclusion of materials in the collection, e.g., defense of selection decisions for materials that may be challenged (or, are you ready to face the challenge of possible censorship without the support of the school board?).
4. Involvement of others in the process of developing what the collection is and is not, e.g., public relations.
5. Defense for budget requests.

Further reasons for the adoption of a written selection policy, as given by the Michigan Association for Media in Education, are:

1. A written statement will make it easier for all school personnel — teachers, librarians, principals, supervisors, superintendents, and members of the Governing Board — to be fully informed of the specific selection practices of the district.

2. The responsibilities of participating individuals and the limits of their responsibilities will be explicitly stated.

3. If criteria are clearly detailed, and techniques for applying them are clearly set forth, those persons responsible for doing the actual selection will do a thorough and efficient job. Written criteria will serve as a basis for common agreement for those responsible for the selection of materials.

4. The materials selected by such criteria and procedures will be better and more useful.

5. A written statement of policies and procedures is an aid in keeping the community informed on the selection of library materials. The confidence of the community in its schools will be increased by the knowledge of the thorough and reasoned philosophies and procedures underlying the selection of materials for its school libraries.[5]

Types of Policies

The problems created by trying to follow a combined policy and procedure statement are further complicated when combining three types of policies within one document, usually called a "selection policy." These statements often include policies and procedures relating to 1) collection development, 2) selection, and 3) acquisitions. Using the term "selection policy" for this combined document is misleading; collection development policy leads to selection policy and to acquisition policy as shown in figure 14.

"Collection development" refers to "the process of assessing the strengths and weaknesses in a collection, and then creating a plan to correct the weaknesses and maintain the strengths,"[6] according to Evans. A "collection development policy" provides a broad overview of needs and priorities based on the goals of the media program and school, offering guidance for decisions regarding the procurement of materials on certain subjects and identifying the depth of coverage.

The "selection policy" identifies the criteria by which materials are evaluated for inclusion in the collection and assigns responsibility for selection decisions. An individual item under consideration must meet not only the criteria identified in the selection policy, but it must meet the needs and priorities established in the collection development policy.

The "acquisition policy" addresses the most efficient process for obtaining materials. This policy must reflect both collection

Figure 14. Derivation of Selection and Acquisition Policies

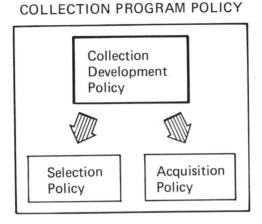

development and selection policies. The acquisition policy establishes the conditions under which materials will be obtained through a jobber, a distributor, or by direct order. For example, if an item meeting the criteria established in the selection policy were needed immediately, the policy would justify direct ordering or local purchasing rather than going through a jobber and receiving a higher discount.

All three types of policies may be combined in one document called a collection program policy. Many policy statements found in schools today emphasize "selection" policies, failing to recognize the importance of collection development and acquisition policies. A combination of the three statements in one document is not meant to diminish the importance of the selection policy but, rather, to stress that selection decisions should include consideration of the collection as a whole as well as consideration of the item itself. Labels for these documents vary from library to library. Regardless of its title, a policy should define the direction of the collection and guide the selection and acquisition processes.

Elements of a Collection Program Policy Statement

Collection program policies must be designed to reflect the goals and needs of the individual media program and its institution. To be effective and responsive to these specific goals and needs, policy statements must be created at both the district and school level. *Media Programs: District and School* notes that collection development should be

guided by a selection policy formulated by media staff, administrators, consultants, teachers, students, and representative citizens, and adopted by the board of education. The district policy is supplemented by selection and acquisitions guidelines formulated by individual schools within the district.[7]

Because of the diversity of building-level educational programs and the changing needs of users, no attempt is made to present a particular school's collection development policy statement. Instead, the following discussion illustrates various components of the collection program policy: the collection development policy, the selection policy, and the acquisition policy with a synthesis of the literature[8] on selection policy statements. This will be integrated with the "Guidelines for the Formulation of Collection Development Policies" in *Guidelines for Collection Development.*

The inclusion and arrangement of the elements of the collection program policy must be determined by the local group responsible for creating the policy statement. A document outlining collection development, along with selection and acquisition policies and procedures, might include:

I. Introduction

II. Statement of Philosophy and Goals of the Institution and the Media Program

III. Analysis of the Institutional Objectives

IV. Detailed Analysis of Subject Areas and Format Collecting, and Criteria for Selection

V. Policies for Acquisition

VI. Evaluation of the Collection

VII. Policies and Procedures for Reconsideration of Challenged Materials

I. *Introduction*

The introduction to the collection program policy statement establishes the uses of the document. This section may outline the theoretical and/or practical reasons for developing the policy; define the scope of the policy (for example, inclusion of all instructional materials, including textbooks, in addition to materials within the media collection); specify the audience for the document, staff, and/or public; state the reasons for publishing the policy; explain how the policy was developed and by whom. The policy should clearly state that the governing body of the district is legally responsible for the selection of materials and should record the date the governing body adopts the policy. The American Association of School Librarians provides an example of how a part of the introduction to a policy might read:

The _____ School Board hereby declares it is the policy of the _____ District to provide a wide range of instructional materials on all levels of difficulty, with diversity of appeal, and the presentation of different points of view and to allow the review of allegedly inappropriate instructional materials through established procedures.[9]

This sentence alerts the reader to several key considerations. It establishes the responsibility of the board, the criteria for selection, and the means to question materials in the collection.

Several writers, including the creators of the Iowa model[10] (presented in chapter 7), recommend that proposed policies be reviewed by legal counsel.

II. *Statement of Philosophy and Goals of the Institution and the Media Program*

This section identifies the philosophy and goals of the institution and the media program, creating a theoretical foundation on which the more practical sections will be built. Many schools endorse other documents in this section as encouraged in *Media Programs: District and School* when it states:

> The selection policy reflects and supports principles of intellectual freedom described in the *Library Bill of Rights*, ... , and other professional statements on intellectual freedom.[11]

Examples of this type of statement are reproduced in chapter 4. If the school or the media program has formal goal statements, they should also be reproduced in this section.

III. *Analysis of the Institutional Objectives*

This section recognizes the principles that will guide the growth of the collection. Much of the information included in this section will be a school document or will have been gathered through "knowing the community." Issues to be addressed include:

A. *Clientele to be served.* A statement of the grade levels, school-sponsored community programs, and children with special needs that are to be served.

B. *General subject boundaries of the collection.* A statement recognizing factors that define subject coverage; for example, limiting coverage to subjects within the curriculum or expanding coverage to subjects of interest to extracurricular programs.

C. *Kinds of programs or user needs supported.* A statement specifying types of subject coverage to be included in the collection; for example, instructional, informational, and recreational materials or those that support particular teaching methods, student organizations, or special user groups.

D. *General priorities and limitations governing selection.* This section provides an overview of the selection policy that will be developed.

1. *Sources of funds that are designated for the collection program.* A statement specifying the role of external institutions in providing funds or materials. Is the collection the sole source of materials to meet the needs of the school? Are instructional materials bought with separate funds? Are funds available from sources outside the regular budget?

2. *Forms of materials to be collected or excluded.* A listing of formats to be purchased or otherwise provided and a statement of the general restriction of subject coverage; for example, subjects or materials to be available in microform and whether supplementary textbooks are to be included.

3. *Languages, geographical areas collected or excluded.* A statement specifying foreign language materials or special geographical areas (for example, city or school publications) to be included in the collection. Policies in a school serving Spanish-speaking children will be different from those in a school that teaches Spanish as a second language. Even if a school doesn't offer classes in foreign languages, this statement should list any appropriate types of language materials.

4. *Other exclusions.* Are there other conditions or factors that will exclude materials from the collection?

5. *Duplication of materials.* A general statement of the circumstances under which duplicate materials will be obtained.

E. *Regional, national, or local collection arrangements that complement or otherwise affect the policy.* This section identifies the programs with which the school is participating and identifies its responsibility in those programs. For example, the district professional collection serves the needs of all teachers within the district; the individual schools will purchase specific journals that are shared among participating libraries.

IV. *Detailed Analysis of Subject Areas and Format Collecting, and Criteria for Selection*

A. *Identification of the types of materials to be collected for specific subjects and types of users.* For each subject, class of clientele, and program discussed earlier, identify the types of materials needed and the depth of coverage (collection intensity) that will be sought. This analysis should consider current levels of collecting and offer guidelines for future collecting.

A level of collection should be defined for each subject, type of user, and program. These levels of collection intensity (or priorities) are derived from the "Guidelines for the Formulation of Collection Development Policies" (see figure 15, page 96).

If at first these definitions may not appear to apply to media programs, consider the example of the school with the revised science curriculum described in chapter 3. In that situation, the priority for science materials was higher (see study level below) than the priority for other materials that may have been collected at the "basic" or "minimal level." It is unlikely that schools will collect at "comprehensive" or "research" levels, but they are included here to illustrate the distinctions between the levels and to encourage a standardized usage of the terminology.

To assign accurate collection intensity levels, the existing collection and the current levels of collecting must be analyzed and compared with what is desired.

B. *Identification of responsibility for selection.* A clear statement of the governing body's legal responsibility for selection, along with the body's delegation of this responsibility to certified library/media personnel, should be followed by a statement delineating who will be involved in the selection decision-making and what their responsibility is. In situations where the policy applies to all instructional materials, a statement should distinguish any differences between those responsible for text materials and those responsible for media program materials. An example of such statements can be found in the Iowa model (see chapter 7).

This section should specify who is responsible for selection decisions. Questions that should be addressed include: Who, other than the professional library/media personnel, will be involved in the selection decisions — teachers, administrators, supervisors, students, community persons? Will they work on a committee-basis, work with approved lists, or work independently? How is responsibility delegated?

C. *Criteria for selection of materials.* This section lists general criteria that apply to all materials under consideration, as well as criteria that apply to materials on specific subjects, for specific users, and in specific formats. Criteria in existing policies include: technical qualities; literary qualities; qualifications of authors/producers; controversial issues, e.g., sex, profanity, cultural pluralism, political ideologies, religious beliefs; intended use, e.g., textbooks, supplementary classroom materials, free materials, and replacements. Additional criteria will be discussed in chapters 8-14.

Figure 15.   Levels of Collection Intensity*

(Author's comments appear in italic typeface.)

"The codes defined below are designed for use in identifying both the extent of existing collections in given subject fields (collection density) and the extent of current collecting activity in the field (collecting intensity)."

1. Comprehensive level. A collection in which a library endeavors, so far as is reasonably possible, to include all significant works of recorded knowledge (publications, manuscripts, other forms) for a necessarily defined field. This level of collecting intensity is that which maintains a "special collection"; the aim, if not the achievement, is exhaustiveness.

Although this level is more intense than that desired or obtained by most schools, one might consider collecting school publications, i.e., programs, yearbooks, student newspapers.

2. Research level. A collection which includes the major published source materials required for dissertations and independent research, including materials containing research reporting, new findings, scientific experimental results and other information useful to researchers. It also includes all important reference works and a wide selection of specialized monographs, as well as an extensive collection of journals and major indexing and abstracting services in the field.

This level could [be] applied to a district collection supporting a specific research program.

3. Study level. A collection which supports undergraduate or graduate course work, [substitute "the student population"] or sustained independent study; that is, which is adequate to maintain knowledge of a subject required for limited or generalized purposes, of less than research intensity. It includes a wide range of basic monographs, complete collections of the works of important writers, selections from the works of secondary writers, a selection of representative journals, and the reference tools and fundamental bibliographical apparatus pertaining to the subject.

For the Fermi Middle School's revised science curriculum, this level of collection intensity was sought and all other subjects were collected at a lower level.

4. Basic level. A highly selective collection which serves to introduce and define the subject and to indicate the varieties of information available elsewhere. It includes major dictionaries and encyclopedias, selected editions of important works, historical surveys, important bibliographies and a few major periodicals in the field.

If we remove "historical surveys" from the above definition, we have a description of the level of collection intensity of most collections in the school

5. Minimal level. A subject area in which few selections are made beyond very basic works.

This definition describes the level of collecting for a school that wants to have a few works on a subject such as art appreciation, but does not include the subject in the curriculum.[12]

*Reprinted by permission of the American Library Association from *Guidelines for Collection Development* by the Collection Development Committee, Resources and Technical Services Division, American Library Association, edited by David L. Perkins, pp. 3-5. Copyright © 1979 by the American Library Association.

If reviews are to be a factor in the criteria, then the following should be considered for inclusion: "select and replace items found in standard lists and catalogs; select only those items that have been favorably reviewed in at least two review sources; [or] do not select anything that has received a negative review."[13]

The inclusion of a statement about a minimum number of reviews must be weighed against other considerations. For example, should a committee making a selection decision rely on its knowledge of the curriculum, the users, and the collection, or be constrained by a reviewer's opinion? If the priorities are clearly defined and the selection criteria is fully given, a statement about reviews may not be needed.

D. *Other situations.* This section addresses other situations that may occur when working with a school collection. Can teachers expect that materials will be procured solely on their recommendations? How much information or justification do they need to provide before an item will be purchased? Will the works of local authors/illustrators/producers be included when those works do not fulfill the criteria? Will the principal be allowed to make selection decisions without consulting the media specialist? Should criteria for equipment be established?

V. *Policies for Acquisition*

This section addresses the most efficient process for obtaining materials. A general statement may read "all materials will be obtained from the most cost-effective and efficient source. Preference will be given to using a jobber that can supply 80 percent of an order within 60 days." The same statement may go on to read, "when materials are needed sooner than possible from a jobber, such as when monies are received for a memorial gift in memory of a student, the media specialist may use the funds to make the purchase of appropriate book titles at one of the local bookstores." This type of exception provides a way in which the media specialist can procure titles quickly under special circumstances.

The policy may state "magazines will be procured through the services of a subscription agency, except for titles obtained through institutional memberships in professional associations or titles that can only be obtained through direct subscription from the publisher." If other types of materials, such as films or pamphlets, are to be obtained from a specified source or in a particular manner, the acquisition policy should address that.

VI. *Evaluation of the Collection*

To ensure that a collection continues to fulfill the collection levels established in the policy, provision should be made for continual evaluation. This review should result in the removal of physically deteriorated or obsolete materials. The policy statement needs to establish the criteria by which materials will be reevaluated; address the scope, frequency, and purpose of evaluation; and establish disposal procedures.

In some documents, the terms "weeding" and "discarding" are used as the heading for this section. This writer prefers the terminology "reevaluating library collections" because it emphasizes a positive approach to maintaining a collection. Readers may want to consult "Reevaluating Library Collections: An Interpretation of the 'Library Bill of Rights,' "[14] which addresses this function as well as its misuse—the removal of materials to avoid controversy.

In practice, elements of the collection program policy described above may be established at the district level rather than at the building level. However, the sections pertaining to the specific collection (such as the Analysis of Institutional Objectives; the Detailed Analysis of Subject Areas and Format Collecting, and the Evaluation of the Collection) must be developed to describe the needs of the individual building's collection.

If your school district has adopted either an overall collection development policy or just a selection policy, you will need to be familiar with it. Do the district policies reflect the goals of your school or the needs of your collection? Is your principal aware of the policy and its implications? When was the last time that the governing body studied the policy? Do additional guidelines need to be developed for your school to cover the collection development and selection activities? Policies need to be "reviewed at regular intervals to insure that changes in defined goals, user needs and priorities are recognized and that changing budgetary situations are confronted."[15]

VII. *Policies and Procedures for Reconsideration of Challenged Materials*

This section of the document provides directions for handling complaints, focusing the complainant's attention on the principles of intellectual freedom rather than on the material itself. While the position has been taken that policies and procedures should be in separate documents (policies for the public, procedures for internal use), it is recommended for this section that both policies and procedures be combined. This is recommended because the public is directly involved in the procedures. Sharing this information in a forthright manner can alleviate some of the tension that can occur in this situation. The American Association of School Librarians notes that this procedure provides for

> a hearing with appropriate action while defending the principles of freedom of information, the student's right to access of materials, and the professional responsibility and integrity of the certified library/media personnel. The principles of intellectual freedom are inherent in the First Amendment of the Constitution of the United States.... In the event instructional materials are questioned, the principles of intellectual freedom should be defended rather than the materials.[16]

In a recent national survey, three-fourths (75%) of the responding school media specialists had a written selection policy.[17] Unfortunately, the media specialists were not asked if they had a collection development policy, how long ago the selection policies were updated, or how they were used. How will the respondents who were without a written policy react when faced with a request for reconsideration of materials? The Wisconsin plan recommends

> the person expressing concern be treated with respect. Remember that such a person has the *right* to request that material be reviewed. Do not take the inquiry personally.[18]

Without a collection program policy, or even a selection policy as a statement of principles and the basis for selection decision, the media specialist would very likely feel that, indeed, the inquiry was personal.

Advantages of including procedures for handling complaints in the written statement are identified by *The Intellectual Freedom Manual*:

> First, knowing the response is ready and that there is a procedure to be followed, the librarian will be relieved of much of the initial panic which inevitably strikes when confronted by an outspoken and, perhaps, irate library patron. Also important, the complaint form asks the complainant to state his objections in logical, unemotional terms, thereby allowing the librarian to evaluate the merits of his objections. In addition, the form benefits the complainant. When a citizen with a complaint is asked to follow an established procedure for lodging his complaint, he will feel assured that he is being properly heard and that his objectives will be considered.[19]

To focus attention on intellectual freedom in this section, rather than on materials or personnel, many libraries reproduce the national statements endorsed by the school board in Part II of the collection program policy.

Other items to be included in this section of the document are statements establishing:

1. Who may register a complaint: a U.S. citizen, a resident of the community, a teacher, a student, an administrator, or a board of education member.

2. Who should be notified when a complaint is received.

3. Whether complaints must be in writing.

4. A form for the complainant to complete.

5. Procedures for handling a complaint when the complainant is unwilling to fill out the form.

6. A committee to consider the complaint. Questions concerning the committee that need to be addressed include: Who should be represented on it? How long will their terms be? How are voting members to be handled? Under what guidelines will they operate? Is there a specified time period for consideration of any one

complaint? Who is responsible for informing the complainant of the processing of the complaint and final action? To whom should the committee report its decision? The New York State guidelines offer this advice:

> It is recommended that the report be submitted to the Board of Education directly rather than to establish a hierarchy of appeal from principal to superintendent to the Board of Education. The longer the issue remains in question, the more potential exists for creating additional tensions.[20]

7. How challenged materials are to be handled during this process. Do they remain in use or are they removed? Arguments for keeping materials available are that intellectual freedom is being challenged, not specific materials.

8. "Whether ... materials will be put through the entire reconsideration process more than once within a specified time period."[21]

9. Whether an explanation of the final action should be reported in writing to the complainant.

10. Procedures for appealing the committee's decision.

Summary

Written and formally adopted policy and procedure statements are needed to guide collection development, aid in selection decisions, assign responsibilities, and guide acquisition practices. These documents aid in the protection of intellectual freedom by establishing policies and procedures for coping with requests for reconsideration of materials.

The collection development policy elements provide the broad overview of needs and priorities based on goals of the media program and offer guidance for decisions regarding the procurement of materials. Selection policy elements establish criteria by which materials are evaluated and explain how selection decisions are made. The acquisition policy elements address the most efficient process for obtaining materials.

The elements of the collection program policy are: 1) Introduction; 2) Statement of the Philosophy and Goals of the Institution and the Media Program; 3) Analysis of the Institutional Objectives; 4) Detailed Analysis of Subject Areas and Format Collecting, and Criteria for Selection; 5) Policies for Acquisition; 6) Evaluation of Collection; and 7) Policies and Procedures for Reconsideration of Challenged Materials.

Notes to Chapter 6

[1]LeRoy Charles Merritt, *Book Selection and Intellectual Freedom* (n.p.: H.W. Wilson, 1970), p. 26.

[2]Office for Intellectual Freedom of the American Library Association, compiler, *Intellectual Freedom Manual* (Chicago, IL: American Library Association, 1974), Pt. 4, p. 3.

[3]"Try Out This Model School District Policy on Censorship," *American School Board Journal*, 160 (1973): 44.

[4]Lillian N. Gerhardt, "Who's in Charge of School Libraries? A Commentary," *School Library Journal* 23 (November 1976): 28.

[5]Michigan Association for Media in Education, *Selection Policy: A Guide to Writing and Updating* (n.p.: Michigan Association for Media in Education, 1977), p. 6.

[6]G. Edward Evans, *Developing Library Collections* (Littleton, CO: Libraries Unlimited, 1979), p. 122.

[7]American Association of School Librarians, American Library Association, and Association for Educational Communications and Technology, *Media Programs: District and School* (Chicago, IL: American Library Association; Washington, DC: Association for Educational Communications and Technology, 1975), p. 62.

[8]Discussion is based on the following sources:
   a. David Perkins, ed. *Guidelines for Collection Development* (Chicago, IL: American Library Association, 1979), pp. 1-8.
   b. Evans, *Developing Library Collections*, pp. 126-34.
   c. Office for Intellectual Freedom, *Intellectual Freedom Manual*, Pt. 4, "Development of a Material Selection Program," pp. 5-10.
   d. Elizabeth Futas, *Library Acquisition Policies and Procedures* (Phoenix, AZ: Oryx Press, 1977), pp. xi-xvii.
   e. American Association of School Librarians, "Policies and Procedures for Selection of Instructional Materials," *School Media Quarterly* 5 (1977): 109-16.

[9]American Association of School Librarians, "Policies and Procedures," p. 111.

[10]Iowa Department of Public Instruction, *Selection of Instructional Materials: A Model Policy and Rules*, rev. ed. (Des Moines, IA: State of Iowa, Department of Public Instruction, April, 1980): 1.

[11]American Association of School Librarians, *Media Programs*, pp. 64-65.

[12]Perkins, *Guidelines for Collection Development*, pp. 3-5.

[13]Evans, *Developing Library Collections*, p. 131.

[14]Office for Intellectual Freedom, *Intellectual Freedom Manual*, Pt. 1, p. 31.

[15]Perkins, *Guidelines for Collection Development*, p. 5.

[16]American Association of School Librarians, "Policies and Procedures," pp.110-11.

[17]Kay E. Vandergrift, "Selection: Reexamination and Reassessment," *School Media Quarterly* 6 (1978): 105.

[18]Wisconsin Department of Public Instruction, *Suggestions for Dealing with Censorship of Media Center Materials in Schools: A Wisconsin Plan*, Bulletin No. 8232 (Madison, WI: Department of Public Instruction, 1978), p. 3.

[19]Office for Intellectual Freedom, *Intellectual Freedom Manual*, Pt. 4, p. 11.

[20]University of the State of New York, State Education Department, Bureau of School Libraries, *Selection Guidelines: School Library Resources, Textbooks, Instructional Material* (Albany, NY: University of the State of New York, n.d.), p. 8.

[21]Michigan Association for Media in Education, *Selection Policy*, p. 6.

Chapter 6 Bibliography

American Association of School Librarians. "Policies and Procedures for Selection of Instructional Materials." *School Media Quarterly* 5 (1977): 109-16.

American Association of School Librarians, American Library Association, and Association for Educational Communications and Technology. *Media Programs: District and School.* Chicago, IL: American Library Association; Washington, DC: Association for Educational Communications and Technology, 1975.

Collection Development Committee, Resources Section, Resources and Technical Services Division, American Library Association. "Guidelines for the Formulation of Collection Development Policies." *Library Resources and Technical Services* 21 (1977): 40-45.

Evans, G. Edward. *Developing Library Collections.* Littleton, CO: Libraries Unlimited, 1979.

Futas, Elizabeth. *Library Acquisition Policies and Procedures.* Phoenix, AZ: Oryx Press, 1977.

Gerhardt, Lillian N. "Who's in Charge of School Libraries? A Commentary." *School Library Journal* 23 (1976): 27-28.

Iowa Department of Public Instruction. *Selection of Instructional Materials: A Model Policy and Rules.* Rev. ed. Des Moines, IA: State of Iowa, Department of Public Instruction, April, 1980.

Merritt, LeRoy Charles. *Book Selection and Intellectual Freedom.* n.p.: H. W. Wilson, 1970.

Michigan Association for Media in Education. *Selection Policy: A Guide to Writing and Updating.* n.p.: Michigan Association for Media in Education, 1977.

Perkins, David, ed. *Guidelines for Collection Development.* Chicago, IL: American Library Association, 1979.

Taylor, Mary M., ed. *School Library and Media Center Acquisitions Policies and Procedures.* Phoenix, AZ: Oryx Press, 1981.

"Try Out This Model School District Policy on Censorship." *American School Board Journal*, 160 (1973): 44.

Vandergrift, Kay E. "Selection: Reexamination and Reassessment." *School Media Quarterly* 6 (1978): 103-11.

The University of the State of New York. The State Education Department, Bureau of School Libraries. *Selection Guidelines: School Library Resources, Textbooks, Instructional Material.* Albany, NY: University of the State of New York, n.d.

Wisconsin Department of Public Instruction. *Suggestions for Dealing with Censorship of Media Center Materials in Schools: A Wisconsin Plan.* Bulletin No. 8232. Madison, WI: Department of Public Instruction, 1978.

7
DEVELOPING POLICY STATEMENTS

The process of developing policy statements should involve a variety of people. As a media specialist, it is your professional responsibility to develop and review policies. Teachers, administrators, and citizens should also be involved in the process. This chapter:

1. Describes the steps in developing policy statements.

2. Presents a model selection policy.

3. Identifies other model policies and guides.

Steps in Developing Policy Statements

From the discussion in the preceding chapter, it should be apparent that policy statements, particularly selection policies, are rarely the product of one individual. A major benefit of a statement written by a committee is the members' advocacy of the principles on which the policy is based.

If your district does not have a policy, assume the professional responsibility of alerting your administrator and the governing body about the need for a policy. If a policy exists, but has fallen out of use, encourage a review of the policy. Ask the director of the district media program to coordinate the formulation of a district media selection policy.

If you are the only certified media personnel in a one-school district, it is your responsibility to develop a policy. The following steps, based primarily on recommendations provided in "Selection Guidelines: School Library Resources, Textbooks, Instructional Materials" (New York State Education Department)[1] and *Media, the Learner and Intellectual Freedom: A Handbook*,[2] will guide you in this important process (see figure 16). The process begins with the governing body as:

1. They decide to establish and adopt a selection policy.

2. They appoint an ad hoc committee composed of representatives of the school community. These

Figure 16. Process of Policy Formation and Revision

INITIAL PROCESS   ONGOING REVISION PROCESS

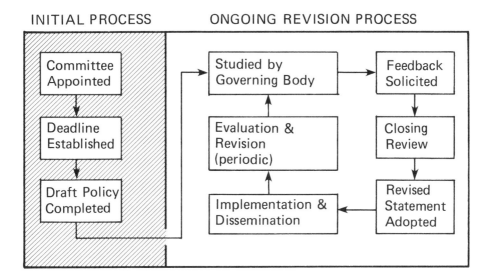

representatives might include parents, students, certified media personnel, administrators, and individuals from other libraries or educational agencies. If the policy is to cover all instructional materials, including textbooks, then subject specialists should be included on the committee.

3. They charge the committee with the responsibility of developing a selection policy, establishing a deadline for presenting its report and policy statement draft. General guidelines should be provided to the committee to facilitate its work.

4. The members of the governing body study the draft prior to discussion with the committee.

5. They solicit discussion and suggestions from legal counsel, from personnel within the school (such as department heads, curriculum committees), and from groups, such as parent-teacher associations and the teachers' association.

6. They conduct a closing review of the committee's recommendations and the comments expressed by others who studied the draft.

7. They adopt a formal written statement as the approved selection policy of that district or local education agency.

8. The governing body provides for implementation of the newly adopted policy. This involves disseminating the

policy to all staff members involved in the evaluation, selection, and use of the materials covered in the policy. A meeting or in-service program could be called to familiarize the staff with the policy so they can respond to any inquiries about the policy. Media personnel and teachers are likely to be the individuals who receive requests that materials be reconsidered.

9. They disseminate the policy to the community. The New York guidelines advise that:

    Activities [be] planned to make school and community personnel aware of the importance of the freedom to read, speak, view, listen, evaluate and learn.[3]

10. The governing body establishes periodic evaluation and revision of the policy. Policy review is recommended at regular intervals of one to three years. It is important that a review be scheduled on a regular basis.

11. Any changes are formally adopted by the governing body.

Sample of a Model Selection Policy

Since the selection aspects of the collection program policy are so important in communicating with the public and in handling complaints, the State of Iowa, Department of Public Instruction, "Selection of Instructional Materials: A Model Policy and Rules,"[4] is included here. This model was selected for inclusion because it 1) shows the format of a separately issued document and 2) clearly addresses the issues that must be raised in creating such a statement. Both policy statements and rules (procedures) have been included within the one statement. The committee's comments (see italicized statements throughout the document) alert the reader to questions or observations that those engaged in writing such a document must consider.

Bartlett, writing about the creation of this document, reports:

The philosophy of our endeavor was established early. Our goal was to develop a model policy and rules which emphasized the ongoing nature of selection, the assignment of responsibility for selection and continued evaluation by school staff members; and which provided for appropriate consideration and review of community concerns.[5]

The term "rules" is used throughout the document for "procedures."

Two of the unique features of this model are 1) the fact that the majority of the committee was composed of lay members and 2) that the committee operates throughout the year, not just in response to a complaint. Bartlett explains the rationale for the membership by stating:

The key to the success or failure of this model is the maintenance of a committee with a majority of lay members and a lay person as chairperson. Many persons ... have told me that appearances before review committees dominated by educational professionals [give] a complainant a feeling of futility. It is very important to establish credibility in the committee through a majority membership of noneducators.[6]

The rationale for the frequency of meetings, which establishes a sense of continuity and credibility, is explained within a comment section of the model (see IV.B.6.d.).

Drawing an illustration of how policies can be misused, Bartlett points out that Section IV.,

> Paragraph A.1. provides that most challenged materials will remain in use until the challenge has been completely processed. This is designed to aid in the elimination of harassment. If materials are removed as soon as an objection is filed, a person merely needs to file an objection to achieve his or her goal of censorship. In one Iowa school district, the absurdity of the absence of such a provision was shown, where in retaliation for the immediate removal of a challenged book, residents opposed to censorship filed challenges to the school's dictionaries and encyclopedias.[7]

Another potential misuse of such policies that unfortunately may even be practiced by media personnel and/or principals is addressed in IV.B.6.e. which

> provides the mechanism by which materials may be removed from use in a rapid manner. The committee intentionally made this procedure difficult to implement so that librarians and administrators could not arbitrarily remove materials from use after an objection has been made. In order to obtain the three-fourths vote of the committee necessary for immediate removal, the material in question will have to appear inappropriate on its face to a good cross-section in the reconsideration committee.[8]

Selection of Instructional Materials:
A Model Policy and Rules*

Introduction

For a number of years the State Department of Public Instruction has demonstrated its concern for careful selection of library media and text materials and for intellectual freedom for teachers and students. In 1968 the department cosponsored a conference concerned with censorship and selection with the Iowa Association of School Librarians. A paper developed for the conference, "Selection Policies for School Libraries," was printed and distributed by the

---

*Reprinted by permission of the Iowa Department of Public Instruction.

department. In 1971 the Department of Public Instruction began distribution of "Policies and Procedures for Selection of Instructional Materials," a paper published by the American Association of School Librarians. And in 1973 the department began helping with the distribution of *Intellectual Freedom Do-line*, published by the Iowa Library Association and the Iowa Educational Media Association (The Iowa Association of School Librarians mentioned above merged with the Audiovisual Education Association of Iowa to form the Iowa Educational Media Association).

Both before and since the distribution of these documents the department has advocated the establishment of selection policy and procedures to help achieve appropriate assignment of selection responsibility, and quality selection, and to guard against unwarranted censorship of materials.

Now the department offers its own model for such policy and procedures statements, emphasizing the ongoing nature of selection, involving assignment of responsibility of selection and continued evaluation by school staff members and providing for appropriate consideration of community concerns.

Local school officials and staffs have responsibility to provide this type of protection and assurance for the schools and communities. The model is intended to provide assistance to schools in developing their own selection policies and procedures. A common approach to the development of such policy statements is for a school board to appoint a committee to prepare a proposal for consideration and adoption by the board.

Model Policy and Rules for Selection of Instructional Media

It is of the utmost importance that a delineation be made between "policy" and "rules." Policy is that general statement of direction given by the board of directors to all concerned. Rule is that procedure developed by the school administration (and under Iowa law, adopted by the board) by which the policy is to be carried out. Rules detail the application of policy to specific circumstances. Proposed policies and rules should always be reviewed by legal counsel.

This model should not be presented for verbatim adoption. It is offered only for local consideration.

Model Statement of Policy

The Board of Directors of the _____ School District hereby declares it the policy of the District to provide a wide range of instructional materials on all levels of difficulty, with diversity of appeal, and the presentation of different points of view and to allow review of allegedly inappropriate instructional materials.

Legal Reference: Code of Iowa §279.8
Ch.301

Model Statement of Rules

I. Responsibility for Selection of Materials

A. The board of directors is legally responsible for all matters relating to the operation of the _____ school district.

B. The responsibility for the selection of instructional materials is delegated to the professionally trained and certificated staff employed by the school system. For the purpose of this rule the term "instructional materials" includes printed and audiovisual materials (not equipment), whether considered text materials or media center materials (media).

C. While selection of materials involves many people (principals, teachers, students, supervisors, community persons and media specialists), the responsibility for coordinating the selection of most instructional materials and making the recommendation for purchase rests with certificated media personnel. For the purpose of this rule the term "media specialist" includes librarians, school media specialists or other appropriately certificated persons responsible for selection of media.

D. Responsibility for coordinating the selection of text materials for distribution to classes will rest with the appropriate department chairperson or with the textbook evaluation committee. For the purpose of this rule the term "text materials" includes textbooks and other print and nonprint material provided in multiple copies for use of a total class or a major segment of such a class.

II. Criteria for Selection of Materials

    A. The following criteria will be used as they apply:

        1. Materials shall support and be consistent with the general educational goals of the district and the objectives of specific courses.

        2. Materials shall meet high standards of quality in factual content and presentation.

        3. Materials shall be appropriate for the subject area and for the age, emotional development, ability level, and social development of the students for whom the materials are selected.

        4. Materials shall have aesthetic, literary, or social value.

        5. Materials chosen shall be by competent and qualified authors and producers.

        6. Materials shall be chosen to foster respect for women and minority and ethnic groups, and shall realistically represent our pluralistic society, along with the roles and life styles open to both women and men in today's world. Materials shall be designed to help students gain an awareness and understanding of the many important contributions made to our civilization by women and minority and ethnic groups.

        Materials shall clarify the multiple historical and contemporary forces with their economic, political, and religious dimensions which have operated to the disadvantage or advantage of women, and minority and ethnic groups. These materials shall present and analyze intergroup tension and conflict objectively, placing emphasis upon resolving social and economic problems.

        Materials shall be designed to motivate students and staff to examine their own attitudes and behaviors and to comprehend their own duties, responsibilities, rights and privileges as participating citizens in a pluralistic, non-sexist society.

        7. Materials shall be selected for their strengths rather than rejected for their weaknesses.

        8. Biased or slanted materials may be provided to meet specific curriculum objectives.

        9. Physical format and appearance of materials shall be suitable for their intended use.

    B. The selection of materials on controversial issues will be directed toward maintaining a balanced collection representing various views.

III. Procedure for Selection

A. Media Center Materials (Media)

1. In selecting materials for purchase for the media center, the media specialist will evaluate the existing collection and the curriculum needs and will consult reputable, professionally prepared selection aids and other appropriate sources. For the purpose of this rule the term "media" includes all materials considered part of the library collection, plus all instructional materials housed in resource centers and classrooms (if any) which are not text materials. For the purpose of this rule, the term "media center" is the space, room or complex of rooms and spaces designated as a library, media center, instructional materials center or similar term. It may include units not contiguous to the center where facilities dictate. These units would include but not be limited to resource centers, production centers, and television studios.

2. Recommendations for purchase will be solicited from faculty and student body.

3. Gift materials shall be judged by the criteria in Section II and shall be accepted or rejected by those criteria.

4. Selection is an ongoing process which shall include the removal of materials no longer appropriate and the replacement of lost and worn materials still of educational value.

5. Selections are forwarded to the office of a superintendent or the superintendent's designee (e.g., the district media director or the business manager) through the principal or other person in charge of the attendance center for purchase throughout the year.

B. Text Material

1. Text materials committees shall be appointed at the time that text adoption areas are determined. Appropriate subject area, instructional level, and media personnel shall be included in each committee.

2. Criteria for text materials consistent with the general criteria for materials selection noted in Section II shall be developed by the text materials evaluation committee.

3. The committee shall present its recommendation(s) to the superintendent or other designated administrator.

4. The superintendent or the superintendent's designee and the text materials committee shall present the recommendation(s) to the board.

IV. Objection

A. Any resident or employee of the school district may raise objection to instructional materials used in the district's educational program despite the fact that the individuals selecting such material were duly qualified to make the selection and followed the proper procedure and observed the criteria for selecting such material.

1. The school official or staff member receiving a complaint regarding instructional materials shall try to resolve the issue informally. The materials shall remain in use unless removed through the procedure in Section *IV. B. 6. e.* of this rule.

a. The school official or staff member initially receiving a complaint shall explain to the complainant the school's selection procedure, criteria, and qualifications of those persons selecting the material.

b. The school official or staff member initially receiving a complaint shall explain the particular place the objected to material occupies in the educational program, its intended educational usefulness, and additional information regarding its use, or refer the complaining party to someone who can identify and explain the use of the material.

(Comment: The vast majority of complaints can be amicably disposed of in the first stages when the school officials and staff are frequently reminded of the school's procedures. A quick personal conference can often solve the problem where a shift into a more formal procedure might inflate the problem. While the legal right to object to materials is not expressly stated, it is implied in such provisions as the right to petition the government for redress of grievances.)

2. In the event that the person making an objection to material is not satisfied with the initial explanation, the person raising the question should be referred to someone designated by the principal or person in charge of the attendance center to handle such complaints or to the media specialist for that attendance center. If, after private counseling, the complainant desires to file a formal complaint, the person to whom the complainant has been referred will assist in filling out a reconsideration request form in full.

3. The individual receiving the initial complaint shall advise the principal or person in charge of the attendance center where the challenged material is being used of the initial contact no later than the end of the following school day, whether or not the complainant has apparently been satisfied by the initial contact. A written record of the contact shall be maintained by the principal or other person in charge of the attendance center.

4. The principal or other person in charge of each attendance center shall review the selection and objection rules with the staff at least annually. The staff shall be reminded that the right to object to materials is one granted by policies enacted by the board of directors and firmly entrenched in law. They shall also be reminded of ethical and practical considerations in attempting to handle resident complaints with courtesy and integrity.

B. Request for Reconsideration

1. Any resident or employee of the school district may formally challenge instructional materials used in the district's educational program on the basis of appropriateness. This procedure is for the purpose of considering the opinions of those persons in the schools and the community who are not directly involved in the selection process.

2. Each attendance center and the school district's central office will keep on hand and make available reconsideration request forms. All formal objections to instructional materials must be made on this form.

3. The reconsideration request form shall be signed by the complainant and filed with the superintendent or someone so designated by the superintendent.

4. Within five business days of the filing of the form, the superintendent or person designated by the superintendent shall file the material in question with the reconsideration committee for

re-evaluation. The committee shall recommend disposition position to the office of the superintendent.

5. Generally, access to challenged material shall not be restricted during the reconsideration process. However, in unusual circumstances, the material may be removed temporarily by following the provisions of Section *IV. B. 6. e.* of this rule.

6. The Reconsideration Committee

    a. The reconsideration committee shall be made up of eleven members.

        (1) One teacher designated annually by the superintendent.

        (2) One school media specialist designated annually by the superintendent.

        (3) One member of the central administrative staff designated annually by the superintendent. (This position will normally be filled by the supervisor or person responsible for the district's media services.)

        (4) Five members from the community appointed annually by the executive committee of the parent-teacher-student association.

        (5) Three high school students, selected annually from and by the student advisory committee.

(Comment: Subsections (4) and (5) represent a departure from the traditional approaches of handling challenged school materials and may well be the key to the success or failure of this model. A committee with a majority of lay members who are representative of the community should be viewed by the community as being objective and not automatically supportive of prior professional decisions on selection. Much of the philosophy regarding the committee structure was borrowed from the policy of the Cedar Rapids Community School District, Cedar Rapids, Iowa.

Use of the parent-teacher-student association in this model is merely illustrative. Whether the non-educators are selected from the P.T.S.A. or other groups interested in the community's schools is not important. The important thing is the establishment and maintenance of the committee's credibility with the community through a majority of nonprofessionals. The policy or rule statement should designate the lay group or groups which will select the community lay members to serve on the committee. An appointed committee will generally be more objective than a voluntary committee.

The method of selecting students for the committee will depend greatly upon the size and organization of the district. A district with several high schools may want to have one student from each on the committee while a district with one high school may want one student representative from each grade. Student selection of the representatives to this committee is very important. Any responsible student group or groups may be used when a student advisory committee does not exist in the district.)

    b. The chairperson of the committee shall not be an employee or officer of the district. The secretary shall be an employee or officer of the district.

(Comment: It is vital to the operation of this model that a community member chair the reconsideration committee. Credibility is the watchword.)

c. The committee shall first meet each year during the third week in September at a time and place designated by the superintendent and made known to the members of the committee at least three school days in advance.

d. A calendar of subsequent regular meetings for the year shall be established and a chairperson and a secretary selected at the first meeting.

(Comment: While many districts may not feel the need to hold regular, perhaps monthly meetings, it is important to establish a sense of continuity and regularity about the committee. The notoriety and excitement caused by emergency meetings when challenges arise in a community may be the unnecessary fuel to cause an ordinary healthy situation to become distorted beyond proportion. It is wiser to cancel unnecessary meetings than to call unexpected ones. Lack of frequent challenges to school materials probably means that one or more of the following is present: (1) satisfaction with the selection process; (2) lack of community interest; (3) belief in the futility of communication with school district officials; or (4) undue influence on the selection and weeding processes.)

e. Special meetings may be called by the Superintendent to consider temporary removal of materials in unusual circumstances. Temporary removal shall require a three-fourths vote of the committee.

f. The calendar of regular meetings and notice of special meetings shall be made public through appropriate student publications and other communications methods.

g. The committee shall receive all reconsideration request forms from the superintendent or person designated by the superintendent.

h. The procedure for the first meeting following receipt of a reconsideration request form is as follows:

(1) Distribute copies of written request form.

(2) Give complainant or group spokesperson an opportunity to talk about and expand on the request form.

(3) Distribute reputable, professionally prepared reviews of the material when available.

(4) Distribute copies of challenged material as available.

i. At a subsequent meeting, interested persons, including the complainant, may have the opportunity to share their views. The committee may request that individuals with special knowledge be present to give information to the committee.

j. The complainant shall be kept informed by the secretary concerning the status of the complaint through the committee reconsideration process. The complainant and known interested parties shall be given appropriate notice of reconsideration committee meetings.

k. At the second or a subsequent meeting, as desired, the committee shall make its decision in open session. The committee's final decision will be, (1) to take no removal action, (2) to remove all or part of the challenged material from the total school environment, (3) to allow students to use alternate titles, approved by school personnel involved, or (4) to limit the educational use of the challenged material. The sole criteria for the final decision is the appropriateness of the material for its intended educational use. The written decision and its justification shall be forwarded to the superintendent for appropriate action and to the complainant and the appropriate attendance centers.

(Comment: The state open meeting law should be reviewed for its application to this provision.)

l.   A decision to sustain a challenge shall not be interpreted as a judgment of irresponsibility on the part of the professionals involved in the original selection or use of the material.

m.   Requests to reconsider materials which have previously been before the committee must receive approval of a majority of the committee members before the materials will again be reconsidered. Every reconsideration request form shall be acted upon by the committee.

n.   In the event of a severe overload of challenges, the committee may appoint a subcommittee of members or nonmembers to consolidate challenges and to make recommendations to the full committee. The composition of this subcommittee shall approximate the representation on the full committee.

o.   Committee members directly associated with the selection, use, or challenge of the challenged material shall be excused from the committee during the deliberation on such materials. The superintendent may appoint a temporary replacement for the excused committee member, but such replacement shall be of the same general qualifications of that person excused.

(Comment: The committee should never be placed in the position of appearing to defend itself, its members, or the school staff. The committee must maintain a nonadversarial position.)

p.   If not satisfied with the decision, the complainant may request that the matter be placed on the agenda of the next regularly scheduled meeting of the board.

(Comment: These requests should comply with existing board policy and rules regarding the board agenda.)

q.   Any person dissatisfied with the decision of the board may appeal to the State Board of Public Instruction pursuant to state law.

(Comment: Subsections p. and q. are implicit and expressly provided for, respectively, in Iowa law. Some persons might feel that it would be more inappropriate to use p. and q. as they may encourage appeals. The provisions of q. would be applicable to decisions of AEA boards, area community technical college boards, and school district boards.)

* * *

FORM I

RECONSIDERATION REQUEST FORM
REQUEST FOR REEVALUATION OF PRINTED OR AUDIOVISUAL MATERIAL
(SUBMIT TO SUPERINTENDENT)

Item Description (fill in all applicable information)

Author _____
Title _____
Publisher or Producer (if known) _____
Date of Publication or Production _____
Type of Material (book, filmstrip, motion picture, etc.) _____
Request Initiated by _____
Telephone _____ Address _____
City _____ Zip _____
School(s) in which item is used _____

Person making the request represents   her/himself   group or organization
Name of group _____

Address of group _____

1. Did you review the entire item? If not, what sections did you review?

2. To what in the item do you object? (Please be specific; cite pages, or frames, etc.) _____

3. In your opinion what harmful effects upon pupils might result from use of this item? _____

4. Do you perceive any instructional value in the use of this item?

5. Should the opinion of any additional experts in the field be considered?
_____ Yes Please list suggestions if any: _____

_____ No
6. In the place of this item would you care to recommend other material which you consider to be of equal or superior quality for the purpose intended?
_____
_____

7. Do you wish to make an oral presentation to the review committee?
_____ Yes (a) Please call the office of the superintendent _____
Telephone No.
Please be prepared at this time to indicate the approximate length of time your presentation will require.
_____ No

DATE _____   _____ SIGNATURE

* * *

FORM II

INSTRUCTIONS FROM THE BOARD TO THE
RECONSIDERATION COMMITTEE

The policy of this school district related to selection of learning materials states that any resident or employee of the district may formally challenge instructional materials used in the district's educational program. This policy allows those persons in the school and the community who are not directly involved in the selection of materials to make their opinions known. The task of the reconsideration committee is to provide an open forum for discussion of challenged materials and to make an informed decision on the challenge.

The most critical component of the reconsideration process is the establishment and maintenance of the committee's credibility in the community. For this purpose, the committee is composed primarily of community members. The community should not, therefore, infer that the committee is biased or is obligated to uphold prior professional decisions. For this same reason, a community member will be selected to chair the committee.

The presence of the school media specialist and the administrative staff member on the committee will assure continuity from year to year and will lend professional knowledge of the selection process. Student members are essential since they are the closest to the student body and will be immediately affected by the decision of the Committee.

The reconsideration process, the task of this committee, is just one part of the selection continuum. Material is purchased to meet an educational need. It is reviewed and examined, if possible, prior to purchase; it is periodically reevaluated through updating, discarding, or reexamination. The committee must be ready to acknowledge that an error in selection may have been made despite this process. Librarians and school personnel regularly read great numbers of reviews in the selection process, and occasional errors are possible.

In reconsidering challenged materials, the role of the committee, and particularly the chairperson, is to produce a climate for a free exchange of ideas. The committee should begin by finding items of agreement, keeping in mind that the larger the group participating, the great the amount of information available and, therefore, the greater the number of possible approaches to the problem.

The complainant may choose to make an oral presentation to the committee to expand and elaborate on the complaint. The committee will listen to the complainant, to those with special knowledge, and any other interested persons. In these discussions, the committee should be aware of relevant social pressures which are affecting the situation. Individuals who may try to dominate or impose a decision must not be allowed to do so. Minority viewpoints expressed by groups or individuals must be heard, and observers must be made to feel welcome. It is important that the committee create a calm, nonvolatile environment in which to deal with a potentially volatile situation. To this end, the complainant will be kept continuously informed of the progress of the complaint.

The committee will listen to the views of all interested persons before reaching a decision. In deliberating its decision, the committee should remember that the school system must be responsive to the needs, tastes, and opinions of the community it serves. Therefore, the committee must distinguish between broad community sentiment and attempts to impose personal standards. The deliberations should concentrate on the appropriateness of the material. The question to be answered by the committee is, "Is the material appropriate for its designated audience at this time?"

The committee's final decision will be: (1) to take no removal action, (2) to remove all or part of the challenged materials from the total school environment,

(3) to allow students to use alternate titles, approved by the school personnel or (4) to agree on a limitation of the educational use of the materials.

The committee chairperson will instruct the secretary to convey the committee's decision to the office of the superintendent. The decision should detail the rationale on which it was based. A letter will be sent to the complainant and to the appropriate attendance centers, outlining the committee's final decision.

Other Model Policies and Guides

Examples of model policies or wording for policies can be found in a variety of sources. The following list provides a sampling of these sources and also indicates the types of agencies and associations that can provide guidance in policy development:

1. American Association of School Administrators, Association for Supervision and Curriculum Development, National Association of Elementary School Principals, and National Association of Secondary School Principals. "Censorship: The Challenge to Freedom in the School." April, 1975. 9 pages.
   Available from Association for Supervision and Curriculum Development, Suite 1100, 1701 K. Street NW, Washington, DC 20006. Single copy $.50, multiple copy rates available. Or from ERIC, ED 115 520, MF - $.76 plus postage.

   Includes the 1970 version of the American Association of School Librarian's "Policies and Procedures for Selection of Instructional Materials," examples of textbook evaluation forms, and discusses the use of complaint forms.

2. American Association of School Librarians. "Policies and Procedures for Selection of Instructional Materials." Rev., 1977. 8 pages. $.50 from the American Association of School Librarians, 50 East Huron Street, Chicago, IL 60611. 0-8389-6317-X. Reprinted from *School Media Quarterly*, Winter 1977, pp. 109-16.

   Provides guidelines for the statement of selection policies and procedures, includes a model policy. The appendices include "Request for Reconsideration of Instructional Materials (Sample)," "Checklist for School Media Advisory Committee's Reconsideration of Instructional Materials — Nonfiction (Sample)," and "Checklist for School Media Advisory Committee's Reconsideration of Instructional Materials — Fiction and Other Literary Forms (Sample)." Also includes a model for the selection process.

3. Association for Educational Communications and Technology. *Media, the Learner, and Intellectual Freedom: A Handbook.* Washington, DC: AECT, 1126 Sixteenth

Street NW, Washington, DC 20036.

Includes the AECT "Statement on Intellectual Freedom," describes the components of a selection policy, and provides samples of evaluation guides, reconsideration request forms, and checklists for the school media advisory committee on reconsiderations. Also includes listings of organizations and contacts for help in intellectual freedom matters.

4. Florida Department of Education. School Library Media Services Section. *Suggested Principles, Policies, and Procedures for Selection and Reconsideration of School Library Media Center Materials in Florida.* March 1976, 22 pages.

Includes suggestions, sample forms, and policy.

5. Michigan Association for Media in Education. *Selection Policy: A Guide to Writing and Updating.* MAME, 1977. 69 pages. Available from Executive Secretary, MAME, 401 South Fourth Street, Ann Arbor, MI 48109. Cost $3.50.

Some unique features of this publication are the samples of components from existing selection policies. An annotated bibliography and the full text of the National Council of Teachers of English's "Students' Right to Read" are included.

6. Kenneth L. Donelson, "The Students' Right to Read," 1972 edition. National Council of Teachers of English. Available from National Council of Teachers of English, 111 Kenyon Road, Urbana, IL 61801. Order No. 48174R, $.70 ($.60 for members); 3 for $1.50; 10 or more, $.35 each.

Although the statement is addressed to teachers of English, the advice is applicable to media personnel. Parts of this document are frequently quoted in selection policies or by other professional associations. A revision is planned for publication in the early 1980s.

7. NCTE Committee on Bias and Censorship, "Censorship: Don't Let It Become an Issue in Your Schools." Reprint from *Language Arts.* February 1978. Available from the National Council of Teachers of English. Order No. 05211R up to 14 free; 15 or more $.15 each.

Describes forms of censorship, factors to be considered in selecting materials, strategies for the classroom teacher in dealing with censors, sample complaint form, and ways to develop community support for a wide range of children's materials in schools and libraries.

8. The State Education Department, the University of the State of New York, Bureau of School Libraries, "Selection

Guidelines: School Library Resources, Textbooks, Instructional Material." The Bureau, no date. 11 pages. Address: The University of the State of New York, the State Education Department, Bureau of School Libraries, Albany, NY 12234.

   Offers advice about the creation of a selection policy and provides a model.

9. Wisconsin Department of Public Instruction, "Suggestions for Dealing with Censorship of Media Center Materials in Schools: A Wisconsin Plan." Bulletin No. 8232. Rev. October 1978. 16 pages. Available from Bureau of Instructional Media Programs, Wisconsin Department of Public Instruction, 126 Langdon Street, Madison, WI 53702.

   Offers practical advice on the provisions of public information and the use of selection policies and requests for reconsideration. Lists and describes agencies and associations concerned with intellectual freedom and the specific assistance that they offer.

10. Pennsylvania School Librarian's Association, Shirley A. Pittman, ed. *The Pennsylvania Guide for School Library Media Specialists.* 1978. Available from Shirley A. Pittman, 186 McIntyre Road, Pittsburgh, PA 15237. $5.00 plus $.50 mailing/handling per copy.

   This unbound guide includes a model letter to parents requesting their permission for a middle school student to read a specific title for mature readers; recommendations for and models of selection policies; and procedures for handling challenged materials. The guide provides information about selection criteria and covers many aspects of the media program.

This list of 10 sources illustrates the range of organizations and agencies that can provide assistance. As you examine guidelines or suggestions, ask yourself what application they have to your situation. Would you recommend their adoption for your school?

Summary

Involving others in the development of policies is important to assure students the right to read, speak, view, listen, evaluate, and learn. The media specialist has a professional responsibility to ensure that policies are developed and reviewed. The governing body has responsibility to develop policies and ensure their implementation.

A sample model selection policy was presented in this chapter to illustrate the types of issues that must be addressed in creating a policy. Such models should be examined for application to the local situation and used as a guide, not adopted verbatim.

Education associations and agencies provide other examples of model policies and offer guidelines for their development.

Notes to Chapter 7

[1]University of the State of New York, State Education Department, Bureau of School Libraries, *Selection Guidelines: School Library Resources, Textbooks, Instructional Material* (Albany, NY: University of the State of New York, n.d.).

[2]Intellectual Freedom Committee, *Media, the Learner, and Intellectual Freedom: A Handbook* (Washington, DC: Association for Educational Communications and Technology, 1979).

[3]University of the State of New York, *Selection Guidelines*, p. 3.

[4]Iowa Department of Public Instruction, *Selection of Instructional Materials: A Model Policy and Rules*, rev. ed. (Des Moines, IA: State of Iowa, Department of Public Instruction, April, 1980).

[5]Larry Bartlett, "The Iowa Model Policy and Rules for Selection of Instructional Materials," in *Dealing with Censorship*, edited by James E. Davis (Urbana, IL: National Council of Teachers of English, 1979), p. 204.

[6]Bartlett, "The Iowa Model," p. 212.

[7]Ibid.

[8]Ibid.

Chapter 7 Bibliography

Bartlett, Larry. "The Iowa Model Policy and Rules for Selection of Instructional Materials." In *Dealing with Censorship*, edited by James E. Davis, pp. 202-14. Urbana, IL: National Council of Teachers of English, 1979.

Intellectual Freedom Committee. *Media, the Learner, and Intellectual Freedom: A Handbook.* Washington, DC: Association for Educational Communications and Technology, 1979.

Iowa Department of Public Instruction. *Selection of Instructional Materials: A Model Policy and Rules.* Rev. ed. Des Moines, IA: State of Iowa, Department of Public Instruction, April 1980.

The University of the State of New York. The State Education Department, Bureau of School Libraries. *Selection Guidelines: School Library Resources, Textbooks, Instructional Material.* Albany, NY: University of the State of New York, n.d.

PART II

Selection of Materials

Selection sounds like a simple task, but it has far-reaching implications for the quality of education offered in an individual school. The needs of one person or program are often in conflict with those of another. For example, one sixth-grade social studies teacher prefers to have students collect data, analyze it, and draw conclusions. She wants materials that collectively present different opinions about topics. In another sixth-grade social studies class, however, the students need structured information with constant reinforcement. For these students, open-ended presentations are confusing. The two classes need the same content presented in quite different ways. Without sufficient materials of both types, the desired learning cannot take place.

Requests for information create conflict. The collection program policy identifies the priorities for the collection and offers selection guidelines. The media specialist has an item in hand and needs to make a decision. Who can use it and when might they use it? How will they use it? Does it duplicate materials already in the collection? Factors such as these must be weighed when making selection decisions.

If the media specialist does not know the teaching methods used, the goals of school programs, and the needs and interests of students, decisions may result in the expenditure of funds for items that are shelf-sitters. If the media specialist does not know the materials in the collection, decisions can lead to duplication. Without knowing what materials are available, items of limited value may be selected. It is disheartening to purchase an item and then learn about a better one.

The burden of selection is not the media specialist's alone; teachers, administrators, and students can participate in the decision-making process. But the media specialist is the one individual who knows the collection and the needs of the school and, ultimately, is the individual responsible for making wise selection decisions.

8
SELECTION PROCEDURES

In the process of choosing materials, a media specialist plans and carries out certain activities that culminate with the evaluation of materials. This chapter describes these activities, including:

1. Identifying and assessing evaluative information about materials.

2. Arranging for personal examination of materials through previewing, arranging exhibits, and visiting examination centers.

3. Involving others in the evaluation of materials.

Appendix 2 provides a listing of the tools mentioned in this chapter.

Overview of the Selection Process

Selection is the process of deciding what materials are to be added to a collection. Potential materials will be identified through many sources. Administrators, teachers, and students request specific items or types of materials; items in the collection wear out or are lost and need replacement; the specialist becomes aware of materials through reading reviews, seeing publishers' announcements, and previewing materials. People may also donate materials to the collection. These suggestions, requests, and gifts should be recorded in a consideration file.

The media specialist should record as much information about the item as can be obtained at this stage, including the identifying source. Check to see if the item is already in the collection and, if not, that it has not been ordered. Many libraries place a copy of the order slip in the card catalog by title entry to facilitate this procedure. At this point, obtain full bibliographic information.

Once an item has been fully identified, a decision must be made whether to include it in, or exclude it from, the collection. This selection decision is based on a number of considerations, including: 1) collection development policy; 2) budget; 3) selection criteria (content, format, and use); and 4) immediacy of need. Once a decision is made to select an item, its record is moved from the consideration file to the desiderata file. The actions following this step comprise the acquisition process.

Information about Materials

A rereading of the opening-day scene in chapter 1 reveals many requests for materials. Are there recommended filmstrips that present general information about light? Where do you find music activity records for kindergarten children? Which plays, science fiction titles, and mysteries are appropriate for Marie's fourth-grade class? Is there a film or videotape the principal can use for his talk on mainstreaming? These requests demand information about:

1. Specific formats: recordings, filmstrips, books, films, and videotapes.

2. User groups (audiences): kindergarten children, fourth-graders, and adults.

3. Subjects: light and mainstreaming.

4. Literary forms and genres: mysteries, plays, and science fiction.

This analysis of the requests establishes the necessary coverage of selection tools and suggests entry points for locating information within the tool.

Bibliographic tools are a basic source for this information. Two types of bibliographies will be especially useful. Trade bibliographies provide information about the availability of materials, such as *Children's Books in Print* and *NICEM Index to Educational Video Tapes.* The second type, referred to as "selection tools," evaluates materials and may include purchasing information. Two examples of selection tools are *Children's Catalog* and *Elementary School Library Collection.*

Whether you, the media specialist, use a bibliography to check if materials are available or are recommended, familiarize yourself with the bibliography by reading the introduction and examining several entries. These should indicate the following characteristics of the work, including:

1. The purpose given for compiling the bibliography: Is your need met by that purpose?

2. The extent of coverage: Does it include information on a variety of formats? Does it provide information for a large number of items, or is it limited in coverage? Does it include materials for a wide range of audiences, preschool through adult? What periods of publication and production are included?

3. The method for collecting the information and who is responsible: Who is responsible for writing the annotations? What are the writers' qualifications?

4. The criteria for inclusion of items: On what basis are items included? Are the criteria stated? Check the introduction for this information.

5. The information listed and format of each item: Is the information clearly presented? Are symbols and abbreviations used? Symbols may indicate levels of recommendation, reviewing sources, interest level, readability level, and type of media. What ordering and bibliographic information is given? Are the annotations descriptive or evaluative? Are all items recommended equally? Are items recommended for specific situations, uses, or audiences? Are comparisons made with other titles or formats? Are materials included only when they have received favorable reviews in other tools?

6. The organization of the entries: Are the indices necessary to locate an item? Do cross-references help you locate related items? Are there indices that provide access by author, title, series title, audience, level, subject, and analytics (sections of materials)?

7. Date of publication: Is the compiler's closing date provided? How often is the bibliography revised or cumulated? Are supplements provided?

8. The cost of the bibliography.

Examining the bibliographies in light of these general questions can provide you with information about the scope, coverage, layout, cost, and limitations of the tools.

Selection tools include an evaluative or a critical annotation for each item, providing:

1. Recommendations for specific items.

2. Specified bibliographic informaton for each item.

3. Purchasing information.

4. Access entries by author, title, subject, format, and even audience approaches to aid in locating recommended materials.

5. Analytical indices, appendices, or other special features useful in helping students and teachers locate portions of works that may be in the collection.

For example, analytical entires in the index to *Children's Catalog* are useful for locating materials on specific subjects and information about individuals named in titles. These tools are not limited to the selection process, as Johnson notes:

Too often the selection tools and review journals purchased by the school are viewed as the librarian's property, to be shelved in office or workroom shelves rather than to be housed and publicized for maximum accessibility to all users.... We need to invest more of our available budgets in reliable selection tools that can support not only the selection of materials but also, often, fuller utilization of materials once they are acquired.[1]

The multiple uses of these resources should be considered when justifying their cost and when deciding where to shelve them.

Selection Tools: Books

Selection tools exist in a variety of formats: books, reviewing periodicals, and bibliographic essays. Commonly used, general selection tools that appear in book format are *Children's Catalog, Elementary School Library Collection, Core Media Collection for Elementary Schools, Junior High School Library Catalog,* and *Canadian Books for Young People.* The cut-off date for inclusion in books creates a time gap between the publication of the last item reviewed and the publication date of the bibliography. As a result, books are not as current as reviewing journals. It is difficult to know whether a new title was not recommended or was simply not received in time for review in that edition.

Book format selection tools provide a means of checking recommendations on "backlist" titles, those items published or produced prior to the current revision. These selection tools are especially useful for checking if titles listed in the teacher's edition of textbooks are available and recommended.

Selection Tools: Reviewing Journals

Reviewing journals evaluate currently published and produced materials. There are a wide range of these journals, each with some unique and valuable feature. Reviewing journals are produced by publishers (commercial firms, professional associations, education agencies) and are aimed at a specific audience (media personnel or classroom teachers). The coverage of materials reviewed by journals may be limited by: 1) format: print materials, audiovisual materials, text and instructional materials; 2) potential users: children in kindergarten through sixth grade, junior high school students, preschoolers through adult; and 3) subject: all materials that may be in a media collection, or materials on a specific subject or curriculum area.

Reviews may be written by journal staff members or by professionals in the field, and it is preferable that reviews are signed by the reviewer. Reviewing journals may also include articles, directories, or columns of interest to media personnel. A sampling of journals and their unique characteristics can be found in figure 17.

Figure 17.   Characteristics of Reviewing Journals

JOURNAL	Commercial	Professional Association	Education Agency	Teachers	Media Specialists	Print	Non-print	General	Instructional	Practitioners	Journal Staff
Booklist		X				X	X	X			X
Bulletin of the Center for Children's Books			X			X	X	X			X
Canadian Children's Literature		X				X	X	X		X	
Children's Book Review Service	X					X	X	X		X	
Curriculum Review	X				X	X	X	X	X	X	
Horn Book	X					X	X	X	X	X	X
In Review: Canadian Books for Children			X	X	X	X		X		X	
Interracial Books for Children Bulletin		X		X	X	X	X	X	X	X	
Kirkus Reviews	X					X	X	X			X
Media and Methods	X				X	X	X	X	X	X	
Reviewing Librarian		X				X	X	X	X	X	
School Library Journal	X					X	X	X		X	
	Publisher			**Audience**		**Format**		**Use**		**Reviewers**	

Trying to locate two or more reviews on a current title can be frustrating. The problem is often caused by the limited number of items reviewed on an annual basis and by the time lag[2] between the appearance of the first review and one in another journal. Nemeyer and Paul report "that only approximately 10 percent of the books published in this country ever get reviewed."[3] Audiovisual materials, reviewed less extensively than books, can present even more difficulties. Figure 18 (page 128) shows the number of juvenile books reviewed annually by the major reviewing journals.

There are legitimate reasons why journals may not review a specific title. One journal has a policy that a work will not be reviewed unless it can be reviewed within a specific time from its publication date. It can be difficult to determine whether an item was received too late to be reviewed, was outside the scope of coverage, or did not meet some other criteria. Time gaps between reviews of the same work may be caused by policies of the journal. When practitioners write reviews, an advantage is gained by testing material in real situations, but time is needed to ship the materials to the reviewer.

Even if the media specialist is able to find the reviews, the value of the assessments can vary in quality or applicability to your collection. Note the position and geographical location of the reviewer to determine

**Figure 18.   Number of Juvenile Books Reviewed by
Major Book-Reviewing Publications, 1978 and 1979**

PUBLICATION	*1978*	*1979*
Booklist [1]	1,075	1,280
Bulletin of the Center for Children's Books	453	452
Horn Book	420	334
Kirkus Reviews	1,250	904
New York Times Sunday Book Review	319	300
Publishers Weekly [2]	562	545
School Library Journal	1,962	2,085
Washington Post Book World	50	137
West Coast Review of Books	110	78

[1] In addition, *Booklist* published reviews on nonprint materials: 1,906 in 1978; 1,534 in 1979. All figures are for a 12 month period from September to August.

[2] Includes reviews of paperback originals and reprints.

Source:*The Bowker Annual of Library and Book Trade Information,* 24th ed. (New York: R.R. Bowker, 1980), p. 447.

if his or her situation is similar to your own. The journal, *Appraisal*, offers a unique feature. Items are reviewed both by a librarian and a subject specialist. A comparison of reviews can offer more and better information about the item than can be obtained from a single review. Cumulated indices in the journals can be helpful in the search for reviews; but a more comprehensive approach to review indexing can be found in a tool such as *Media Review Digest.* The cost of such tools may require that they be shared by all libraries in the district.

Bibliographic Essays

Bibliographic essays describing materials on a particular subject, theme, use, or audience are another source of recommendations. These essays can be very helpful, but demand careful analysis. Some essays are written under the unannounced condition that only recommended items can be included. An omitted item may not be recommended, but it may also have been overlooked. Bibliographic essays usually focus on a specific component of an item and often do not provide an overall assessment of the material.

Reliance on Reviewing Media

Media specialists today regularly use reviewing media because they seldom have the opportunity to examine materials. The lack of selection committees in the schools places the entire burden of selection on the media specialist. To examine every item published or produced within a given year would be a staggering task. Belland writes:

> It is intriguing, then, to notice that both media program personnel and publisher/producer respondents ranked favorable reviews as being the most important selection factor. This would tend to imply that school personnel have neither the time nor the commitment to analyze materials in terms of a particular curricular need. They defer judgment to those persons who are professionally involved in reviewing a wide variety of materials.[4]

Vandergrift suggests one solution:

> Perhaps school media specialists need to allocate their school days more carefully to provide some time for reading reviews and previewing what materials are available, without worrying about taking time away from the students, or worrying that classroom teachers or the principal will think they just sit around on the job. An emphasis on selection will reap benefits for the entire school community, and it deserves more concentration than most of us can muster while sitting in front of the TV set at the end of a long, busy day.[5]

Belland goes on to point out if media programs are to be integrated with school programs, materials must be evaluated accordingly.

The review user must remember that reviews are expressions of the writer's opinion based on her or his knowledge of materials and children. Realize that whether you personally examine items or rely on reviews as you engage in evaluation, there will be occasions when materials, for one reason or another, will remain unused or be inappropriate; these situations will be learning experiences.

Information about materials can also be obtained from publishers, producers, distributors, and wholesalers. The information may be in catalogs, flyers, or other announcements and is not evaluative. These sources of information are discussed in the chapter on acquisitions.

Personal Examination

There are many ways to obtain materials for personal examination; however, the most practical ways include visits by sales representatives, formal previewing arrangements, and visits to examination centers, traveling exhibits, or conferences.

Previewing

Previewing is one of the most efficient ways to examine materials personally prior to purchase. This is the practice of borrowing nonprint materials from an examination center, a producer, or a distributor for a specific time for the purpose of evaluation.

Levy observes that this is both a privilege and a responsibility.[6] Previewing is the most effective way to involve students and teachers in the selection process. If there is a committee evaluating materials on a specific subject, make arrangements with several companies so their materials can be examined at the same time. When arranging previewing sessions, however, consider the needs and limitations of the committee.

In one school, teachers had expressed a need for filmstrips on the Civil War, so arrangements were made with several companies to preview their materials during a particular week. Throughout that week, a group including teachers, students, and the media specialist compared the filmstrips. Although this experience was an excellent opportunity to evaluate and compare materials, fatigue from overexposure to the same format and content was experienced by the participants. This problem could have been avoided by scheduling shorter viewing periods, such as during the lunch period.

Spirt suggests:

The media specialist need only set up a single plan with the approval of the principal, chief administrator, or director. the plan depends upon cooperation and, therefore, should include everyone in the planning stage. The objectives should be kept brief, e.g., the media center should: 1) serve as a clearinghouse for the requests for preview for all materials, 2) ask for evaluations of the materials for possible purchase, 3) hold regular group screenings on materials that have been selected from previewing journals.[7]

Previewing is not a free way to supplement the collection, nor should several teachers within one building request the same item for use at different times. The media specialist will be responsible for returning these materials in good condition to the producer within the specified time. Levy warns that misuse of previewing privileges could force producers to impose rental fees.[8] You will find that requesting materials you are seriously considering for purchase, and planning for their systematic evaluation, is an excellent way to make informed selection decisions.

Exhibits

Arrangements can be made for materials to be brought to your school or district for display. Check with your district media supervisor or the state media consultant for the names of companies or agencies in your area that offer these services. You can contact a jobber or distributor to arrange for specific titles to be exhibited.

An example of an effective use of exhibits occurred when the media specialists of a district evaluated the social studies sections of their collections, worked with teachers in examining the gaps in the collections, and requested a copy of each recommended title. The materials were displayed for a two-week period during which teachers and students examined the materials and made selection decisions. The district supervisor anticipated that each title would be ordered by at least one school, but agreed to purchase for the system collection any titles not so selected. This careful preselection and financial backing prevented costs involved in returning unwanted items to the jobber.

Some companies have media mobiles that visit schools so teachers can examine materials, and many educational conferences include exhibits. Plan to attend with teachers from your building, so you will be familiar with the materials they see. You may be able to point out that the collection already has specific titles or to suggest similar ones. You can also ensure that you have the correct ordering information.

Combined Book Exhibit,[9] a commercial book-exhibiting venture, is currently investigating the feasibility of sponsoring an annual program of exhibits within states or other geographically defined areas. If their plans are implemented, this service will have the advantage of prepared catalogs so teachers and students can record their selections. One disadvantage in this type of exhibit is that the items exhibited are selected by the commercial, rather than the professional, sponsors.

Examination Centers

Another way to evaluate materials personally is to visit an examination center. These centers may serve district, regional, or state levels and be housed in the district media center, at a university, or in a state agency. In some centers, you can examine materials ranging from curricular and instructional materials to trade book and audiovisual materials. Other centers focus on materials for specific users or specific formats. The Anne Arundel County Review and Evaluation Center provides

> a setting where education personnel and others can evaluate materials, and it also has available a "placemat" with selection criteria. Copies of reviews are provided for individual items that have been reviewed by Anne Arundel County staff or by the professional review media.
>
> Because the Center concentrates on providing current materials and because it does not include a circulating collection, it functions as an aid in the selection process.[10]

The "Educational Media Selection Center Program" (EMSC) project identifies two key purposes for examination centers:

1. A comprehensive collection of teaching and learning resources that serves as a depository for examination and selection.

2. A place where in-service training programs are conducted.[11]

The EMSC project was never fully realized, but the specific suggestions for developing such centers are still valid.[12]

Although examination centers do not yet serve all parts of the country, a list of existing ones can be found in *Children's Media Marketplace.* A 1977 national survey[13] reported that 78 of the 211 respondents had access to a book examination center, while only 52 had access to an examination center for nonprint materials.

At the national level, EDMARC (Educational Materials Review Center of the Office of Education) is an examination center open to the public in Washington, DC. Newly published trade books are kept on display for one year, while textbooks and related curricular materials are displayed for three to four years.

In the United States and Canada, publishers have created centers to display current titles, promote books, and disseminate information. Add your school to the mailing list for information from the Children's Book Council (United States) or the Children's Book Centre (Canada).[14]

Involving Others

The idea that teachers, students, administrators, and curriculum specialists should be involved in making selection decisions is not new, but, in practice, it is not as common as one would expect. Yet, the idea is one of the "guiding principles" for "Collections" in *Media Programs: District and School.* The following discussion focuses on the role of teachers and students in the selection process.

Teachers

It is beneficial to involve teachers[15] in the selection process because:

1. They bring knowledge of their specializations, teaching methods, the students, and instructional needs.
2. Their participation increases their knowledge of the materials and leads to more and better use of materials in the classroom.
3. They can provide opportunities to test materials in the classroom and encourage students to evaluate materials.

Teachers can contribute a great deal to the selection process; however, some problems must be anticipated.

Plan to acquaint teachers with the collection. Explain to them, or involve them in developing, the criteria to be used in the selection process, and have reviews available for reference. Any group, made up of people with diverse views, will experience conflict in some form. As the media specialist, you will often be providing in-service education on how to evaluate materials. Jealousies may occur over who is serving on the committee. When you ask teachers to make suggestions or to participate on selection committees, some may respond that they "don't have time" or do not view the center as having "teaching" materials in their area of specialization. They may be expressing feelings of inadequacies about their knowledge of materials. Others may express the view that selection is your responsibility, not theirs. However, when approached as a subject specialist or an effective user of materials, many teachers will be glad to participate.

The situation in your school may be such that an advisory committee to identify needs in the present collection, to establish priorities for acquisition, and to plan for evaluation of the collection is a more effective way to involve teachers. Johnson notes that:

> Achievement of joint responsibility of this order, coupled with opportunities for in-service education of teachers in materials evaluation, can lead to the development of media center collections that serve as the backbone, rather than an enrichment source, for the instructional program.[16]

It has been this writer's experience that sincerely soliciting a teacher's opinion, acting on it, and informing the teacher of the results — why you purchased a specific item or didn't, and notifying the teacher when the requested materials arrive — brings about a positive and cooperative response from the teacher.

As you work with selection committees, record the reasons for decisions. Forms listing criteria with places, names of the evaluators, and their ratings can simplify record-keeping. Keeping this information on file can prevent duplication of effort; it is easy to forget which items have already been evaluated. The record also provides a means for accountability when a decision is challenged. Ideally, one format should cover all types of materials. In practice, however, one finds it may be easier to develop separate forms for books, nonprint materials, and instructional materials. A sample form is provided in figure 19 (page 134).

Teachers may also be involved in selecting free and inexpensive materials, such as maps, pamphlets, booklets, charts, etc., for the "information file" (vertical file). At Rolling Hills Elementary School, the principal is required to have periodic meetings with the entire faculty. However, at one session, he felt it would be beneficial to meet separately with the teachers of primary and intermediate students. He asked the media specialist to work with one group of teachers while he worked with the other. She recognized this as an excellent opportunity to involve teachers in the development of an information file.

The media specialist started the meeting with each group of teachers by describing the characteristics of an information file, what it consists of, and how it can be used by teachers and students. Next, she described guides to free and inexpensive materials, such as *Educators' Guide to Free Social Studies Materials* and *Free and Inexpensive Learning Materials* (George Peabody College for Teachers). The guides were

Figure 19.   Sample Evaluation Form

MATERIALS EVALUATION FORM

Title _____ Author/Producer_____
Edition_____ Series Title _____
Publisher/Distributor_____ Place_____ Date_____
Format:☐Book,☐8mm Film,☐Filmstrip,☐Phonodisk,☐Tape,☐Other____
Appropriate Users (circle): P   K   1   2   3   4   5   6   7   8   Adult

Curriculum Uses Include:

Information Uses Include:

Personal Uses Include:

CRITERIA	RATING				WHY? Please Comment
	Poor	Fair	Good	Superior	
Authoritativeness					
Accuracy or Credibility					
Organization					
Appropriateness of Content					
Aesthetic Quality					
Technical Quality					
Overall Rating					

Recommendation: ☐ Add 1 copy, ☐ Add __copies, ☐ Do not recommend,
                ☐ Uncertain, Why?_____

Evaluator(s): _____
Evaluation test group: _____
Date: _____

distributed to the teachers for identification of items pertinent to their instructional purposes.

A problem arose when teachers indicated items they wanted solely for their individual teaching purposes. In their enthusiasm, the teachers thought of their classroom collection needs rather than the needs of the school's collection. An agreement was reached that the teachers would be notified as the materials arrived so they could decide if they wanted a separate copy for their classrooms. The arrival notices prompted teachers to visit the media center and to participate in the use and evaluation of other types of materials. Both the media specialist and principal considered the postage bill a small financial commitment to the heightened awareness of the media center collection and program.

Similar types of experiences and benefits can occur through cooperatively working with teachers in the identification, description, and evaluation of community resources, human resources, field trips, etc.

Students

Children as young as first- and second-graders can begin learning about the selection process. Memories come to mind of groups of young children coming to the media center to select materials for their classrooms. The children were encouraged to consider questions such as: Do all your classmates share your interests? Are there children who like more pictures in their books? Are there times when you want something to read in a short time? Are there children in your class who prefer facts over stories? Didn't Jennifer get a new puppy? Do you think she would like this filmstrip about taking care of a puppy? Questions such as these start children thinking critically about the materials they use.

The idea of using children as book reviewers is not new. One program had 17 children, grades four through eight, periodically reviewing several books. The children were given titles compatible with their interests and reading level and were expected to review 25 to 50 books within the year. The reviewers recorded comments about the book but were not asked to provide a synopsis. A study reported the following benefits:

1. Users helped run the school system; the opportunity offered "a place for the pupil in the Establishment."[17]

2. Positive attitudes about reading were strengthened.

3. Pride was developed.

4. Participation fostered the child's sense of responsibility: "The development of responsibility for one's own behavior and relationships to others is obviously a current national problem and an area which must be stressed especially from the earliest grades."[18]

5. Communication took place among the adults involved with the child in this project (teachers, principals, and media specialist).

These benefits seem timely even a decade after they were reported. How reassuring to the adults in this project to find that children, unaware of the adult's evaluation of a title, frequently agreed with them.

An elementary school media specialist in Indianapolis writes of children evaluating audiovisual materials:

> I ... have access to audiovisual materials which may be borrowed from the Materials Preview and Evaluation Center (MPEC). Teachers know that I will look for materials for them once a week if they let me know in advance what they need. The students found out about this service to teachers and started making similar requests.... I told them I would fill their requests if they would spend a few minutes with me after using the material to help in filling out the evaluation forms. I was surprised to find that students are highly critical of materials ... their main criterion is that the audiovisual materials contain accurate, precise information.[19]

School districts wanting to involve students in the educational process might want to adopt guidelines similar to the Montgomery (Maryland) County schools. Two students are appointed by the student council to serve on the advisory committee, which advises the principal and head librarian on student requests and establishes priorities for purchase of materials. The guidelines state that "an allotment of 15 percent of these funds for new materials will be designated for student requested materials."[20] This policy is in keeping with a board of education policy that students be involved in the educational program.

Children involved in the selection process can help alert other children to materials and opportunities in the media center. A classmate's recommendation often carries more weight, certainly more appeal, than the same recommendation from an adult.

A final example concerns the Cooperative Children's Book Center[21] at the University of Wisconsin in Madison. This collection is an examination center for researchers and professionals. First-graders used this collection when participating in the selection of books. The teachers and librarian prepared the class by discussing qualities of various books.

> Among the criteria the children considered were attractiveness, the size of the print, space between lines, the interest and worth of the author's "message," meaningful illustrations, and the inclusion of an index. Or from a child's point of view, "The outside and the inside of the book look good to me."[22]

During the six-week selection period:

> School-sponsored activities included previewing books from among the titles included in Books on Exhibit and visiting the local ... branch library, the central Milwaukee Public Library, and the Cooperative Children's Book Center.[23]

Children arranged their reviews in order of preference and influenced the selection of over 1,300 titles. Names of student selectors were indicated in the books, and each class was offered the opportunity to be the first to check out their selections.[24]

These examples highlight a few ways to involve others in the selection process and point out the advantages, insights, and excitement that can be so easily generated.

Summary

The selection process calls for professional knowledge and judgment about materials, as well as the sources that review them. One needs to be a knowledgeable consumer of the sources that evaluate materials: selection tools, reviewing journals, and bibliographic essays.

Careful planning and initiative are needed to involve others effectively in the personal evaluation of materials through previewing or visiting exhibits and examination centers.

Notes to Chapter 8

[1]Mary Frances K. Johnson, "Media Selection: Six Concerns," *Catholic Library World* 47 (1976): 416.

[2]For an analysis of reviews of 30 titles chosen from the 1972, 1973, and 1974 lists of Notable Children's Books, see Virginia Witucke, "A Comparative Analysis of Juvenile Book Review Media," *School Media Quarterly* 8 (1980): 153-60.

[3]Carol A. Nemeyer and Sandra K. Paul, "Book Publishers and the School Library Market," *School Media Quarterly* 6 (1978): 174.

[4]John Belland, "Factors Influencing Selection of Materials," *School Media Quarterly* 6 (1978): 117.

[5]Kay E. Vandergrift, "Selection: Reexamination and Reassessment," *School Media Quarterly* 6 (1978): 109.

[6]Phyllis Levy, "The Review Privilege," *Previews* 1 (1973): 3.

[7]Diana L. Spirt, "A Plan for Previewing," *Previews* 2 (1973): 3.

[8]Levy, "The Review Privilege," p. 3.

[9]If you are unable to learn about this program from someone within your state, write Mr. Edward A. Malinowski, Managing Director, the Combined Book Exhibit, 12 Saw Mill River Road, Hawthorne, NY 10532.

[10]Division of Library Development and Services, Maryland State Department of Education, "Focus: Recent Developments in Materials Selection," *Library Keynotes* 7 (1977): 3.

[11]John Rowell and M. Ann Heidbreder, *Educational Media Selection Centers: Identification and Analysis of Current Practices.* ALA Studies in Librarianship, No. 1 (Chicago, IL: American Library Association, 1971), p. 4.

[12]Cora Paul Bomar, M. Ann Heidbreder, and Carol A. Nemeyer, *Guide to the Development of Educational Media Selection Centers.* ALA Studies in Librarianship, No. 4 (Chicago, IL: American Library Association, 1973).

[13]Summarized data from the 1977 survey conducted by the Association of American Publishers, the Resources and Technical Services Division (American Library Association), and the American Association of School Librarians (American Library Association).

[14]Children's Book Council, Inc., 67 Irving Place, New York, NY 10003; and the Children's Book Centre, 229 College Street, 5th Floor, Toronto, Ontario M5T 1R4.

[15]This discussion is based in part on the following sources: 1) Frederic R. Hartz, "Selection of School/Media Materials," *Catholic Library World* 47 (1976): 425-29; 2) Blanche Woolls, "Who Reviews What ... In What Way ... For What Purpose ... With What Results," *AV Guide: The Learning Media Magazine* 51 (1972): 4-7; 3) Mary Frances K. Johnson, "Media Selection: Six Concerns," *Catholic Library World* 47 (1976): 416-17.

[16]Johnson, "Media Selection," p. 417.

[17]Wes Measel and L. Lucille Crawford, "School Children and Book Selection," *American Libraries* 2 (1971): 956.

[18]Ibid., p. 957.

[19]Carol Birdsong, "Students Select Materials for Their Media Center," *Hoosier School Libraries* 14 (1974): 25.

[20]Department of Educational Media and Technology, Evaluation and Selection, *Evaluation and Selection of Instructional Materials Equipment* (Rockville, MD: Montgomery County Public Schools, Summer, 1974), p. 7.

[21]Elizabeth Burr and Mary Carr, "Happy Birthday to the CCBC: Ten Years of Cooperative Service to Those Who Serve Youth," *Wisconsin Library Bulletin* (69 (1973): 167-70.

[22]Based on information supplied by Jerry Hubert and Sister Mary Ann Breuer, "Children's Book Selection," *School Library Journal* 20 (1973): 35.

[23]Ibid.

[24]Ibid., p. 36.

Chapter 8 Bibliography

Baker, D. Philip and Bender, David R. "Marketing, Selection, and Acquisition of Materials for School Media Programs, Part I and II." Theme Issues. *School Media Quarterly* 6 (1978): 97-122, 127-32; and 6 (1978): 171-87, 197-201. Includes Belland, John, "Factors Influencing

Selection of Materials," 6 (1978): 112-19; Nemeyer, Carol A., and Paul, Sandra K. "Book Publishers and the School Library Market," 6 (1978): 173-78; and Vandergrift, Kay E. "Selection: Reexamination and Reassessment," 6 (1978): 103-11.

Birdsong, Carol. "Students Select Materials for Their Media Center." *Hoosier School Libraries* 14 (1974): 24-26.

Bomar, Cora Paul; Heidbreder, Ann M.; and Nemeyer, Carol A. *Guide to the Development of Educational Media Selection Centers.* ALA Studies in Librarianship No. 4. Chicago, IL: American Library Association, 1973.

Burr, Elizabeth and Carr, Mary. "Happy Birthday to the CCBC: Ten Years of Cooperative Service to Those Who Serve Youth." *Wisconsin Library Bulletin* 69 (1973): 167-70.

Based on information supplied by Jerry Hubert and Sister Mary Ann Breuer. "Children's Book Selection." *School Library Journal* 20 (1973): 35.

EPIE Institute, Educational Products Report: An In-Depth Report, Number 54. *Improving Materials Selection Procedures: A Basic "How To" Handbook.* New York, NY: Educational Products Information Exchange Institute, 1973.

Grover, Robert and Gonzalez, Sharon. "A Study of Children's Film Reviews." *Top of the News* 37 (1981): 248-57.

Hartz, Frederic R. "Selection of School/Media Materials." *Catholic Library World* 47 (1976): 425-29.

Hatfield, Frances S. "How to Promote Your Books to School Libraries." *Catholic Library World* 47 (1976): 416-17.

Levy, Phyllis. "The Review Privilege." *Previews* 1 (1973): 3.

Maryland State Department of Education. Division of Library Development and Services. "Focus: Recent Developments in Materials Selection." *Library Keynotes* 7 (1977): 1-3.

Measel, Wes, and Crawford, L. Lucille. "School Children and Book Selection." *American Libraries* 2 (1971): 955-57.

Miller, Marilyn L. "Collection Development in School Library Media Centers: National Recommendation and Reality." *Collection Building* 1 (1978): 25-48.

"Reviews, Reviewing, and the Review Media." Theme Issue. *Top of the News* 35 (1979): 121, 123-73.

Rowell, John, and Heidbreder, M. Ann. *Educational Media Selection Centers: Identification and Analysis of Current Practices.* ALA Studies in Librarianship, No. 1. Chicago, IL: American Library Association, 1971.

Spirt, Diana L. "A Plan for Previewing." *Previews* 2 (1973): 3.

Witucke, Virginia. "A Comparative Analysis of Juvenile Book Review Media." *School Media Quarterly* 8 (1980): 153-60.

Woodbury, Marda. *Selecting Materials for Instruction: Issues and Policies.* Littleton, CO: Libraries Unlimited, 1979.

9
GENERAL SELECTION CRITERIA

Selection is a complex decision-making process, not a simple, gut-level "I-like-this" reaction. Responsible collection development requires that broad considerations govern the evaluation and choice of a single item. As a media specialist, you are responsible for the collection as an entity as well as for individual items. The reasons for choosing a specific item must be based on your evaluation of the item itself and its relationship to the collection. Justification for the choice of an item should be formulated from an assessment of its contribution to the fulfillment of the policies and goals of the collection program.

Selection decisions reflect, in part, the evaluator's ability to judge materials against given criteria. However, selection decisions are often subjective. Criteria must be identified and established to guide decisions and lend consistency to this activity. Criteria can be used to evaluate content, physical form, or potential value of materials to users or programs. All criteria must be considered in the final decision to select an item for the collection. This chapter describes general criteria that can be applied to all types of materials, criteria related to:

1. Intellectual content and its presentation
2. Physical form
3. Equipment

Later chapters will discuss criteria for specific formats and for instructional, informational, and personal needs.

Intellectual Content and Its Presentation

The fundamental selection criterion is the quality of the content, which Asheim notes "is considerably affected by the extent to which the format is properly used in relation to the content and to the needs of the audience to whom it is addressed."[1] Spirt suggests the following criteria:

1. What is the idea, intellectual content, etc. in the material, and how is it presented?

2. Is the medium that is used to present the idea the most suitable one for its treatment?[2]

Analysis of these questions provides a framework for this discussion. The criteria provided are offered as guides, not absolutes. The collection, the users, and the resources outside the collection influence the applicability of each criterion to specific items.

How can one evaluate an idea, the intellectual content of a work? Criteria can include 1) authority; 2) appropriateness of content to users; 3) scope; 4) accuracy of information; 5) treatment; 6) arrangement and organization; 7) literary quality; 8) materials available on the subject; 9) durability of information; 10) reputation of author, artist, or filmmaker; 11) special features; and 12) value to the collection.

1. Authority

The basis for the criterion of authority is formed by the qualifications and abilities of the people responsible for the creation of the work. Authority can be judged through consideration of the qualifications of the author or director, the quality and acceptance of other works by the same person, and dependability of the publisher or producer. Does this work meet the standards you expect from this person or organization?

2. Appropriateness of Content to Users

Appropriateness of content focuses on the content in relation to its intended use and audience. The concepts must be presented at the user's developmental level. In other words, is the presentation geared to the maturity and interest level of the intended users? The content should not be presented in a manner that talks down to users, nor should it extend beyond their capability to understand, regardless of whether the content is factual or imaginative. An item should be appropriate to the children for whom it is intended, not to some arbitrary standard established by adults.

3. Scope

Scope refers to the overall purpose and depth of coverage of the content being presented. Examine the introduction or the teacher's guide to an item to determine the intended purpose and coverage. Evaluate whether the stated purpose meets a need of the collection and, if so, whether the material fulfills its purpose. The material being reviewed should present the content from a different perspective if there is sufficient coverage of the same content already in the collection.

4. Accuracy of Information

Information presented in materials should be accurate. Facts and opinions should be distinguished and, as much as possible, should be impartially presented. Recency is a large part of accuracy, especially in technological subjects where changes occur rapidly. Check with a subject area specialist, if necessary, to be sure the information is up-to-date. Remember, recent date of publication does not necessarily indicate that material is current.

5. Treatment

The treatment of style of presentation can affect the potential worth of an item. Is the style appropriate for the subject and use? In the best items, the presentation catches and holds the user's attention, draws on a typical experience, and stimulates further learning or creativity. Are signs (pictures, visuals) and symbols (words, abstractions) necessary to the content and helpful to the user? The treatment of an item must also be appropriate to the situation in which it will be used. Some materials will require an adult to guide the student's use of the material; in other cases, a teacher's guide will be necessary to present the information fully. Does the length of time necessary to use the item lend its use to class periods? The use of a 60-minute film may be limited if the longest possible viewing period is 55 minutes.

6. Arrangement and Organization

How the material is presented in terms of sequence and development of ideas influences the ease with which the information can be understood. Content should develop logically, flowing from one section to another, emphasizing important elements. Does the arrangement of information facilitate use? A chronologically arranged work may present difficulties when searching for specific information if there is no subject index to guide the user. A summary or review of major points will often help the user shape the information into a usable form.

7. Literary Merit

The components of literature serve as another area of evaluation. What theme or idea is the author trying to communicate? The theme should be presented in a coherent manner and be relevant to the child's real or imaginary world. Organization of plot, setting, characterization, and style should be consistent. Is the user's interest captured early? The plot should provide actions in related sequences to arrive at a logical outcome. Does the story have a beginning, a middle, and an end? Are changes and developments plausible but not predictable? Does the description of the time and place of the action evoke a clear and credible setting? The characters should be convincing in their actions. Is the work presented in a style that is appropriate to the theme? The choice of words and syntax can create a mood and help convey ideas. Is the point of view appropriate for this work? What is the total effect of the work? One component should not stand out from the others, except for emphasis, creating a unity of literary elements.

8. Materials Available on the Subject

When selecting materials for the collection to fill a need for a particular subject, program, or user, the factor of availability may overweigh other criteria. This occurs frequently with current events, such as the election of a new president. Biographic information may be needed quickly, and there are few, if any, materials available for children. By the time the president finishes his first four-year term, there is usually a wide range of titles and formats from which to select, but fewer requests from users. Other examples include the continuing lack of fiction works for children reading at the third- and fourth-grade level and the scarcity of "high interest-low vocabulary" materials.

9. Durability of Information

Durability of information is often related to the scarcity of materials. The concept or subject may be stable or may change rapidly (such as political boundaries, fashions, or automobiles). Thus the subject presented, as well as the information about the subject, may change. An automobile assembly line today may be similar to one 10 years ago, but the automobiles produced, the materials used, and the processes have changed. For rapidly changing subjects, less expensive formats (books, filmstrips) may be preferred to more expensive formats (films) so replacements can be obtained more economically.

10. Reputation of Author, Artist, or Filmmaker

A particular author, artist, or filmmaker and specific titles may be considered important ones for children to know. One might consider the "classics" an important part of the collection. Does the particular work being evaluated exemplify the contribution of its creator? If children should know a particular work, purchase it for the collection even if it hasn't been requested.

11. Special Features

Information that is peripheral to the main content of a work may be important to the collection. Distinctive characteristics of the item being evaluated—maps, charts, graphs, glossaries, and other features—can be used independently. A record album may contain biographic information about the composer or performer; the teacher's guide to a filmstrip may offer suggestions of follow-up activities or lists of related materials that would be useful without the use of the filmstrip. Is the information accurately and completely indexed? These special features can be a decisive factor in selection decisions that are less than clear-cut.

12. Value to the Collection

After evaluating the specific qualities of the item, the media specialist needs to consider the item in its relation to the collection. Does the item meet any need of the school program or the users? Is there more than one way the item can be used? Who is likely to use the item? How often will the item be used? Could the item be used by an individual for informational or recreational purposes and also be used by a teacher in an instructional situation?

13. Other Considerations

Series: Each item within a series must be judged independently in terms of its value and known needs. Books in a series may be written by different authors, but all authors may not write equally well. If the same author is responsible for the entire series, is that individual equally knowledgeable about all subjects presented in the series? Even with fictional works, the author may not be able to sustain the interest of the reader. Can the works be used independently, or must they be used in sequence?

If the item is a filmstrip, must the entire set of filmstrips be purchased? The presentation and production quality should be satisfactory in each filmstrip. Does the collection need the content offered in each of the filmstrips in the series? Frequently, it is more economical or convenient to purchase an entire set. This problem also occurs when purchasing study prints and kits.

Cost: The price of an item and the expense involved in obtaining it can influence the selection decision. Is the item within the range specified by the budget? Is it more expensive than a satisfactory substitute? If the material requires new equipment, the price of equipment must be added to the cost of the item. Will purchasing the new equipment provide for the use of other materials in the collection? The item should receive enough use to justify its cost.

The intellectual content of an item and its presentation are important considerations in the process of selecting materials. Criteria relating to content form one basis on which to evaluate an item. The packaging of that information, or its physical form, also must be evaluated.

Physical Form

The quality of the content can be weakened if it is not presented through the appropriate medium. How does one determine which medium presents the content most effectively? If this appears to be a simple question, it is not. One of the primary criteria to be evaluated is the compatibility of content and format. In speaking of Michelangelo's *David*, Wehmeyer suggests that

> had a reader never seen the sculpture (or its model or photo), a purely verbal description, without visuals, would not likely enable him to envision more than a vague image. Just as the David must be seen, so must Beethoven's Ninth Symphony be heard, corduroy be touched, lilacs must be smelled, or wonton be tasted before a learner can begin to understand them.[3]

This example demonstrates characteristics of formats and identifies ways in which people learn. Inherent qualities of the message may suggest a specific format. If motion is needed, a film can most effectively show that action. If an object is being discussed in detail, a drawing, photograph, or model might best show the detail. Although later chapters will discuss criteria for specific formats, there are general criteria that apply to all materials including: 1) technical quality, 2) aesthetic quality, and 3) safety and health considerations.

1. Technical Quality

The physical characteristics of the item must be judged independently and collectively. Are illustrations and photographs clear and eye-catching; is there a reason for soft-focus effects? Sound, visual materials, and narrative should be used to focus attention. Is the sound clearly audible? Are filming techniques, such as close-ups, animation, or flashbacks, used to focus attention or reveal information? Colors should be chosen which express the theme or message. Are line, shape, and texture used effectively? Is there balance in the arrangement of illustrations and text? The selection of typeface can be expressive and provide clarity. The typeface used in projected images, such as transparencies or captioned filmstrips, should project clearly.

2. Aesthetic Quality

Both the external design and the presentation of the content need to be aesthetically pleasing: separate elements combining to form an aesthetic whole. Is the item attractively packaged? Book jackets and album covers should attract the user.

3. Safety and Health Considerations

Safety and health features are particularly important when selecting tactile materials, but should be considered for all materials. Is the item constructed of nonflammable materials? Can an item be cleaned? Realia present a challenge in terms of cleanliness. What can you do with a piece of salt from the Great Salt Lake that will probably be licked by 905 of the 1,000 students in the school? Materials with movable parts also present problems. Models and kits may have parts that can cut fingers or be swallowed. Live animals can also create health and safety problems.

4. Other Considerations

Is the material to be used by an individual or a group? The potential number of simultaneous users must be considered in selection decisions. A filmstrip of a book might be preferred to using the actual book with most groups. The variety of purposes for using the material also should be considered. For motivation, games and live specimens invite participation. Films bring distant places to the user more dramatically than a map does. Videotapes of the landing on the moon, photographs of that event, or even a piece of the moon have more impact than reading a text or viewing a filmstrip. If creativity is to be encouraged, then a programmed text may be limiting. For example, a programmed package for the microcomputer can introduce a student to the basic principles of computer programming, but can limit the creativity of a student who has reached an advanced level.

People have preferences that should also be considered, although they may be hard to assess. Will the viewer who first saw "The Tap Dance Kid" on the ABC Afterschool Special telecast find its print version (Fitzhugh's *Nobody's Family Is Going to Change*) equally acceptable? Does the person who first met the content as a book, appreciate the motion picture? A television newscast may be preferred over a radio broadcast or a newspaper.

Translating a work from one medium to another can affect the treatment of the subject and the impact of the message. Verbal language differs from visual language. This difference can result in two seemingly unrelated works, drawn ostensibly from the same content.

Ease of use, storage, and maintenance are also important selection criteria. Can the item be used easily by an individual child or a group? Does it require special storage? Is the item durable? Can it be easily replaced or repaired? Does the item include more than one part, such as kits that may include print and nonprint materials? Must all the items be used together? If a single item or part is lost, can the remaining parts be used? Can missing items, such as game parts, be replaced locally? Can they be purchased separately? These practical criteria can be just as important as the more aesthetic considerations.

Equipment

Many materials found in media collections require equipment if they are to be used. Without proper equipment and conditions, such as darkened rooms or rearview projection for example, a medium such as film cannot be used effectively. There are general criteria that should be considered when selecting equipment.

1. Ease of Use

If the equipment is too complicated, people may be discouraged from using it. In any case, proper conditions and facilities should be provided. Projection areas should have permanently mounted screens and adjustable light controls. Are rear screen units needed? Multiple outlets will be needed in the area where the equipment will be used.

The equipment itself needs to be examined with the potential users in mind. What level of manual dexterity is needed to operate the equipment? How many steps are involved to run the equipment? Does the equipment have numerous controls? How "operator-proof" is the equipment? Some filmstrip projectors have lenses that are manually pulled in order to focus and can easily pull off. How much time will be needed to teach students and faculty how to use the equipment? Are visual explanations of how to run the equipment included with each item? Are the directions complete and easy to follow? Are automatic operations dependable? Is there an option for manual or remote control? Are shut-off or cooling-down features automatic?

2. Size, Weight, Design

Physical properties of the equipment can also deter use. Does the size, weight, or design of the equipment require that it be used and stored in one location? Can the equipment be moved on a cart? Equipment that circulates needs to be lightweight and compact. If equipment is circulated to students' homes, the equipment will need to be weatherproof. If equipment is used in a two-story building, is it too heavy or bulky to carry up stairs? Carrying cases may be needed. Are there straps or handles that aid in moving the equipment? The straps and handles should be strong enough to withstand the weight of the item carried any distance. Are strong materials used in the construction of the equipment? Durability is a key criterion.

3. Performance

Equipment should operate efficiently and consistently at a high level of performance. Poor-quality projection or sound reproduction can negate the technical quality so carefully sought in selection. What is the quality of mechanical constructions? The noise or light from the equipment should not interfere with its use. Is the equipment subject to overheating? Evaluations of equipment performance can be found in *Library Technology Reports, Consumer Reports*, and *EPIE Report.*

4. Availability of Software

As new technologies are developed, there is often a time lag between the introduction of equipment and the production of appropriate software. The recent addition of microcomputers to media collections can serve as an illustration of this problem. Most programs for microcomputers have been developed by the manufacturer of a specific piece of equipment and cannot be used with equipment from another manufacturer. The range of subjects offered by the manufacturer of your equipment may not meet the needs of your program or be directed to the age group you serve.

5. Compatibility

Equipment needs to be compatible with other equipment in the collection. Will the equipment being reviewed require different replacement parts than items already in the collection or additional in-service training to operate it? Is the equipment limited to those materials produced by the manufacturer of the equipment?

6. Versatility

Equipment that can be used in a variety of ways may be desirable. Can the equipment be used by an individual or a group? Can it be used with more than one medium, such as a slide/filmstrip projector? If attachments or adaptors are needed to accomplish this versatility, how easily can these changes be made?

7. Need

The long-range use of the equipment needs to be considered. Will the equipment be used often enough to justify its purchase? If the item is not purchased, what will be the consequences? Will teachers not be able to present materials they want to use? If only one teacher working with one class on one subject wants the equipment, is there sufficient justification to purchase the item?

8. Safety

Safety features should be considered, especially when young children are to use equipment. Rough or protruding edges should be avoided. Is the equipment balanced so it won't topple easily? Users should be protected from dangerous parts, such as a moving fan or heated element, and electrical connections should be suitably covered and grounded. If the equipment generates heat or fumes, these need to be ventilated. The item should carry the Underwriters Laboratory (UL) or Canadian Standards Association (CSA) seal.

9. Maintenance and Service

The equipment should be built to withstand hard usage, but systematic planning for maintenance and service must be provided. Can minor repairs or bulbs replacement be handled quickly and easily? Does the distributor or manufacturer deliver, unpack, and test new equipment? Does the manufacturer offer in-service training on operating or repairing the equipment? The media staff of the district or school may have a person assigned to do repairs. Some distributors and manufacturers provide "on-the-spot" repairs, while others require that the item be sent to a factory.

10. Reliability of Dealer and Manufacturer

The reputation of the distributor and manufacturer is a significant criterion. What conditions are covered in warranties or guarantees? Does the manufacturer honor warranties? Does the distributor or manufacturer deliver on time? How quickly do they respond to requests for assistance? Are they located geographically close to the school?

11. Cost

Quality should be weighted over cost, but budget must also be considered. Does a competitor offer a similar, less-expensive item? Does the lower price represent less quality in terms of performance standards, warranties, or service? Are trade-ins allowed by the distributor or the school? Should the equipment be leased rather than purchased?

12.   Sources of Information

Photographs and uniform specifications for equipment can be found in the annually revised *Audio-Visual Equipment Directory*. Criteria for specific types of equipment and a dictionary of technical terms are presented in *Media Equipment: A Guide and Dictionary*.

Summary

Making selection decisions is a subjective activity for which the media specialist is responsible and, therefore, held accountable. As the individual responsible for a collection, ensure that the collection, as an entity, will fulfill its purposes of meeting the schools' goals and the instructional, informational, and user needs. Within this context, one must judge the value of individual items to the collection. Although selection decisions are subjective, one should be able to justify why the item is chosen for the collection.

Why is an item added to the collection? A basic criterion for evaluating any material is the impact of its intellectual content. What will that item add to the collection? Will it add information in a new dimension? Will it appeal to the users?

Another criterion is the compatibility of the medium to the message. Have the purpose and the use of the message been considered by the creator?

These are the two basic criteria against which all items must be judged. Additional criteria relating to specific formats, uses, and needs must also be considered and will be discussed in the following chapters. Selection is a complex process, demanding skills and knowledge of the media specialist if wise selection decisions are to be made.

Notes to Chapter 9

[1]Lester Asheim, "Introduction," in *Differentiating the Media: Proceedings of the Thirty-Seventh Annual Conference of the Graduate Library School, August 5-6, 1974*, edited by Lester Asheim and Sara I. Fenwick (Chicago, IL: University of Chicago Press, 1975), p. 4.

[2]Diana L. Spirt, "Criteria, Choices, and Other Concerns about Filmstrips," *LJ/SLJ Previews* 1 (1973): 6.

[3]Lillian B. Wehmeyer, "Media and Learning: Present and Future, Part I: Present," *Catholic Library World* 50 (1978): 150.

Chapter 9 Bibliography

Asheim, Lester, and Fenwick, Sara I., eds. *Differentiating the Media: Proceedings of the Thirty-Seventh Annual Conference of the Graduate Library School, August 5-6, 1974*. Chicago, IL: University of Chicago Press, 1975.

Brown, James W.; Lewis, Richard B.; and Harcleroad, Fred F. *AV Instruction: Technology, Media, and Methods.* 5th ed. New York, NY: McGraw-Hill, 1977.

Brown, James W.; Norberg, Kenneth D.; and Srygley, Sara K. *Administering Educational Media: Instructonal Technology and Library Services.* New York, NY: McGraw-Hill, 1972.

Clarke, James P. "Equipment Evaluation." *Catholic Library World* 46 (1975): 305-306.

Cullinan, Bernice E. *Its Discipline and Content.* Literature for Children Series. Dubuque, IA: Wm. C. Brown, 1971.

Evans, G. Edward. *Developing Library Collections.* Littleton, CO: Libraries Unlimited, 1979.

Fast, Betty. "The Case for Multipurpose Media." *Wilson Library Bulletin* 50 (1976): 634-35.

Gerlach, Vernon S., and Ely, Donald P. *Teaching and Media: A Systematic Approach.* Englewood Cliffs, NJ: Prentice-Hall, 1971.

Gillespie, John T., and Spirt, Diana L. *Creating a School Media Program.* New York, NY: R. R. Bowker, 1975.

Grove, Pearce S., ed. *Nonprint Media in Academic Libraries.* Chicago, IL: American Library Association, 1975.

Hicks, Warren B., and Tillin, Alma May. *Developing Multi-Media Libraries.* New York, NY: R. R. Bowker, 1970.

Huck, Charlotte S. *Children's Literature in the Elementary School.* 3rd ed. updated. New York, NY: Holt, Rinehart, and Winston, 1979.

Levitan, Karen M. "Resource Development and Evaluation: A Focus on Research." *School Media Quarterly* 3 (1975): 316-18, 323-26.

Prostano, Emanuel T., and Prostano, Joyce S. *The School Library Media Center.* 2nd ed. Library Science Text Series. Littleton, CO: Libraries Unlimited, 1977.

Spirt, Diana. "Criteria, Choices, and Other Concerns about Filmstrips." *LJ/SLJ Previews* 1 (1973): 6.

Sutherland, Zena; Monson, Dianne L.; and Arbuthnot, May Hill. *Children and Books.* 6th ed. Glenview, IL: Scott, Foresman, 1981.

Wehmeyer, Lillian B. "Media and Learning: Present and Future, Part I: Present." *Catholic Library World* 50 (1978): 150-52.

10
CRITERIA BY FORMAT: VISUAL MATERIALS

When evaluating materials for inclusion in a collection, the unique qualities of the format often suggest the criteria to be used. The next two chapters focus on the characteristics of the different formats and how they should be considered in selection decisions. Formats (print, projected still images, graphs, moving images, auditory, tactile and instructional (systems) will be described in terms of their:

1. Physical characteristics
2. Advantages
3. Disadvantages
4. Selection criteria
5. Implications for collection development
6. Sources of bibliographic information and reviews

Children acquire knowledge through their senses: seeing, hearing, touching, tasting, and smelling. This chapter discusses materials in which the sense of sight predominates, although other senses may be used. Specifically, this chapter covers: print materials (books, periodicals, newspapers, pamphlets, microforms), projected still images (filmstrips, slides, transparencies), graphics (posters, graphs, charts, tables, diagrams, cartoons, art prints, study prints), moving images (motion picture, video).

Although this chapter concentrates on format criteria, remember that the decision to select an item is based on an evaluation of all of its various components and on the value it adds to the collection. Who will use the item? Under what circumstances will it be used? Does it fulfill a unique need? Selection decisions must be made not only on judgments about the physical item, but also on its content, potential use, and audience appeal.

Print Materials

Print materials include books (hardback and paperback), periodicals, newspapers, pamphlets, and microforms (microfilm, microcard, and microfiche).

Books

Hardback and paperback books share similar characteristics but can fulfill different selection needs. Variations in size of type and placement can affect potential use; layout, graphics, and photographs can enrich a text.

Advantages

1. Books are usually designed for individual users.
2. The user can set the pace and stop in the process to recheck information or reread a section.
3. The table of contents and index can provide ready access to information contained in a book.
4. Books are portable and inexpensive.

Disadvantages

1. Use of colored artwork or photography, while adding to appeal or clarity of explanation of text, increases the cost of a book.
2. Movement is difficult to illustrate on the printed page.
3. Use with large groups is impractical.
4. Contact with books is a personalized, internal experience; interaction and feedback for the learner are difficult to achieve except in programmed texts.

Selection Criteria for Hardbacks and Paperbacks

1. Is the shape and weight of the book appropriate for the intended audience?
2. How opaque is the paper? A young reader may be confused by print that shows through the page.
3. Is the typeface suitable for the intended audience?
4. Is the spacing between words and between lines adequate for the young or reluctant reader?
5. Do the page layouts and color add appeal and clarity to the text?
6. Is the book jacket attractive? Does it reflect the content of the book?
7. Are the illustrations placed within the text where they can be used easily, or are they bound together in an inconvenient location?
8. Is the medium used for illustrations (e.g., line drawing, watercolor, block prints) appropriate to the setting and mood of the story?
9. When a readability formula, such as Fry or Spache, is applied, is the text appropriate to the intended audience?[1]

Additional Criteria for Hardbacks

1. Are the bindings durable and covers washable? Are reinforced bindings available for titles that will be used by very young children or for ones that will be frequently circulated?

2. Will the hardcover books lie flat when open?

Collection Considerations

While selections should cover a wide range of subjects and genres, the reading and maturity levels of students should also be considered. Additional copies of popular materials should be ordered. Paperbacks are an inexpensive way to meet these demands. Remember that a paperback book may have more appeal to some users than the same title in hardback.

Sources of Information

Children's Books in Print, Subject Guide to Children's Books in Print, and *Paperbound Books for Young People*, all published by Bowker, list available items. Reviews can be found in selection tools, reviewing journals, and bibliographic essays as discussed in chapter 8.

Periodicals and Newspapers

There are two types of periodicals and newspapers: general, such as *Ranger Rick's Nature Magazine*, and instructional, such as *Scholastic Sprint*.

Advantages

1. Periodicals and newspapers provide the only source of current events information for some children.

2. Juvenile periodicals offer short stories and participatory activities and are extensively illustrated.

3. Several juvenile periodicals solicit contributions of writing or illustrations from children.

4. Many periodicals suggest activities that adults can use with children.

5. Indices, such as *Children's Magazine Guide* and *Abridged Readers' Guide to Periodical Literature*, provide access to information for students preparing reports.

Disadvantages

1. Circulation controls are difficult to establish. Many magazines on popular topics disappear from collections when students take them or teachers borrow them for a "great" bulletin board pattern.

2. When a large number of children are involved, reader participation activities (such as "fill in the blanks," "connect the dots," or puzzles) need to be copied or laminated so they can be used more than once.

3. Storage space that provides easy access to several volumes of a journal may be difficult or expensive to provide.

4. If fold-outs and cut-outs, such as calendars and photographs of sport figures or animals, are removed, they may eliminate portions of the text.

5. The amount and quality of advertisements in journals may detract from their usefulness in schools.

Selection Criteria

1. Is the content of interest to students or teachers?

2. Are subjects treated clearly in a well-organized manner?

3. Is the illustrative matter pertinent and adequately reproduced?

4. Is the format appropriate for the purpose of the magazine and the intended audience?

5. Are large-print items needed by any users?

Collection Considerations

Local, state, national, and international newspapers should be represented in the collection. If classes subscribe to instructional newspapers, the media specialist may find it useful to have a copy of the teacher's edition in the media center. The length of time periodicals are kept will depend on patterns of usage and availability of storage facilities. It is a common practice to acquire microform editions for items needed after five years and to clip the others for the vertical file or to discard them.

Source of Information

Periodicals for School Media Programs by Selma K. Richardson is an annotated listing of over 500 periodicals appropriate for grades kindergarten through 12.

Pamphlets

The definition of pamphlet varies, but the term will be used here to denote multiple-paged printed materials that are housed in the vertical file rather than shelved with books. Pamphlets may be published by local, state, and national governments as well as associations, businesses, etc. Pamphlets and other vertical file materials can provide a wealth of current and specialized treatments of a subject. Teachers find that government documents frequently provide concise and up-to-date information on a topic, although the vocabulary level may be beyond the child's comprehension.

Advantages

1. Pamphlets are inexpensive or free. Duplicate copies can be readily obtained on topics of high interest.
2. Information found in pamphlets is often more current than that found in other media, except magazines and newspapers.
3. Pamphlets can provide a variety of viewpoints on a subject.
4. Pamphlets often discuss subjects unavailable elsewhere in the collection. Their treatment is usually brief, focusing on a specific subject.

Disadvantages

1. Because of their size and format, pamphlets are easily misfiled.
2. Pamphlets need to be checked periodically for accuracy.
3. The flimsy construction of pamphlets limits repeated use.

Selection Criteria

1. Since many pamphlets are sponsored by groups or businesses, the extent of advertising must be considered. Does advertising dominate the presentation?
2. Regardless of whether the item contains advertising, is the message presented without bias and propaganda?
3. Is the information already provided elsewhere in the collection?

Collection Implications

Pamphlets are an inexpensive means to have information on both sides of an issue. Materials should be readily accessible and reviewed periodically for currency of information.

Sources of Information

Shirley Miller in *The Vertical File and Its Satellites* discusses the management of vertical files and suggests many sources for such materials. Tools such as *Free and Inexpensive Learning Materials* list a wide range of such materials. *Selected U.S. Government Publications*, available free from the Superintendent of Documents, U.S. Government Printing Office, Washington, DC 20402, lists pamphlets, books, maps, and other materials produced by the U.S. government. *U.S. Government Publications for the School Media Center* by Alice Wittig identifies recommended publications and lists the U.S. Government Printing Office bookstores. Reviews for a limited number of government publications can be found in *Booklist.*

Microforms

Microforms, including microfilm, microcards, and microfiche, present both advantages and disadvantages to the collection. These formats require expensive viewing equipment and often have less user appeal than identical content in hard copy. However, storage and retrieval of magazines and newspapers, a continual challenge to media specialists, is no longer a problem in schools where extensive use is made of microform materials. Some media specialists find that subscribing to the microfilm edition of a newspaper such as the *New York Times* is more economical and efficient than the paper edition. If a collection includes professional materials and the proper equipment is available, microform documents, such as those provided through ERIC Clearinghouse on Information Resources, can be obtained and stored at a lower cost.

Advantages

1. A microform copy of a title is less expensive than the hardcover version.
2. Microforms can be converted to hard copy with proper equipment.
3. Primary source materials can be protected and stored.
4. Microforms have the highest storage density of any media.

Disadvantages

1. The cost of equipment needed to use a small collection of microforms outweighs the low cost of the microforms.
2. Many users spend more time trying to locate specific sections of the material than they do when using hard copy.

Selection Criteria

1. Does the collection contain the equipment needed to use the specific type of microform being considered?
2. Does the material meet the criteria for other print formats? Is the reproduction clear?
3. Is the equipment easy to use?

Collection Implications

The choice of negative or positive reproduction should be based on the equipment available and the user preference. Newspapers and magazines may be easier to store in microforms, but books may be easier to use in their hardback version. Consideration should be given to equipment that can project both microcards and microfiche if both formats are in the collection.

Sources of Information

Listings of available microforms, including microfiche and microfilm, can be found in *Guide to Microforms in Print* and its companion work *Subject Guide to Microforms in Print*; evaluations can be found in *Microform Review*.

Projected Still Images

Visual materials that project still images include filmstrips, slides, and transparencies.

Filmstrips

The 35mm filmstrip, black and white or color, silent or sound, has become one of the most heavily used forms of media in schools. Its high use may be explained by the characteristics of the material and equipment, which lend themselves to individual group use, often in full room light.

Advantages

1. Filmstrips can be shown on individual viewers or projected for large groups.
2. They are small, easy to store and distribute.
3. The fixed sequence of the frames ensures that visuals will not be lost or shown out of order and allows the instructor to control the speed of the presentation and to point out critical items while holding a single frame on the screen.
4. Sound tracks can be operated manually or automatically if the filmstrip and projector are properly equipped.
5. Sound tracks are often available in several languages for the same filmstrips.
6. A wide variety of subjects and presentation levels are available in this format.
7. Compact size and easily manageable equipment make this format one that can be readily circulated for home use.

Disadvantages

1. Editing and updating is more difficult and expensive than with slides.
2. Effective use of sound filmstrips requires audio-equipped projectors and compatible synchronization methods.
3. The fixed sequence does not permit flexibility in presentation.

4. Filmstrips are unable to simulate movement as in motion pictures and television, which are more familiar to students.

5. With each showing, the film is subject to physical damage, such as scratches or ripped sprocket holes.

Selection Criteria

1. Is the treatment designed for self- or teacher-directed presentation?

2. Is the length appropriate for the purpose and audience?

3. Is the item packaged for convenient use?

4. Is the sound or silent version needed by the users?

5. Which types of sound synchronization are available?

6. Are the captions well written and easily readable?

7. Do the visuals support the verbal message?

8. Are visuals consistent in style?

Collection Implications

The emphasis given to sound versus silent filmstrips in the collection is dependent on use patterns and user needs. Narration or captions may be needed in English and Spanish, which may mean Mexican Spanish, Cuban Spanish, and/or Puerto Rican Spanish. Media specialists face the problem of meeting the needs of their students, while producers face the problem of determining which dialect will be purchased by most schools.[2] Thus, the producers' decision may limit distribution of the dialect needed by the individual school.

Whether you purchase cassettes or disc recordings will depend upon the equipment available and user preferences.

Filmstrips should be packaged in containers the size and shape of books if they will be intershelved within the collection.

Sources of Information

Booklist and *School Library Journal* regularly review filmstrips. The *NICEM Index to 35mm Filmstrips* and the *Educators Guide to Free Filmstrips* list available items.

Angie LeClercq in "The Filmstrip Industry—A Guide to the Production, Distribution, and Selection of Educational Filmstrips" (*Library Technology Reports* 12, May 1976, pp. 257-59) describes additional reviewing sources, as well as the production process and subjects covered by major producers.

Slides

Three types of slides are commonly found in media collections: 1) the 2x2-inch slides used in projectors with trays, carousels, or cartridges, and on slide sorters or in individual viewers; 2) stereo reels, such as those used with the Viewmaster; and 3) microslides of biological specimens used with the microprojector. Most collections do not contain the 3¼x4-inch lantern slides because they break so easily.

Advantages

1. Color visuals can be produced economically.
2. Their size permits compact packaging and storage and ease of distribution and circulation.
3. Instructors can adapt sequencing and edit according to their needs.
4. Sound can often be ordered or can be added with the proper equipment.
5. Microslides permit an entire class to view microscopic materials, rather than requiring each student to have a microscope.
6. Slides can be projected for an indefinite time to accommodate discussion.

Disadvantages

1. Single slides are difficult to access rapidly.
2. Although slides can be processed or duplicated inexpensively, this takes time and is dependent upon the quality and speed of local laboratory services. Fast service is often available but at substantially higher costs.

Selection Criteria

1. Are art slides faithful to the original work?
2. Are mountings durable?
3. Is there continuity to the set of slides?
4. Are content and length of presentation appropriate for the intended purpose and audience?

Collection Implications

Effective group use of slides may require remote control features and projectors of lenses of appropriate focal length. Ensure that slide storage and display units are compatible with the equipment. Slides produced by students and teachers to be considered for inclusion in the collection should be of the same quality as those purchased.

Sources of Information

Reviews of slides are found in *School Library Journal* and *Booklist*, and available items are announced in NICEM *Index to Educational Slides.*

Transparencies

Transparencies are single sheets of acetate or plastic containing visual or verbal information that may be used in multiple sets as overlays. They are shown with an overhead projector. Some books and reference materials also use transparencies as overlays on illustrations to illustrate relationship or sequence.

Advantages

1. The instructor or presenter can face the audience in a lit room, thus facilitating interpersonal exchange and note-taking.
2. The user can quickly edit, sequence, and review the presentation.
3. The presenter can write on the transparency while it is being projected for use, or use a pencil-size pointer with ease.
4. Local production is relatively inexpensive and can be accomplished with a minimum of skill.
5. Overlays can be used to add information to a base visual.
6. Within certain limits, motion can be simulated.
7. The equipment is simple to operate and involves little maintenance except bulb replacement.

Disadvantages

1. Storage and circulation of transparencies may be more complex than with slides and filmstrips.
2. Multicolored transparencies may be more expensive than 35mm slides.
3. A special tilted screen may be needed to avoid a distorted visual image.
4. Unless equipment is properly positioned, it may obstruct the view of the screen.
5. There is a lack of standardization in size and packaging of transparencies.
6. Complex overlays may create problems during presentation.

Selection Criteria

1. Does the subject lend itself to transparency form rather than to illustration as a poster, mounted picture, slide, or other medium?
2. Is the lettering clear?
3. Is the information uncluttered?
4. Is the mounting secure?

5. Is the set logically sequenced and organized?
6. Is the transparency clearly labeled?
7. Are overlays easily manipulated?

Collection Implications

A greater number of overhead projectors will be needed in schools where teachers use the lecture method than in schools where individualized instruction is given. An overhead projector in each classroom is desirable in schools where many teachers use them during the same time period. If local production is done by either students or teachers, provision must be made for materials, equipment, and work areas.

Sources of Information

Transparencies are reviewed in *Booklist.* Their availability is listed in NICEM *Index to Educational Overhead Transparencies.*

Graphics

Graphics are nonmoving, opaque, visual materials that provide information through verbal and visual images (drawings, photographs). These materials include posters, graphs, charts, tables, diagrams, cartoons, art prints, and study prints.

Posters relate a single specific message or idea and should be selected on the basis of their clarity of design and attractiveness.

Graphs illustrate the relationship of numerical data. Four major types of graphs include: 1) line graphs, which present data on a simple continuous line in relation to a horizontal and vertical grid; 2) bar graphs, which show relationships through use of proportional bars; 3) circle or pie graphs, which show relationships as percentages of whole; and 4) pictograph or picture graphs, in which symbols present information.

Charts include tables and diagrams and are used to present data that have been classified or analyzed in some way. Tables list or tabulate data, usually with numbers. Diagrams show relationships between components, such as in a process or device.

Cartoons are stylized drawings, often part of a series, that tell a story or make a point quickly. The symbols used in political and satirical cartoons may require explanation to students.

Pictures include flat prints, study prints (one or both sides may have drawings or photographs with accompanying text or guide book) and art prints (reproductions of art works).

Advantages

1. Graphic materials are fairly inexpensive and widely available.
2. Physical detail can be illustrated with media such as X-rays, electron microscope photographs, and enlarged drawings.

3. Carefully selected pictures can help to prevent or correct students' misconceptions.

4. Graphic materials are easy to use, and some are easy to produce.

Disadvantages

1. Sizes and distances are often distorted.

2. Lack of or poor quality of color may limit proper interpretation.

3. Students need to develop "visual literacy" in order to use these materials effectively.

4. The size of the material must be large enough for all members of a group to see the same detail.

5. Motion cannot be simulated, only suggested.

6. If an opaque projector is used, the room must be completely darkened.

Selection Criteria

1. Is the information presented in an uncluttered manner?

2. Are nonrelevant elements either deemphasized or omitted?

3. Is there unity of presentation? Are the basic artistic principles of balance and harmony observed?

4. Is the lettering clear and legible?

5. Is the size large enough for the intended audience?

6. Does an art print give an accurate reproduction of color and detail?

7. Are the framing and mounting durable?

8. Are there sufficient individual pictures in a series to show a sequence of information?

Collection Implications

If you anticipate that the textual information on the back side of a study print will need to be displayed, consider ordering two copies of the set. The teacher's guide to the series may also provide this information. Graphics that are circulated, especially for home use, should be laminated, mounted, or protected in some way. Special storage units may be needed to permit students to examine the materials without damaging them.

Sources of Information

Donna Hill in *The Picture File* describes sources of pictures and selection aids. The catalogs of art reproduction distributors, such as the New York Graphic Society's *Fine Reproductions of Old and Modern Masters*, provide ordering information and serve as visual reference works. Prints are reviewed in tools such as *School Library Journal, Booklist*, and *Elementary School Library Collection.* The ALSC (Association for Library Service to Children) Print and Poster Evaluation Committee offers criteria and suggestions for these materials in "Planning for a Print and Poster Collection in Children's Libraries" (*Top of the News* 37, Spring 1981, pp. 283-87).

Visual Materials: Moving Images

Motion Picture

Motion pictures, including 16mm, 8mm, and super 8mm films, are available on reels or in cartridges. Movies can add the dimensions of motion and sound to presentation of information. The format options (black and white, color, silent, sound, reel, and cartridge) provide alternatives that can help meet the needs of individual users or groups.

Advantages
1. Special visual effects can be produced to encourage learning; examples include compression or extension of time, multiple images on one screen, distortions and illusions, and smooth transitions from one scene to the next.
2. Films can be used with front- and rear-screen projection for individual or group use.
3. Content is locked into a fixed sequence.
4. Motion picture equipment is, at present, more available than video equipment, fairly portable, and simple to operate.

Disadvantages
1. Production costs are high. Even film rental can be costly.
2. Film production lacks the instant feedback capability of video.
3. Film stock cannot be erased and reused.
4. A film's usefulness is limited by the recency of its content and amount of its physical deterioration. Care must be taken to prevent film breakage; films must be cleaned regularly. Film maintenance involves considerable time and cost.
5. Format options (16mm and 8mm, standard and super, optical or magnetic sound, silent, reel-to-reel, cassette, and cartridges) require compatible equipment.
6. If films are rented, bookings may need to be made as much as six months before the desired date of use.

7. 16mm films require darkened or, at least, dimmed rooms, or rear-screen projection equipment.

8. Equipment for 16mm films may be too difficult for the user to operate.

9. Ready access to information is difficult.

Selection Criteria

Witt offers seven questions to aid in the evaluation of films:

> (1) Is the film an integrated, organized set of ideas?... (2) Does the film prepare the learner for upcoming information?... (3) Does the film offer learners strong encoding/retrieval cues?... (4) Does the film allow time for rehearsal of the material?... (5) Does the film have a strong visual component?... (6) Is the film interesting? Does it hold your attention?... (7) Does the film include prescreening materials?[3]

These questions are directed at films designed "to teach specific verbal/visual information or concepts; they aren't quite as effective for evaluating films teaching motor skills, problem solving, or attitude change."[4]

Other criteria to be evaluated include:

1. Are content and treatment available in a less-expensive form?

2. If considering purchase, how often will the film be used and by how many people?

3. What is the quality of the acting, the scenario, the presentation techniques (photography, sound, and color)?

Collection Implications

In many schools, 16mm films are borrowed from the district media center or a film rental agency rather than purchased for the building-level collection. The 8mm film collection should include items covering a wide range of subjects in order to meet the needs of students and teachers.

Sources of Information

Reviews can be found in *Booklist, School Library Journal, EFLA Evaluations* and *Landers Film Review.* Available items are listed in NICEM *Index to 16mm Educational Films,* NICEM *Index to 8mm Motion Cartridges,* and the *Educators Guide to Free Films.* Further suggestions for selecting films are found in Emily S. Jones' *Manual on Film Evaluation* (Educational Film Library Association). The *Educational Film Locator* provides a comprehensive union list of holdings of the 50 Consortium of University Film Centers (CUFC), with information about lending policies. EFLA's *Film Library Quarterly* frequently has articles about children's films. A useful bibliography is Maureen Gaffney's *More Films Kids Like.*

Video

Video materials include materials transmitted by broadcast or open-circuit television and those transmitted within a closed-circuit television system. The use of broadcast programs brings people, places, and events that could not otherwise be seen to the user. Live television adds a dimension of immediacy. Since children enter school as experienced television consumers, the school can capitalize on the child's background while helping the child become a more critical viewer. At the same time, "The very familiarity of TV sometimes contributes to habits of inattentiveness and passivity. Students do not know how to learn from TV."[5]

Telecasts from the open-circuit television system have the advantages of films. Scheduling to ensure viewing time is a problem. The basis for evaluation is similar to that used with films, but the opportunity for previewing is almost nonexistent. Media specialists can alert teachers to programs by sharing information provided in the sources at the end of this section.

Advantages of Videotaping and/or Television Broadcasts

1. Videotaping of a performance can provide instant replay for criticism and evaluation.

2. Many of the visual effects used in filmmaking to enhance presentations can be used in the production of television programs.

3. As in films, the content and sequencing of the program is locked in, but the recorded program can be stopped or replayed.

4. Systems can be created to allow viewing of the same information simultaneously in more than one location in the school.

Disadvantages

1. Small monitor screens limit audience size unless multiple monitors or video projector systems are provided.

2. Equipment, although easy to use, must be compatible with the videotape. Consideration must be given to reel versus cassette, tape size, cartridge, and development of discs.

3. Production costs are high and include supplies, equipment, and production areas.

4. The amount of lettering on graphics for video is limited to about one-half that of film or still visuals.

5. Black-and-white television affects the use of color in presentations.

6. Because of rapid changes in video technology, many standard video systems will soon be obsolete.

7. Rapid access to information is difficult. However, Heuston points out that videodiscs with "Chapter Stop" provide "a fast forward or reverse tab key that goes rapidly to predesignated locations in the videodisc that may be thought of as chapters"[6] and foresees that an index could be used to help move a viewer efficiently through the disc.

Selection Criteria

1. Do the programs reflect adequate planning and effective presentations, creating a unified whole?
2. Does the telecast make use of the full range of television production techniques, or is it a filmed lecture?
3. Is the picture clear and undistorted?
4. Are the details easily discernible?
5. Is the same content available in a different format for less money?

Collection Implications

Materials produced by students, teachers, and staff that meet the selection criteria should be retained as part of the collection. Receiving and video playback equipment should be chosen for ease of use and durability.

Sources of Information

NICEM's *Index to Educational Video Tapes* lists available items. Study guides to forthcoming broadcasts are available from a number of sources, including commercial networks, *Teachers' Guide to Television*, and groups such as Prime Time School Television. Journals, such as *NCCT Forum: Quarterly Journal of the National Council for Children and Television*, include articles and list sources of further information.

Booklist reviews videotapes; *School Library Journal* reviews videocassettes; *EPIE Report* and *Library Technology Reports* review equipment.

Children's Media Market Place lists program distributors (companies that lease, sell, rent, and/or syndicate children's television programs). *School Library Journal* has a regular column "Video Watch."

Summary

This chapter discussed the formats that present information through the sense of sight. The next chapter discusses formats that utilize other senses. Later chapters describe individuals who have limited or no access to information presented in specific formats. A collection must contain a variety of formats if it is to meet the needs of all users.

Notes to Chapter 10

[1]The Fry readability formula can be readily applied by teachers and media specialists (see Edward B. Fry, "A Readability Graph for School Libraries, Part I," *School Libraries* 19 [1969]: 13-16 and "The Readability Principle," *Language Arts* 52 [1975]: 847-51). The Spache Readability Formula provides a finer distinction than Fry and is found in George D. Spache, *Good Reading for Poor Readers*, 10th ed. (Champaign, IL: Garrard, 1978).

[2]Daphne Philos, "Selection and Acquisition of Nonprint Media," *School Media Quarterly* 6 (1978): 183-84.

[3]Gary A. Witt, "How to Find and Use a Good Film," *Instructional Innovator* 25 (1980): 43-45.

[4]Ibid., p. 43.

[5]Vernon S. Gerlach and Donald P. Ely, *Teaching and Media: A Systematic Appraoch* (Englewood Cliffs, NJ: Prentice-Hall, 1971), p. 389.

[6]Dustin Heuston, *The Promise and Inevitability of the Videodisc in Education* (Washington, DC: National Institute of Education, 1977), p. 36.

Chapter 10 Bibliography

American Association of School Librarians, American Library Association, and Association for Educational Communications and Technology. *Media Programs: District and School.* Chicago, IL: American Library Association; Washington, DC: Association for Educational Communications and Technology, 1975.

Anderson, Ronald H. *Selecting and Developing Media for Instruction.* New York, NY: Van Nostrand Reinhold, 1976.

Brown, James W.; Lewis, Richard B.; and Harcleroad, Fred F. *AV Instruction: Technology, Media and Methods.* 5th ed. New York, NY: McGraw-Hill, 1977.

Brown, James W.; Norberg, Kenneth D.; and Srygley, Sara K. *Administering Educational Media: Instructional Technology and Library Services.* New York, NY: McGraw-Hill, 1972.

Cummins, Julie. "Children's Films: Secondhand, Secondrate, or Second Wind?" *Library Trends* 27 (1978): 45-49.

Eisley, H. Michael. "A Primer of Projectuals," *Previews* 3 (1974): 7-9.

Evans, Arthur. "An Evaluation Form that Makes Sense." *Instructional Innovator* 26 (1981): 32-33.

Fry, Edward B. "A Readability Graph for School Libraries, Part I." *School Libraries* 19 (1969): 13-16.

Gerlach, Vernon S., and Ely, Donald P. *Teaching and Media: A Systematic Approach.* Englewood Cliffs, NJ: Prentice-Hall, 1971.

Gillespie, John T., and Spirt, Diana L. *Creating a School Media Program.* New York, NY: R. R. Bowker, 1975.

Heuston, Dustin H. *The Promise and Inevitability of the Videodisc in Education.* Washington, DC: National Institute of Education, 1977.

Kaczmarek, Carol. "Government Publications for Elementary Libraries." *Hoosier School Libraries* 15 (1975): 18-23.

Kemph, Jeff. "Videodisc Comes to School." *Educational Leadership* 38 (1981): 647-49.

Maryland State Department of Education. Division of Library Development and Services. Office of School Media Services. *Evaluating and Selecting Media.* Baltimore, MD: The Office, 1976.

Miller, Shirley. *The Vertical File and Its Satellites: A Handbook of Acquisition, Processing, and Organization.* 2nd ed. Library Science Text Series. Littleton, CO: Libraries Unlimited, 1979.

"Paperback Explosion." Theme Issue. *Top of the News* 34 (1977): 35-71, 75-77, 79-83, 85-88.

Philos, Daphne. "Selection and Acquisition of Nonprint Media." *School Media Quarterly* 6 (1978): 179-87.

Rosenberg, Kenyon C., and Doskey, John S. *Media Equipment: A Guide and Dictionary.* Littleton, CO: Libraries Unlimited, 1976.

Schultz, Kathryn. "The Development of a Vertical File in an Elementary School Library—A True Story with a Happy Ending." *California School Libraries* 48 (1977): 16-25.

Spache, George D. *Good Reading for Poor Readers.* 10th ed. Champaign, IL: Garrard, 1978.

Witt, Gary A. "How to Find and Use a Good Film." *Instructional Innovator* 25 (1980): 43-45.

Wittich, Walter A., and Schuller, Charles F. *Instructional Technology: Its Nature and Use.* 6th ed. New York, NY: Harper and Row, 1979.

11
CRITERIA BY FORMAT: MULTISENSORY MATERIALS

As noted at the beginning of chapter 10, children learn through their senses. This chapter describes materials in which several senses may be used simultaneously or where the predominant senses used are hearing, touching, tasting, or smelling. Specifically, this chapter covers cartographics (maps and globes), auditory formats (sound recordings, educational radio broadcast), tactile formats (games, toys, models, sculpture, specimens), and instructional systems (textbooks and related materials, multimedia packages or kits, computer programs). These materials will be described in terms of their:

1. Physical characteristics
2. Advantages
3. Disadvantages
4. Selection criteria
5. Implications for collection development
6. Sources of bibliographic information and reviews

Some of the materials described in this chapter (such as kits) include materials described in chapter 10 (such as filmstrips). The reader will need to refer back to the appropriate section as this information will not be repeated.

Maps and Globes

Materials included in this discussion are flat maps, wall maps, and globes. When a map is projected in a book, consider both the following discussion and the information presented in the previous chapter.

Advantages

1. Maps can provide a wide range of information: place locations and spellings; significant surface features;

distances between places; scientific, social, cultural, political, historical, literary, and economic data.

2. Wall maps can be studied by groups.

3. Outline maps or globes that are unmarked encourage students to learn the names, shapes, and locations of political and topographical features.

4. Maps are readily available at a wide range of prices.

Disadvantages

1. If a group of students is to examine the same detail in a map, multiple copies or a transparency may be needed.

2. Cartographics, especially those on geographical, scientific, or political topics are quickly outdated.

Selection Criteria

1. Is the map aesthetically pleasing? Is color used to help the user interpret the information?

2. Is the depth of detail suitable for the intended audience?

3. Is the map legible? Are symbols representational and clearly typed?

4. Is the item durable? Has plasticized or cloth-backed paper been used?

5. Is the surface glareproof?

6. Do details obscure essential information?

Collection Implications

The collection should include different sizes of maps to meet the different needs of individuals and groups. Simple neighborhood, community, and state maps should be available to students as should more complex geographical, political, and literary maps. Maps should be easily accessible; those used frequently should be reinforced.

Sources of Information

The catalogs of map and globe publishers are the easiest to use and least expensive source of information about availability. James Coombs' "Globes: A Librarian's Guide to Selection and Purchase" (*Wilson Library Bulletin* 55 [1981]: 503-508) describes the types of globes available and offers additional criteria for selection. Federal and state agencies are common sources of highway and historical maps. Reviews are scarce.

Auditory Formats

Auditory materials include sound recordings (disc, tape, audiocards, and radio broadcasts). The most commonly used disc is 12 inches in diameter and 33⅓ rpm (revolutions per minute). Talking books use 16-inch, 3¼ rpm discs. Cassettes are usually recorded at 1⅞ ips (inches per second) and may lack the quality that can be obtained with reel-to-reel recordings at 3¾ or 7½ ips. Audiocards have a strip of magnetic tape containing up to 15 seconds of recorded sound, enabling the user to see the words as the sound is heard.

Recordings

Advantages

1. Recordings are portable and easy to use.
2. A wide range of content is available in this format.
3. Equipment is fairly easy to use and relatively inexpensive.
4. Music and sound effects can create moods or draw attention to specific information.
5. Use can be more easily scheduled than with radio broadcasts.
6. Information is locked into a fixed sequence. Easy retrieval can be achieved through use of bands on discs or counters on tape recorders.
7. Since record players and tape recorders are found in many homes, most children are familiar with their use as a listening or recording device.

Disadvantages

1. People may become bored if they use only audio materials for extended periods of time.
2. Discs can be easily damaged by scratching, warping, or lack of cleaning.
3. Sound quality on discs deteriorates with use.
4. Equipment malfunction can lead to tape jamming.
5. Different equipment is needed to accommodate the variety of tape speeds and arrangements of tracks.
6. Use with large groups may be limited without amplification systems.

Selection Criteria

1. Does narration begin with attention-getting words to draw the listener's attention? Are key words or key statements emphasized to aid the listener? Are the sentences short and simple?
2. Is the sound distortion-free?
3. Are the length and quality of the performance appropriate to the intended audience?

4. Do labels give enough information to distinguish one item from another and give playback information?
5. Are tapes and discs compatible with available equipment?
6. Is equipment easy to use and portable?
7. Does the equipment ensure accurate, high-quality reproduction?

Collection Implications

Provision should be made for individual and group use of music, documentaries, narrations, and drill masters. Storage for discs should be easily accessible and prevent warping.

Sources of Information

Available items are listed in NICEM *Index to Educational Audio Tapes*, NICEM *Index to Educational Records*, and *Educators Guide to Free Audio and Video Materials.* Reviews can be found in *Booklist* and *School Library Journal.*

Educational Radio Broadcasting

Since the times of radio programs are established by the broadcaster, classroom schedules may need to be rearranged to make use of a desired program. Scheduling problems and the difficulty of providing adequate listening conditions for large groups have deterred widespread use of radio broadcasts. When the school or district owns a radio station, such problems are easier to overcome. Guides to daily programming or series broadcasts from your local National Public Radio station can alert you to forthcoming programs of interest.

Tactile Formats

Students learn through touch with tactile formats such as games, toys, models, sculpture, and specimens. Although games and toys are not new to the learning process, it is only recently that they have been accepted as a legitimate part of the collection.

Games

A game "is a simplified, operational model of a real-life situation that provides students with vicarious participation in a variety of roles and events."[1] Games encourage participation but are usually limited to a small number of players at any one time. Players are given rules within which they must operate, a sequence and structure for their actions, and, sometimes, a time limit. Some games require use of computer or other equipment. At present, games available for use with microcomputers tend to be designed for specific pieces of equipment and cannot be used with equipment from other manufacturers.

Advantages

1. Participants become involved in solving the problems.
2. Games can simulate a more realistic environment than other media.
3. Participation usually generates a high degree of interest.

Disadvantages

1. Games can be time-consuming, lasting as long as several days. The intense involvement in a problem-solving situation is often interrupted by the bell and lost by the next day.
2. The limited number of players can create problems when others want to be involved.
3. Games can distort the social situation they attempt to simulate through omitted details or creator bias.

Selection Criteria

1. Is the packaging designed for control of the pieces? If a piece is lost, can it be replaced locally?
2. Are the items durable?
3. Are the directions clear?
4. Are the content, reading level, time requirements, and required dexterity appropriate for the intended audience?
5. Does the game require a computer? Is it compatible with existing equipment?
6. Is the game too costly or elaborate for its intended uses?

Collection Considerations

Commercially produced and locally developed games should be considered for inclusion in the collection. They serve many uses: educational purposes, practice of manipulative skills, opportunities for interacting with others, and relaxation.

Sources of Information

Social Education, the official publication of the National Council for the Social Studies, contains reviews of games. *Booklist* also reviews games occasionally.

Toys

As with games, toys such as blocks, puzzles, and construction materials allow the student an opportunity to develop coordination and to learn through touch, manipulation, and sight.

Advantages

1. Play is a way of exploring natural laws and relationships.
2. Toys can be used to develop perceptual motor skills. Toys such as dolls can be used to develop affective skills.
3. Toys can be used by individuals or groups.
4. Toys are inexpensive and can be made locally.

Disadvantages

1. Directions and parts may be lost.
2. The various shapes of toys can create different storage problems.

Selection Criteria

1. Can the child use the toy independently, or is adult guidance needed?
2. Has the user's developmental stage been considered in the selection?
3. Is color used to guide the use of the toy, or is it mere decoration?
4. Is the toy constructed of solid materials?
5. How breakable is the toy?
6. Can it be used without all of its parts? Can replacement parts be purchased or made in-house?
7. Is the material nonflammable?
8. Can the toy be washed or cleaned?

Collection Implications

Selection should be based on knowledge of the developmental needs of children served. You may need to provide duplicate items so that the same toy can be used by more than one student or can be used in the media center and also circulated.

Sources of Information

A practical guide to the selection and use of toys is *Toys to Go: A Guide to the Use of Realia in Public Libraries*, edited by Faith H. Hektoen and Jeanne R. Rinehart. The Consumer Products Safety Commission lists toys not considered safe for children to use.

Models

Representations of real things are found in models, dioramas, and mock-ups. A model is a three-dimensional representation of an object and may be smaller or larger than the real object. Cut-away models show the inside of an object. Dioramas provide an impression of depth with their realistic replicas of objects placed in the foreground against a curved background. Mock-ups stress important elements of the real object.

Advantages

1. These formats offer a sense of depth, thickness, height, and width.
2. They can reduce or enlarge objects to an observable size.
3. They can simplify complex objects.
4. The model and mock-up can be disassembled and reassembled to show relationships between parts.

Disadvantages

1. The size of models may limit their use with a group.
2. Some models are difficult to reassemble.

Selection Criteria

1. Are size relationships of the part to the whole accurately portrayed?
2. Are parts clearly labeled?
3. Are color and composition used to stress important features?
4. Will the construction withstand handling?

Collection Considerations

The size of many of these materials creates storage and distribution problems. Packaging models for circulation may also be difficult. Materials produced by the school staff and students may lack the durability needed for permanent inclusion in the collection.

Sources of Information

Bibliographic and review information is hard to locate for these materials. Suppliers of scientific equipment, such as Ward's Scientific Establishment, list their products in catalogs.

Sculpture

Sculpture and sculpture reproductions add another means for learning through touch and for developing aesthetic tastes.

Advantages

1. Sculpture reproductions are becoming more readily available and are fairly inexpensive.

2. The use of sculpture is not limited to art study but can be used in social science classes, mathematics, language arts, science, etc.

Disadvantages

1. An item may be too small to be used by a group.
2. Storage may pose a problem. Displaying the pieces about the media center can add to the atmosphere of the room and solve a storage problem.
3. The size and weight of some pieces may make circulation awkward.

Selection Criteria

1. Is the item made of durable material to withstand the touching that sculpture invites and which is necessary to fully appreciate the work?
2. Are the sculpture reproductions true to the original?

Collection Implications

The range of subjects should reflect the various areas of the curriculum as well as interests of the students.

Sources of Information

Many museums, such as the Metropolitan Art Museum, and some commercial firms make reproductions of sculptures. You will probably find examples on display at state and national conferences.

Specimens

Specimens may be alive, preserved in containers, or imbedded in plastic. They carry a special impact because they bring a piece of the real world into the hands of inquisitive users.

Advantages

1. Specimens can be handled and closely examined by students.
2. Specimens, such as stamps and postcards, can be acquired inexpensively from a wide range of sources, including the students themselves.
3. Live specimens may be borrowed from zoos, museums, and local breeders.
4. The handling and care of live specimens has many benefits for students and can provide an area of lively interest in the media center.
5. Live specimens, such as plants and cocoa beans, provide means for children to learn through smell.

Disadvantages

1. Specimens preserved in glass containers can be easily dropped and broken.
2. Some items may be too fragile or too small for more than one person to use at a time. Items, such as birds' nests and stuffed animals, are hard to keep clean.
3. Live specimens need proper care; aquariums, terrariums, or cages may need to be provided, and special growing conditions may need to be simulated.
4. Live specimens are most successful in media centers where adults share the children's appreciation of plants, fishes, reptiles, and animals. Are you prepared to find the snake that slipped out of someone's hand or to track down the hamster scurrying in and out of the shelving units?

Collection Considerations

Display areas where specimens can be observed by several students at the same time should be provided. Care should be taken not to duplicate materials found in other parts of the school, such as the science laboratory.

Sources of Information

Journals, such as *Science and Children*, have articles about the use of specimens and sometimes have reviews of these materials. Scientific supply houses sell specimens and storage units. Local museums, zoos, and botanical gardens may loan materials to schools and provide speakers or slide-tape programs about the materials.

Instructional Systems

Instructional systems include a broad range of materials designed to meet precisely defined instructional objectives. Materials include textbooks (basic and supplementary), workbooks, multimedia packages, and programs (courseware) developed for computers. These materials have been developed by commercial companies, manufacturers of equipment, school districts, and educational agencies.

Textbooks and Related Materials

Textbooks may be used as the chief source of information in the classroom or as supplementary information sources.

Advantages

1. Instruction is in a fixed sequence but can be reorganized by the instructor.

2. The table of contents and index provide rapid access to information.

3. Each student may have a copy.

4. The teacher's editions offer suggestions for related materials and activities.

5. Textbooks are field-tested, and the results of those tests can be requested and evaluated.

Disadvantages

1. Adoption of textbooks often implies they will be used over a number of years.

2. Textbooks can limit the creativity of a teacher.

3. Textbooks may encourage rote learning rather than stimulate exploration.

4. The content to be covered can be imposed by the limitations of the text.

Selection Criteria

The selection of textbooks or other instructional systems is usually done by teachers in consultation with media specialists. In some situations, the media specialist may not be involved, but the criteria presented here provide basic information necessary for selection. A media specialist may want to purchase a single copy of a particular text even though it is not used in the classroom setting.

1. Is the content accurate and objective?

2. Does the content represent a broad spectrum of viewpoints on a given topic?

3. Is the text correlated to the visual materials?

4. Are bibliographies up-to-date, and do they include multimedia materials?

5. Is the treatment appropriate for the intended purposes and audiences?

6. Is the arrangement chronological or systematic?

7. Is the presentation free of racial or sexual stereotyping?

Collection Implications

In some schools, media specialists are responsible for the organization, storage, distribution, and inventory of textbooks. Whether you have this responsibility or not, you need to be aware of the content, the material recommended in the bibliographies, and the potential use of textbooks as information sources.

Sources of Information

Available textbooks and related teaching materials, such as charts and workbooks, are listed in *El-Hi Textbooks in Print.*

Reviews can be found in *Curriculum Review* and the journals of professional teacher associations, such as *Reading Teacher* (International Reading Association). The Association for Supervision and Curriculum Development frequently has publications related to this topic. One useful example is *Eliminating Ethnic Bias in Instructional Materials: Comment and Bibliography*, edited by Maxine Dunfee, which includes a checklist for evaluating the treatment of minority groups and women.

Multimedia Packages or Kits

Multimedia packages or kits contain a variety of formats within one package. The materials may be preselected for the purpose of presenting information in a fixed sequence for use by an individual; they may be designed for user self-evaluation. Other kits and packages are less structured, a collection of related materials that can be used singly or in any combination by an individual or group.

Advantages

1. A variety of formats on a specific subject are combined into one package.
2. Programmed kits are designed to bring users to the same level of development.
3. Kits that include sound recordings of accompanying text mateirals can aid the learner who has difficulty with reading.

Disadvantages

1. One kit may include material designed for several grade levels.
2. Some kits may include materials that duplicate items in the collection.
3. The prices of kits cover a wide range and may require special equipment.

Selection Criteria

1. Does the kit create a unified whole? Is there a relationship between parts?
2. Is special equipment needed to use the materials? Does the collection include the equipment?
3. Do each of the items in the kit meet the criteria for that format?
4. Is the kit difficult to use?
5. Are the directions clear? Is adult guidance needed?

6. Does the kit fulfill a unique purpose not met by other materials within the collection? Is there room to store the materials?

Collection Implications

Kits should be selected on the basis of their potential use and appeal, or can be created from materials existing within the collection.

Sources of Information

Kits are reviewed in *Booklist, School Library Journal,* and *Curriculum Review.*

Computer Programs

Of the materials discussed in this chapter, computer programs and their equipment are the most rapidly changing. The advances in technology, particularly with microcomputers, have led to their increased availability for the schools. Computer software and courseware (instructional software) are available through five sources: in-house programming, commercial vendors, computer magazines, user groups, and researchers.

Advantages

1. Microcomputer programs can be used for creative problem-solving, drill and practice, testing, recreation, and guidance purposes.
2. Individualization and self-paced interaction are special instructional features of these systems. Programs can provide the reinforcement and stimulation needed by students who have learning disabilities.
3. For students who move frequently from one school to another, programs can provide remedial coursework.
4. Microcomputer networks, such as the ones being developed by IEU (Intermediate Education Units), are gaining popularity and presently can be found in Michigan, Colorado, and New York.[2]
5. Microcomputers are small, portable, and provide fast machine response time.
6. Increased attention is being given to the need for schools to help students develop computer literacy. Children as young as third-graders are now enrolled in computer courses.[3]
7. Use of microcomputers can be a highly motivating experience for disabled and gifted, as well as average, learners.

Disadvantages

1. There are few programs of consistently high quality presently available.

2. Teachers need to develop computer literacy—a skill not required by most teacher-certification programs. This lack of knowledge can create an initial negative response to using microcomputers in teaching.

3. Lack of compatibility of software and equipment limits use.

4. Ignorance of special qualities of microcomputers and poor programming can lead to improper use of the medium. Referring to computers, Gerlach and Ely point out that:

> There is a danger with any new instrument that it will be considered a panacea for educational ills. With almost every new device that has been invented, a group of zealots has promoted the new invention as the solution to many educational problems. This type of media myopia prevents an honest assessment of possible alternatives to solving the problems. Some researchers have found, for example, that the computer was being used to teach material that could have been taught just as well (and much less expensively) using traditional programmed instruction. In effect, the computer had become an electronic page turn.[4]

Selection Criteria

One of the chief considerations in selection will be the compatibility of software and equipment. Three types of software recording media are cassettes, cartridges, and floppy discs (standard floppy disc—8-inch diameter or microfloppy discs—5¼-inch diameter).[5] Criteria include:

1. What is the transmission speed?

2. Is the program fixed, or can it be modified?

3. Which computer language is used?

4. What is the capacity of the storage medium? How many bits per second?

5. How and with what ease can the user replay a program or record data?

Collection Considerations

As with other instructional systems, media specialists will want to work closely with teachers in selection and development of these materials. Changes are occurring so rapidly that it will be difficult to keep up-to-date without constantly monitoring growth in the industry. Remember that with any new technology, there is a time lag between the development of equipment and the availability of appropriate software.

Sources of Information

Creative Computing and *Compute* are examples of two magazines that list names of user groups, prime sources of software programs. A useful overview of the development and implications for education is found in the special issue of *Educational Technology* entitled "Microcomputers in Education" (19, October 1979, pp. 7-67). Franz J. Frederick's *Guide to Microcomputers* provides listings of networks, magazines, companies, and ongoing projects in schools. His guide provides a clearly written introduction to the subject, including how microcomputers can be used in media center operations.

A number of states are investigating or developing computer-based educational programs. One example is the Minnesota Educational Computing Consortium that provides in-service programs, technical advice, and software to member schools that pay a fee for services.

Summary

The last two chapters discussed the wide range of materials that a collection may contain if it is to meet the needs of its users. When selecting materials, consider who will be using the materials, what formats they prefer, how the materials will be used, and whether appropriate equipment is available. Few collections will include every format described. Some materials may be outside the scope of a school's collection program policy; others may not be suitable for a particular group of users.

Advances in technology will bring new formats to the market. As these advances and refinements occur, consider their application to your collection. Does a new format meet needs not met by earlier formats? Will sufficient subject coverage be available in the new format to justify purchasing the necessary hardware? Does the new format add a dimension to content, unavailable in other media? If not, it may not be a good investment. Future developments in media will bring new horizons to the school media center if they are truly advantageous and if the products they generate are selected and implemented with the user in mind.

Notes to Chapter 11

[1]Vernon S. Gerlach and Donald P. Ely, *Teaching and Media: A Systematic Approach* (Englewood Cliffs, NJ: Prentice-Hall, 1971), p. 340.

[2]Charles L. Blaschke, "Microcomputers Software Development for Schools: What, Who, How?" *Educational Technology* 19 (1979): 28.

[3]Lynn Schoen, "Survey of Micros Shows Common Goals, Problems," *Media Review* 3 (1980): 1.

[4]Gerlach and Ely, *Teaching and Media*, p. 329.

[5]For a fuller discussion of the characteristics and advantages of each, see Emile E. Attala, "Mass Storage Media for Microprocessor-Based Computer Assisted Instructional Systems," *Educational Technology* 19 (1979): 53-55.

Chapter 11 Bibliography

American Association of School Librarians, American Library Association, and Association for Educational Communications and Technology. *Media Programs: District and School.* Chicago, IL: American Library Association; Washington, DC: Association for Educational Communications and Technology, 1975.

Anderson, Ronald H. *Selecting and Developing Media for Instruction.* New York, NY: Van Nostrand Reinhold, 1976.

Brown, James W.; Lewis, Richard B.; and Harcleroad, Fred F. *AV Instruction: Technology, Media and Methods.* 5th ed. New York, NY: McGraw-Hill, 1977.

Brown, James W.; Norberg, Kenneth D.; and Srygley, Sara K. *Administering Educational Media: Instructional Technology and Library Services.* New York, NY: McGraw-Hill, 1972.

Gerlach, Vernon S., and Ely, Donald P. *Teaching and Media: A Systematic Approach.* Englewood Cliffs, NY: Prentice-Hall, 1971.

Gillespie, John T., and Spirt, Diana L. *Creating a School Media Program.* New York, NY: R. R. Bowker, 1975.

Hektoen, Faith H., and Rinehart, Jeanne B., eds. *Toys to Go: A Guide to the Use of Realia in Public Libraries.* Chicago, IL: American Library Association, 1975.

Lopez, Antonio M., Jr. "Microcomputers: Tools of the Present and Future." *School Media Quarterly* 9 (1981): 164-67.

Kaczmarek, Carol. "Government Publications for Elementary Libraries." *Hoosier School Libraries* 15 (1975): 18-23.

Kemph, Jeff. "Videodisc Comes to School." *Educational Leadership* 38 (1981): 647-49.

Maryland State Department of Education. Division of Library Development and Services. Office of School Media Services. *Evaluating and Selecting Media.* Baltimore, MD: The Office, 1976.

"Microcomputers in Education." Theme Issue. *Educational Technology* 19 (1979): 7-67.

Miller, Inabeth. "The Micros Are Coming." *Media and Methods* 16 (1980): 32-34, 72-74.

Miller, Shirley. *The Vertical File and Its Satellites: A Handbook of Acquisition, Processing, and Organization.* 2nd ed. Library Science Text Series. Littleton, CO: Libraries Unlimited, 1979.

"Paperback Explosion." Theme Issue. *Top of the News* 34 (1977): 35-71, 75-77, 79-83, 85-88.

Philos, Daphne. "Selection and Acquisition of Nonprint Media." *School Media Quarterly* 6 (1978): 179-87.

Rosenberg, Kenyon C., and Doskey, John S. *Media Equipment: A Guide and Dictionary.* Littleton, CO: Libraries Unlimited, 1976.

Report to the Commissioner's Advisory Committee on Instructional Computing. *More Hands for Teachers.* Tallahassee, FL: State of Florida, Department of Education, 1980.

Schoen, Lynn. "Survey of Micros Shows Common Goals, Problems," *Media Review* 3 (1980): 1, 8.

Schultz, Kathryn. "The Development of a Vertical File in an Elementary School Library—A True Story with a Happy Ending." *California School Libraries* 48 (1977): 16-25.

Spache, George D. *Good Reading for Poor Readers.* 10th ed. Champaign, IL: Garrard, 1978.

Witt, Gary A. "How to Find and Use a Good Film." *Instructional Innovator* 25 (1980): 43-45.

Wittich, Walter A., and Schuller, Charles F. *Instructional Technology: Its Nature and Use.* 6th ed. New York, NY: Harper and Row, 1979.

Zamora, Ramon. "Computer Town, USA! Using Personal Computers in the Public Library." *School Library Journal* 27 (1981): 28-31.

12
MEETING CURRICULAR AND INSTRUCTIONAL NEEDS

A major purpose of the collection lies in its support of school programs. The variety of instructional programs and practices found within a school creates diverse demands upon its collection. To be well versed about instructional programs, the media specialist must:

1. Understand the approaches to education emulated within the school.

2. Be familiar with the curriculum plans used in the school.

3. Be knowledgeable about the purposes and demands of the various teaching models used by teachers.

This chapter discusses the assumptions underlying four commonly held views of education and the ways that each view uses resources to achieve its goals. Teaching support systems include human and material resources. The underlying principles of a particular teaching model provide a basis for selecting material resources with appropriate content and formats.

Each school is unique. The subjects covered in one school may be identical to those found in another school, but classroom situations may bear no resemblance to one another if the approach to teaching differs. This discussion highlights some of the differences, providing an overview of educational models on which the media specialist can begin to analyze the teaching methods and educational goals of a school. Some of the questions to explore are:

1. Does the school have a unified approach to the educational process?

2. Is there a similarity in teaching methods?

3. Do some teachers prefer one method over another?

4. Are specific methods recommended in the curriculum plans, or do teachers have freedom to choose their own method?

As you work with teachers, learn about their attitudes and teaching methods so that the media center can best serve their needs.

Approaches to Education

People view the purpose of educating children in different ways. Society values different goals for education at different itmes. An example in the United States is the recent attention directed at basic education. This example illustrates the call of society for changes in education. While the principal and teachers with whom you work may share this educational goal, it is likely that some will not.

The faculty at Jefferson Elementary School are in agreement that basic education is an important goal; however, they do not agree on how to achieve that goal. Several teachers prefer to use the Basal Reading Series that details teaching strategies and prescribes student activities. In contrast, Irene, a teacher at the school, uses the individualized reading approach that builds on the individual child's interests and abilities. The media specialist at Jefferson Elementary School must recognize that the formally adopted goals statement does not reflect each teacher's individual perspective of education. Knowing how teachers view education can help the media specialist work with them. The discussion that follows describes four perspectives that are likely to be encountered.:

1. Basic Education
2. Personalized Education
3. Learning What the Scholar Does
4. Engaging in a Dialogue on the Critical Problems of Society[1]

By examining these four commonly held perspectives shown in figure 20 (page 188), the media specialist can identify their characteristics, the implications for the media program, and the demands on the collection.

Basic Education

The basic education approach emphasizes skills and basic knowledge. The perspective described here is broader than the "basics" or reading, writing, and arithmetic; the goal is to provide society with informed citizens who can function economically and socially within a democratic society.[2] The goal is achieved by providing all students with a common background and knowledge base and is pursued without consideration of the child's interests.

Thus, the basic education curriculum is designed to prepare children to perform functions needed by society. The curriculum includes the traditional subjects of reading, writing, arithmetic, history, geography, government, and economics. Contemporary technology is also an important part of the curriculum, teaching students to communicate and to be informed consumers of various media. As future citizens of the world, children need to understand differences of other cultures and the economic, political, and social problems faced by nations throughout the world.

Figure 20.   Perspectives of Education

PERSPECTIVE • GOAL	ROLE OF STUDENT	ROLE OF TEACHER	ROLE OF SUPPORT SYSTEM
Basic Education • Informed citizenry	• Achieve a predetermined level of performance or acquire a common background or knowledge	• Evaluate progress Prescribe learning activities	• Reinforce basic concepts and skills
Personalized Education • Development of the individual	• Pursue individual interests	• Guide the development of the individual	• Provide wide-ranging information in a variety of formats
Learning What a Scholar Does • Transmit knowledge of a discipline	• Apply the tools of scientists	• Scientific role-model Offer counsel and advice	• Provide data and equipment for collecting data
Dialogue on the Critical Problems of Society • Improve society	• Explore the nature of society	• Suggest issues and guide the examination of alternatives	• Offer differing viewpoints on a variety of issues

To ensure that all children leave their schooling with the same level of competency in specified skills and knowledge, attention is given to each individual's progress. Diagnostic programs prescribe remedial learning experiences. Children use self-instructional materials or study in small groups to learn specific skills. Individuals acquire these skills at different rates, moving quickly through some developmental activities and taking more time with others.

Media specialists acquire commercial materials that facilitate reinforcement of learning and assist in the design and production of self-instructional materials. Programmed materials in print, machine, or computer formats need to be collected. Single-loop films can help reinforce concepts. Games can be used for study of social issues or political processes. In the basic education process, individualization of instruction is based on the child's level of performance, not on the child's interests.

Personalized Education

The child is the key in this approach. Attention is given to the individual's talents and interests, encouraging unique personal development. A typical setting for this approach is a school that holds humanistic values and provides resources so the student can grow intellectually and develop his own personality. The curriculum is designed around the needs and interests of the individual child, not the needs of society or academic disciplines.

The teacher works on a one-to-one basis to guide in the full exploration of each student's capabilities and interests. In practice, few schools have the personnel or facilities to implement such a plan for every student. Existing examples can be found, however, in programs designed for gifted or disabled children.

In a school that practices personalized education, students can engage in a wide range of activities. One student may produce a film about his neighborhood, study a foreign language and geography to correspond with a student in another country, conduct scientific experiments, or work on mathematical puzzles. At another time, this child may be found reading a favorite book or listening to music.

A wide range of resources on many subjects and in many formats is necessary to support this type of program. In addition,

> some of these resources need to be other teachers, who might work at the school on a full or part-time basis, as artists, musicians, and writers. Good libraries are essential, and can include banks of motion pictures that the student can use to teach himself, television courses, particularly short courses that he can draw on when he needs them, laboratory materials, shops, and so on.[3]

The collection must cover a wide range of subjects presented at different levels. Listings of community and human resources are also valuable. The media specialist must know each student, be involved in his/her development, and serve as a motivator to bring resources and students together.

Learning What the Scholar Does

The goals of teaching academic inquiry—how scholars work—are focused outside the child and are aimed at meeting the needs of academic disciplines by introducing the child to the knowledge and methodology of various disciplines.

Students work in small groups to analyze critical problems, applying tools of the social and natural sciences. Teachers need skill and interest in the inquiry method to offer adequate counsel and advice. Investigation and analysis require sufficient time for students to acquire the techniques of inquiry involved in a discipline. thus, the student will develop abilities in 1) generating data (e.g., experimenting), 2) organizing data (e.g., charting), 3) using data (e.g., theorizing), and 4) using theories (e.g., predicting).[4] Subjects covered in this curriculum are the natural and social sciences (e.g., economics, anthropology, sociology, mathematics, biology). In elementary schools, distinctions become blurred by grouping several disciplines into one subject (e.g., social studies).

Materials developed by scientists and social scientists, help children develop these models of analysis and are part of the curriculum. The community serves as a place to gather data. Students use the tools of the scientists to collect oral history or to study local government or ecology. Other learning activities take place in laboratory centers equipped with necessary tools.

The media center should have spaces and laboratory areas for small groups to work together in their investigations. The collection should include materials introducing the basic knowledge of the discipline, information about how scholars carry out scientific inquiry, and the tools necessary for research. In this situation, one should find not only the usual information sources and formats, but also materials and equipment that students can use in investigations. Circulating tape recorders will facilitate the collection or oral history. Scientific and mathematical equipment will also be needed.

Engaging in a Dialogue on the Critical Problems of Society

The fourth educational perspective focuses on critical issues and values of our culture by introducing students to a dialogue on the nature and future of society. Students deal with controversies, identifying issues and values and debating alternative solutions to collective problems. This experience allows children to engage in the democratic process. It is the ultimate goal that students gain the necessary skills to participate in society effectively. Political and social issues make up units of study. A problem in the local community, such as flooding due to lack of planning for housing developments, provides a basis for investigation. Another group may study the value and limits of dissent in the democratic political process.

The nature of the subjects and the use of time for such investigations may make adults uneasy. Many teachers may think that skills are not being taught; parents may say that values should be taught in the home. Some adults will think that students are not ready or able to cope with such problems. Instructional materials for school-age children often avoid these types of issues.

This approach calls for information that not only helps children identify the issues, but also presents different viewpoints. Newspaper accounts, journal accounts, and videotaped discussions need to be timely, reflecting current thinking on the topic. In their investigations, students may interview community members or observe local government in operation. The media specialist must be knowledgeable about government agencies, community resources, and people who may be interviewed by students or invited to the school.

Effective teachers in this school are those who enjoy dialogue and encourage students to think deeply and creatively about issues. The media specialist should share these traits and must be willing to defend the child's right to information.

As you visit schools, look for evidence of these four approaches to education. In an effort to achieve different goals, a single teacher may, at one time or another, adopt one or more of the approaches. By looking at the perspectives of education, one can begin to identify the school's goals that have implications for the curriculum, the teachers, the students, and the collection.

The Curriculum

A school achieves its purposes through its educational program, the curriculum. Typical elements in a curriculum include: 1) a statement of goals and objectives, 2) the content to be covered, 3) the organization (or sequencing) of that content, 4) teaching strategies selected to meet the objectives or organizational requirements, and 5) a program for evaluation.[5] Curriculum plans may give particular emphasis to one or more of these elements. Each element of the curriculum has implications for the media program and its collection.

Examine the curriculum plans for your school. This task may be time-consuming for curriculum plans vary in scope, and many schools will have plans for all subject areas. Some plans are comprehensive, covering all educational programs; others cover specific subjects; still others cover specific learning situations.

Curriculum plans can be general in tone or give very specific directives for teachers. The general approach often outlines the broad tasks of the school and identifies the teacher's responsibility. More specific curricula specify when, how, to whom, with what, and under what conditions the teacher is to function. The more specific curriculum offers more direct practical information for the media specialist than does the general curriculum. However, both plans will be helpful guides to the types of materials to be added to the collection.

An analysis of the curriculum can indicate the content or subject matter to be covered, when it will be covered, to what depth, and how it will be presented. If several classes will be simultaneously studying the same unit, duplicate copies of specific materials will be needed. Otherwise, work with teachers to decide whether specific units can be taught at different times of the year. The curriculum may indicate why a unit is recommended at a specific time and if altering its sequence would be detrimental to the learning process.

Teaching Models

The discussion of the perspectives of education pointed out that people hold diverse views of the goals of education. The role of the teacher varies from one perspective to another. Even within a particular perspective, a teacher may use a variety of approaches. Media specialists need to know what approaches will be used to know resources needed.

Joyce and Weil's book *Models of Teaching* offers a guide to understand the range of approaches that can be used. Of particular interest to media specialists is the concept of "support system," which Joyce and Weil define as:

the conditions necessary for ... [a teaching model's] existence. What support, we ask, is needed in order to create the environment specified by the model?... Suppose that a model postulates that students should teach themselves, with the roles of teachers to consultation and facilitation. What support is necessary? Certainly a classroom filled only with textbooks would be limiting and prescriptive. Rather, support in the form of books, films, self-instructional systems, travel arrangements, and the like is necessary or the model will be empty.[6]

This concept directly involves the media specialist in the teaching process. An understanding of teaching methods is necessary to communicate effectively with administrators about what implications various teaching methods will have for the media program and what demands will be made on the collection. Joyce and Weil warn "many able educational programs fail because of failure to consider or anticipate the support requirements."[7]

Teachers use different models to achieve desired results. Diversity also occurs as teachers and administrators personally interpret the models. Specifically, the following characteristics of the teaching models shown in figure 21 can be examined:

Figure 21. Characteristics of Teaching Models

TEACHING MODEL	ROLE OF STUDENT	ROLE OF TEACHER	ROLE OF SUPPORT SYSTEM
Group Investigation	• Participate in group problem-solving	• Promote and guide group interaction	• Provide a wide range of information and opinion
Inductive Model	• Explore problems using the scientific method	• Non-directive Encourage clear thinking processes	• Provide factual information
Operant Conditioning	• Demonstrate specified responses	• Provide structured learning experience	• Instructional package provides all necessary support materials

1. The purposes they serve
2. The role of the teacher
3. The role of the students
4. The support systems needed

The discussion that follows does not attempt to cover all models described by Joyce and Weil. One model "group investigation" is used as an example of how examining a particular model can reveal information needed to be considered in a collection program. Three other models are described briefly in terms of the role of the teacher, role of student, and support system.

Group Investigations

This model, usable for all subject areas and at every age level, blends the goals of academic inquiry, social interaction, and social process learning. The components of this model include:

1. Presentation of problem situations in which students participate, observing themselves as inquirers and as interactors with others.
2. The diagnostic process, in which the student identifies and formulates problems and pursues solutions.
3. A consciousness of method of inquiry as the student collects data, associates and classifies ideas, formulates and tests hypotheses, studies consequences, and modifies plans.
4. Development of the capacity for reflection to formulate conclusions and integrate them with earlier ideas.[8]

While applying scientific methods of inquiry, the group approach builds on emotional aspects of inquiry. Each student faces the conflict of personal need versus the group's task requirements. As individuals react to the situation and reconcile their differences, self-awareness is increased while curiosity is stimulated.

Inquiry is the result of the motivation and curiosity of students, not the direction of the teacher. It is the inquiry process, not the product of inquiry, that is important. A major goal of this approach is the transfer of knowledge, the development of the student's ability to draw on past experiences and apply them to the present. The teacher serves as counselor, consultant, and friendly critic, guiding the group experiences through three levels: 1) task level (What is the nature of the problem?); 2) group management level (What information is needed?; and 3) individual meaning level (How does the individual react to the conclusions?).[9]

The classroom application Joyce and Weil describe begins when a sixth-grade social studies class reads an article about a 12-year-old child who dies from an overdose of heroin. The investigation begins with the question: How could this have happened? After interviewing a doctor and reading about drug use by children, the class discovers the complexity of the drug issue. As students broaden their investigation, they explore the relationship that drug use has to housing problems, the welfare system, and racial discrimination.

The support system for group investigation needs to be extensive and immediately responsive to the needs of teachers and students. "A first-class library [is needed to provide] information and opinion through a wide variety of media."[10] Students will often need to go outside the school in their search for information. Media specialists will need to provide access to community resources, including a list of human resources, and access to materials available from other institutions. Joyce and Weil state "one reason cooperative inquiry of this sort has been relatively rare is that the support systems were not adequate to maintain the level of inquiry."[11]

The implications for collections should be obvious. A wide range of current materials must be available to students. Listings of community and human resources will receive high usage. Materials must be readily accessible, or the inquiry will be delayed and the sense of curiosity hindered. Information files of pamphlets can present various views on a subject and supplement the use of newspapers and magazines. Materials that distinguish between fact and opinion can encourage this type of learning.

Other Models

A brief description of three other teaching models illustrates the diversity of demands that can be placed on the collection. In the "inductive model," based on scientific method, three phases are designed to increase thinking capacity. During the first phase, students are required to predict consequences, explain unfamiliar data, or hypothesize. During the second phase, children attempt to explain their predictions; and, in the third phase, children verify their predictions or identify conditions that would verify the predictions.

Under the inductive model, a second-grade social studies class may deal with the concept that the supermarket needs a location, equipment, goods, and services. The unit opens with the question: What does a person need to open a supermarket? Drawing on the children's experience in supermarkets, the teacher poses questions to draw data from their observations. The teacher may use pictures to generate additional observations by the children. The teacher guides the children as they categorize their observations, which constitute the data to be interpreted. As pupils explore dimensions and relationships, they move toward the stage where they can make inferences and predictions. A trip to a supermarket could serve as a means for verifying their predictions. The media center must provide a large amount of raw data to be organized by the children. Unlike the first model, where the materials need to reflect various opinions on the subject, with the "inductive model" students need factual information upon which to make their own judgments.

In the "nondirective" or "student-centered" model, the individual and/or group develop their own goals. The student takes responsibility for initiating and maintaining learning activities. The nondirective teacher understands but doesn't judge the student, speaks only when in the role of participant, and clarifies the student's attitudes by helping him or her reflect and decide what to do next. The support system is dependent on open-ended intellectual resources, those which do not offer solutions. Students need access to thought-provoking resources as they identify their goals. Community and human resources may also be needed to fulfill the needs of this teaching model.

In contrast, the "operant condition" model is highly structured with no open-ended dialogue. The teacher or program controls the action. Stimuli are presented verbally or physically to the learner until the student's response is correct. The correct response is then reinforced or confirmed. This model has application for subject matter as well as behavior modification. In the operant condition model, the support system is the program itself; a design that ensures an organized, logical sequence is critical. Each student selects from several programs and works at an individualized pace. "In traditional educational strategies, the teacher grades [the] student; he is at fault; in programmed instruction the student grades the teacher."[12]

The media program supports the operant conditioning model with three types of activities. First, programs produced or selected by teachers are stored and circulated through the media center. Second, the materials are selected for the collection based on their potential to help students perform specific objectives. Third, the media specialist is involved in the design and production of instructional programs.

Implications for the Collection

The media specialist must know the priorities and understand the constraints of the curriculum and teaching methods in his or her school if the collection is to meet the needs of the school's instructional programs. To support some of these programs, the collection must include materials that traditionally have been considered "instructional" or "classroom" materials. Items already in the collection need reassessment to ascertain how they can contribute to the teaching/learning process.

Many teaching strategies require that so-called library materials will be major sources of information and/or instruction. Selection decisions based on instructional needs can only be achieved through cooperative efforts by teachers and media specialists. General selection tools do not include the type of analysis and evaluation of materials needed to match materials and teaching strategies. However, they provide a starting point for the selection process. As teachers participate in selection decisions and use materials, record their evaluations. Obtain recommendations for materials from publications that are subject- or program-oriented. Examples of this type of information source include journals of subject-oriented professional associations and subject-oriented selection and bibliographic tools. Appendix 2 provides a list of journals that review materials, articles on criteria for selecting materials in a specific subject field, and bibliographies for subject areas.

Summary

Media specialists have a responsibility to ensure that the collection meets the curricular and instructional needs of the school. To carry out this responsibility, they must know the conditions for use of materials: who, how, and for what purposes. Trying to learn why materials are to be used is often harder than finding out who uses them and how they are used. Curriculum plans may provide this information. Teachers and administrators can also provide information about conditions for use.

The challenge of meeting curricular needs is complicated by the different views of what education should be. Teachers and administrators may be unable to articulate their viewpoints. But, if the media specialist sorts through what is seen and heard, the various approaches to education can begin to be understood.

As you work with teachers and grow in your knowledge of their methods, you will begin to understand the changing needs for materials. For one subject, a teacher may use a model that makes heavy uses of specified materials; he or she may later use a different model that makes no demands on the collection.

Throughout your career you will want to learn more about teaching. Professional resources for teachers can provide helpful information. If media programs are to be integrated with the school's programs, the media specialist must understand the why and how of teaching. Professional reading should include literature on educational principles and methods. Take advantage of conversations, observation in classrooms, in-service programs, and other opportunities to further your understanding of teaching. The knowledge gained will enhance your ability to work with teachers and result in more effective use of the collection.

Notes to Chapter 12

[1]Bruce Joyce and Marsha Weil, *Models of Teaching* (Englewood Cliffs, NJ: Prentice-Hall, 1972), pp. 334-40.

[2]Arthur W. Foshay, *Curriculum for the 70s: An Agenda for Invention* (Washington, DC: Center for the Study of Instruction, National Education Association, 1970), p. 3.

[3]Joyce and Weil, *Models of Teaching*, p. 337.

[4]*Teaching toward Inquiry* (Washington, DC: National Education Association, 1971), p. 49.

[5]Hilda Taba, *Curriculum Development: Theory and Practice* (New York, NY: Harcourt Brace Jovanovich, 1962), p. 10.

[6]Joyce and Weil, *Models of Teaching*, p. 16.

[7]Ibid.

[8]Ibid., pp. 39-40.

[9]Ibid., p. 44.

[10]Ibid., p. 46.

[11]Ibid.

[12]Ibid., p. 289.

Chapter 12 Bibliography

Foshay, Arthur W. *Curriculum for the 70s: An Agenda for Invention.* Washington, DC: Center for the Study of Instruction, National Education Association, 1970.

Joyce, Bruce, and Weil, Marsha. *Models of Teaching.* Englewood Cliffs, NJ: Prentice-Hall, 1972.

Kingsbury, Mary. "Priorities for Rounding Out a Century." *Wilson Library Bulletin* 50 (1976): 395-98.

Klein, M. Frances. *About Learning Materials.* Washington, DC: Association for Supervision and Curriculum Development, 1978.

Miller, Marilyn L. "Collection Development in School Library Media Centers: National Recommendation and Reality." *Collection Building* 1 (1978): 25-48.

Payne, Arlene. *The Study of Curriculum Plans.* Washington, DC: National Education Association, 1969.

Saylor, J. Galen, and Alexander, William M. *Planning Curriculum for Schools.* New York, NY: Holt, Rinehart, and Winston, 1974.

Schiro, Michael. *Curriculum for Better Schools: The Great Ideological Debate.* Englewood Cliffs, NJ: Educational Technology Publications, 1978.

Schools for the 70s and Beyond: A Call to Action. Washington, DC: Center for the Study of Instruction, National Education Association, 1971.

Taba, Hilda. *Curriculum Development: Theory and Practice.* New York, NY: Harcourt Brace Jovanovich, 1962.

Taylor, Kenneth I. "Media in the Context of Instruction." *School Media Quarterly* 4 (1976): 224-28, 237-41.

Teaching toward Inquiry. Washington, DC: National Education Association, 1971.

Vandergrift, Kay E. "Are We Selecting for a Generation of Skeptics?" *School Library Journal* 23 (1977): 41-43.

13
MEETING THE TYPICAL NEEDS OF INDIVIDUALS

One purpose of the collection is to meet informational and recreational needs of individuals. To fulfill this purpose, media specialists must know the individuals using the collection.

This chapter focuses on materials and tools designed to help media specialists select materials that meet the typical needs of groups of individuals. For convenience, this chapter is organized by the following categories of user need:

Preschoolers and Kindergarteners

Beginning Readers

Personal and Social Development

Personal Interests

Reference Materials

Foreign Books for Children

Bibliographic information for the tools mentioned in this chapter can be found in Appendix 2.

This chapter provides only a starting point for getting to know users. A work such as this cannot fully explore all the differences in people. You, as a media specialist, will need to know each individual with whom you are working. When you select materials for a collection, however,

> it must never be forgotten that reading, viewing, and listening can all be done for different purposes: factual, educational, cultural, recreational. The purpose differs with the user. In other words, a work in a collection never has a single use or purpose; it is multidimensional, depending on the individual user's needs. Therefore different levels and styles of materials, and different approaches to a subject, are needed.[1]

In addition to format and content, criteria for selecting materials should include consideration of what groups will potentially use the materials. The range of human needs is endless, varying from person to person. As you work with individuals in your school, you will, no doubt, recognize additional characteristics and needs not identified in this chapter or the next (which will focus on the special needs of groups of users).

Students

To select materials that meet the wide range of needs and interests exhibited and expressed by students, the media specialist needs a knowledge of available materials, as well as a knowledge of the individual students. How does one provide a personalized contact for every student? Wehmeyer offers this advice:

> The media center collection is so selected that each student can pursue assigned research topics in the medium he prefers, in materials at a difficulty level appropriate to his needs. But that is only the beginning. In the collection there must be a point of contact for every student, an item on the shelves which lets him know that his personal interests are anticipated by someone. That item may be the Bowmar sound filmstrip on drag racing, or *Model Airplane News* magazine, or a Charlie Brown comic collection—or a recorded Bach organ fugue ... variety is the key to ... a contact collection.[2]

Do you remember Donna, the fifth-grade teacher who visited the media center on the first day of school in chapter 1? Each of the students in her class has individual needs.

Daniel, for example, reads at the second-grade level. He is socially active and enjoys participating in all activities. When concepts or vocabulary are beyond his comprehension, however, he becomes restless, moving about the room looking for something else to do. In the process, he often disturbs others who have longer attention spans. When Daniel is in the media center, his favorite pastimes are feeding the gerbils, flipping through the pages of *World Magazine*, and viewing filmstrips about the lives of sports figures.

After a summer spent on a ranch, Daniel came into the media center and asked for "the" book about horses. The media specialist was surprised for Daniel usually avoided books. What had prompted this request? Daniel's story unfolded—he wanted to know why a horse on the ranch had to be killed. The media specialist knew little about horses, but realized that Daniel was asking for a detailed drawing of the horse's anatomy. After making several telephone calls to other media centers, the media specialist located a technically written but well-illustrated book. Daniel was excited when the book arrived through interlibrary loan. He immediately started studying the drawings. Matching a label on one illustration with a word in the text, Daniel struggled to read the explanation. The media specialist offered to help; both learned through the experience. Daniel's explanation of what he had witnessed helped the media specialist understand the technical language, so she could simplify the explanation. In this incident, Daniel's high interest level increased his attention span.

In contrast, Michael has an inquiring mind and reads at the eighth-grade level. He works effectively whether alone or with a group and always has some project underway. His interests are diverse: history, old maps, science, carpentry, stamp collecting, hiking, swimming, spectator sports, and visiting museums. With Michael, the media specialist is challenged to find detailed information on a wide range of subjects. Michael loses all sense of time when he concentrates on a favorite topic.

The other students in the class are equally unique. Donna has them working in teams on reports about states. One group checks the vertical file for information about California. Another team previews slides to use in a class presentation. A third group produces transparencies for its report. Several children work in the reference area locating illustrations of state flowers and flags. Brian shows John how to use the opaque projector to enlarge an outline map. This class uses every type of resource in the media center.

Other class members have prepared their presentations and are pursuing individual interests. While Rebecca looks for a new horse story, Michelle listens to poetry recordings, and Jeffrey studies a map of the universe. Chris is heard laughing over a new riddle book; Jason and Matthew continue their game of chess; Lisa is trying to organize a group to write a play.

These children also represent different home environments. Magazines, books, newspapers, recordings, and television programs are regular sources of information and entertainment in Michael's home. He has helped his older brother write programs for their microcomputer. Lisa's garage loft is the neighborhood theater. Plays and puppet shows occur whenever there is an interest, enough players, and an audience.

Many class members belong to organized groups such as the Boy Scouts. Other students take music, dance, or art lessons. Daniel's and Chris' experiences, however, center on activities sponsored by the school or in the immediate neighborhood. The cost of more formalized activities is beyond the incomes of their families; their world is limited to where they can ride their bicycles.

The purpose of this look at the members of one class has been to illustrate differences in individuals. Regardless of how students are grouped or classified, one must never forget that each child is a special, unique individual. Each class member represents a different home environment, level of intelligence, degree of motivation, language fluency, and reading ability. Other differences include age, physical and mental health, socioeconomic background, physical coordination, creativity, hobbies, and preferred style of learning.

Coursework in child or adolescent psychology, human growth and development, educational psychology, communications, group dynamics, and human relations provides a background for understanding differences in people. Information about individual students can be obtained through studying their school records, interviewing their teachers and parents, observing students and keeping anecdotal records, conducting interest profiles, and other techniques. Your personal knowledge of each child is important if you are to meet each one's needs.

We must be concerned about the welfare of students and knowledgeable about their behavior. It cannot be demanded of teachers that they love children. Love is a human feeling and cannot be turned on and off at will. Besides, some children are sometimes not very lovable. Professional responsibility, however, requires concern for the persons involved in the process, and such concern can and should be demanded of teachers.[3]

Without this concern for the individual, can media specialists know and meet students' needs? This book and other sources can only provide general guidelines. Only you know the individuals in your school.

Preschoolers and Kindergarteners

Some programs for preschoolers are designed to orient both parent and child to the school prior to the child's enrollment in kindergarten. Although your school may not sponsor such a program, both you and the kindergarten teacher can anticipate questions from parents about materials and experiences recommended for this age group.

During these early years, a child normally displays a rapid development of language skills, taking pleasure in words and rhymes. An interest in written language generally shows itself at the age of four, according to Durkin.[4] Children are curious and enjoy materials that encourage participation and involve naming, touching, and pointing. Manipulative materials, such as games, toys, and puzzles, can also initiate imaginative play. Active play is preferred to sitting or listening. The child is beginning to assert independence as accomplishments are realized.

Questions that should be considered in selecting materials for these age groups are:

1. Are the materials realistic and accurately reported? Taylor notes that children at this age have "much difficulty in distinguishing between what is real and what is fantasy."[5]

2. Does the story or book offer an element of surprise or suspense? Is there humor that appeals to the child?

3. Does the information build on a child's experiences?

4. Is the length of the material designed for the interest and attention span of a young child?

5. Are the words simple, descriptive, and within the understanding of a child?

6. Are the ideas and concepts understandable to a child?

7. Do illustrations closely represent the text?

8. Are materials durable? Can parts be replaced?

Sources of information about materials for this age group also include works for their parents and teachers. In *Babies Need Books*, Butler explains "why" children up to the age of six need books, and suggests ways to use specific titles with children. Taylor's *A Child Goes Forth* provides guidelines on selection and use of materials. Practical suggestions for parents are given in Rogers' "What Books and Records Should I Get for My Preschooler?" The collected essays in *The Kindergarten Child and Reading* discuss the young child and identify criteria for selecting or making instructional materials.

Beginning Readers

The beginning reader is described by Good as "a pupil who is in the preprimer stage of reading development or at the reading readiness stage."[6] Books designed for the child just learning to read are frequently labeled "beginning-to-read" or "beginning readers." The phrase "easy-to-read" may refer to books for the same audience, but it usually designates titles for older children who need a limited vocabulary in their books.

Titles designed for the beginning reader contribute to personal development by providing a child the opportunity to read independently. Such works

> do more than offer children a limited engagement with print and success with a controlled vocabulary ... [they] can reinforce ... background in literary experience. [They can now read what they once heard.] They can help sensitize children to the difference between literary language and spoken language; they can encourage growth in their sense of story; and they can reinforce a positive sense of self and a genuine enjoyment of reading.[7]

Criteria to consider include:

1. Is the vocabulary appropriate for the developmental level?
2. Is repetition of words or phrases handled in an appealing style?
3. Are sentences simple and direct?
4. Does the work have literary quality?
5. Will the story or information appeal to children?
6. Does the format add appeal?

After analyzing the genre, Hains concluded:

> Beginning Readers can offer children a limited engagement with these literary conventions—plot patterns, types of characterization, setting conventions and various stylistic devices. These books can offer a bridge between the

being-read-to engagement with literature and the choosing and reading of literature for themselves. While some of these books are strong in only one area, others like *A Bargain for Frances* and *Seeing Is Believing* encourage a fuller literary experience. As teachers, we should include some of the BEST of the genre on our classroom shelves.[8]

The "Easy Reading" column by Judith Goldberger in *Booklist* provides reviews of books, which indicate interest level and reading level, for beginning readers and older children with reading problems. *Elementary School Library Collection* recommends titles in this genre and indicates reading level in the entries and appendix.

Personal and Social Development

Media specialists have a responsibility to provide materials that help children understand themselves and others. There are a number of tools designed to assist in this effort. Many of the tools identify professional background readings that will help increase the media specialist's personal sensitivity and awareness of children's needs.

The significance of working with children in this manner is described by Dreyer:

> Books have an important role in everyday life. Through well-chosen books, readers may increase their self-knowledge and self-esteem, gain relief from unconscious conflicts, clarify their values, and better understand other people. By identifying with characters in books, people may come to realize that they are part of humanity; that they are not alone in their struggles with reality. Reading increases personal knowledge and invites readers to consider themselves objectively.[9]

As disabled children are being integrated into regular classrooms, adults have become increasingly aware of a need to help children understand each other. Works that accurately portray disabilities can help children understand the needs, and recognize the qualities, of their disabled classmates. Baskin and Harris also realize:

> The promise of full participation for the disabled remains to be met. Translating rhetoric into reality requires the abandonment of inaccurate·and rejecting perceptions and their replacement by enlightened, accepting ones. Literature can help in this quest by presenting models for the restructuring of a more hospitable, supportive society.[10]

On the other hand, when recommending titles to disabled students for their personal development, it should be remembered:

The disabled, unlike the nondisabled, know they are *more* than their guide dog or their wheelchair. Therefore, their role models could be individuals who share, for example vocational or avocational interests, but who do not necessarily share an identical impairment. While reading books about disabled heroes or heroines is of value, restriction to only these models is confining.[11]

Some writers of these tools point out the use of books as therapy. The average media specialist, however, does not have the education necessary to use books in a diagnostic and prescriptive manner. However, others may have such training, and these tools can facilitate our joint efforts.

In *Notes from a Different Drummer: A Guide to Juvenile Fiction Portraying the Handicapped*, Baskin and Harris evaluate the literary quality and the subject treatment in books written about disabilities for readers from five to eighteen years old. Berstein's *Books to Help Children Cope with Separation and Loss* provides descriptive annotations and evaluative statements of books that deal with the new sibling, the new school, death, divorce, desertion, serious illness, war, foster care, stepparents, adoption, and homelessness. The "Developmental Values" index of Sutherland's *The Best in Children's Books* also provides a guide to recommended titles dealing with topics such as adjusting to the new baby or boy-girl relationships.

Dreyer's *The Bookfinder: A Guide to Children's Literature about the Needs and Problems of Youth Aged 2-15* is presented in a unique format. The top half of each page includes a subject, author, and title index including psychological, behavioral, and developmental topics of concern to children and adolescents. The bottom half of each page contains annotations, bibliographic information, main subject headings, synopses, analysis of strengths or limitations of presentation, and a list of works presenting the same content in other formats (films, tapes, paperbacks, Braille, talking books, filmstrips, and recordings). The book is designed with split pages so that the index and annotations can be used at the same time.

In *Children's Literature: An Issues Approach*, Rudman presents a critical guide to professional and juvenile materials arranged by theme, such as siblings, divorce, death, aging, war, sex, blacks, native Americans, and females.

Reading Ladders for Human Relations is designed for teachers, parents, and librarians. The five themes (ladders)—"Growing into Self," "Relating to Wide Individual Differences," "Interacting in Groups," "Appreciating Different Cultures," and "Coping in a Changing World"—have subcategories that describe titles appropriate for preschool through mature high school readers. The essays at the beginning of each section and the annotations are designed to help the user promote sensitivity in human relations.

Media specialists must also select materials that will satisfy the needs of children from diverse ethnic backgrounds. Some of the tools cited earlier in this section include titles dealing with ethnic backgrounds. The following titles represent only a sampling of the many bibliographies designed to help in this area. Bibliographic essays in journals such as *School Library Journal* and the review columns in *Booklist* can be used to update the information provided in these tools.

The New York Public Library has published several useful titles, including *The Black Experience in Children's Books, The Black Experience in Children's Audio-Visual Mateirals*, and *The Chinese in Children's Books.* Discussions of how titles were selected for inclusion in these tools offer valid criteria for your selection activities. *Black World in Literature for Children* recommends materials for readers three years old through adult; this work is unusual in that it also indicates titles not recommended.

Two examples of tools about Native Americans are *Books on American Indians and Eskimos* and *Literature by and about the American Indian.* both works list titles for elementary school through young adult readers.

Building Ethnic Collections is broader in scope, covering over 40 ethnic groups, including reference sources, curriculum materials, books, and audiovisual materials. Another tool by Wynar and Buttlar is *Ethnic Film and Filmstrip Guide for Libraries and Media Centers: A Selective Filmography.*

Additional tools can be found in bibliographies, such as *Selecting Materials for Children and Young Adults.*

Personal Interests

Many of the bibliographies and reviewing sources identified in the chapters about formats can be used when trying to match user and material. The following tools share a common characteristic: recommendations are based on appeal of the titles to children of a specific age group.

Committees within the National Council of Teachers of English periodically revise *Adventuring with Books: A Booklist for Pre-School—Grade 6* and *Your Reading: A Booklist for Junior High Schools.* Recommended titles are grouped by subjects of reader interest, such as "Witchcraft," "Mystery," "Being in Love" (subject headings of appeal to junior high students). The annotations in *Your Reading* are written to be used by the students themselves.

Popular Reading for Children: A Collection of the Booklist Columns covers fantasy, ghosts, humor, mysteries, science, and the "Fourth Grade Connection." The latter deals specifically with titles for the 9- to 11-year-olds. Another restrospective tool, *Best Books for Children: Preschool through the Middle Grades*, annotates over 13,000 fiction and nonfiction titles that have been recommended by at least three review sources.

A current reviewing source that focuses on materials for the adolescent reader is *Kliatt Paperback Book Guide.* Kliatt recommends books for students ages 12 through 19 and includes codes for titles recommended for special groups of students, such as those with low reading abilities or those ready for mature subjects and themes.

Reference Materials

Children's personal interests and classroom activities, may necessitate the use of reference materials. Reference books are those works, such as an encyclopedia, that provide factual information and are not intended to be read from cover to cover. This is not to say that some child won't read an encyclopedia from cover to cover—every school seems to have at least one child who does this or, at least, tries.

Certain reference titles (like *Guinness Book of World Records*) are so popular, you will need a circulating copy as well as one in the reference collection. In schools where groups go on week-long camping trips or nature hikes, the media center should include several copies of nature identification books. These works can be ordered in hardback or paperback depending on how the books will be used.

The whole collection, particularly nonfiction works and materials in the vertical (or information) file, will receive heavy usage when they are being used to answer children's questions.

Children can be introduced to the concept of indexes to articles through the *Children's Magazine Guide.* Adults also find this a useful index to craft ideas, plays, and other activities designed for children.

Criteria used for adult reference materials—authority, scope, treatment of materials, arrangement, format, and special features—apply equally well to reference materials for children. Illustrations, cross-references, and pronunciation guides are especially important features in children's reference materials.

Two useful selection tools are *Reference Books for Children* and *Guide to Reference Books for School Media Centers.* Both tools recommend a wide range of titles on a variety of subjects. *Elementary School Library Collection* includes a section of recommended reference materials. Reviews of current titles are published in "Reference and Subscription Books Review" in *Booklist.*

Indexes to poetry, fairy tales, plays, and music can serve two purposes—to indicate where many short works have been published and to provide a list of source materials that serve as a check for titles of anthologies that could be added to the collection. Reference works that can be used in this way include:

Index to Poetry for Children and Young People: 1970-1975

Folklore: An Annotated Bibliography and Index to Single Editions

Index to Fairy Tales, 1949-1972

Index to Collective Biographies for Young Readers

Index to Children's Songs

Subject Index to Poetry for Children and Young People 1957-1975

Foreign Books for Children

Books from other countries appeal to children, providing them with opportunities to experience different cultures or to use foreign language skills. If your school has a foreign language program, find out what kind of materials the teacher recommends and when they would be most helpful.

When selecting foreign children's books, remember the following tips from Harrison:

Do develop foreign professional contacts through *Bookbird*, Friends of IBBY, and other channels.

Don't use selection tools more than about a year old, except as last resorts.

Don't expect books from foreign countries to meet U.S. standards for library acquisition, either in bookmaking quality or in literary or cultural viewpoint.

Don't promise your users specific titles or types of materials before you receive them.[12]

Bookbird, journal of the International Institute for Children's Literature, contains articles and reviews. The Friends of IBBY, Inc. is the organization in the United States sponsored by the U.S. National Section of the International Board on Books for Young People. Their semiannual *Newsletter* carries news about juvenile titles in the United States and abroad. Another source of information is the Information Center on Children's Cultures, a service of the United States Committee for UNICEF. This agency can be contacted for information about sources of children's books, lists of pen pals and other exchanges, pictorial materials, and information sheets about other countries. *Bulletin of Proyecto Leer* is a free semiannual publication supported by the Books for the People, Inc. and includes annotations of books recommended for children.

Summary

Children are important people in media specialists' lives. They deserve to be known as individuals. This is not an easy task if you work in a large school. When you first join a faculty, it seems that you know only the troublemakers or the children who spend a lot of time in the media center.

When working with groups of children, it is easy to overlook individuals who seem to melt into the crowd. Media specialists are involved with students during important years of development; yet we seldom realize how our brief contact can affect children and their families.

This writer recalls a first-grader who came into the media center one day asking for information about logic and philosophy. "Yes," I replied.

He seemed to know what he wanted. With my fingers crossed, we went to the shelves. I knew we had only three titles on logic and wondered if he would be able to understand them. He did. Years later as a woman was talking to me about the attitudes that media specialists display to children and the rights of children to information, she described how her young son proudly brought home a nonfiction book. His teacher had wanted him to read a picture book rather than a book about logic. As I listened to her story, I wondered if this boy could have been the child I remembered. As it turned out, I had helped the boy in his early quest to study logic. As he grew older, he continued to pursue his interests. He became a champion chess player in his early teens. Every day there are children or adults who are influenced by media specialists, but rarely do we get the opportunity to learn the results of our efforts.

Notes to Chapter 13

[1]Richard K. Gardner, *Library Collections: Their Origin, Selection, and Development* (New York, NY: McGraw-Hill, 1981), p. 197.

[2]Lillian W. Wehmeyer, "The Student-Centered Media Center," *California School Libraries* 45 (1974): 19-20.

[3]Arthur W. Coombs, *Educational Accountability: Beyond Behavioral Objectives* (Washington, DC: Association for Supervision and Curriculum Development, 1972), p. 36.

[4]Dolores Durkin, "Facts about Pre-First Grade Reading," in *The Kindergarten Child and Reading*, edited by Lloyd O. Ollila (Newark, DE: International Reading Association, 1977), p. 2.

[5]Barbara Taylor, *A Child Goes Forth* (Provo, UT: Brigham Young University, 1975), p. 82.

[6]Carter V. Good, ed. *Dictionary of Education*, 3rd ed. (New York, NY: McGraw-Hill, 1973), p. 472.

[7]Maryellen Hains, "Beginning Readers: A Bridge to Literary Conventions," *Ripples* 5 (1980): 5.

[8]Ibid., p. 8.

[9]Sharon Spredemann Dreyer, *The Bookfinder: A Guide to Children's Literature about the Needs and Problems of Youth Aged 2-15*, Vol. 1 (Circle Pines, MN: American Guidance Service, 1977), p. ix.

[10]Barbara H. Baskin and Karen H. Harris, *Notes from a Different Drummer: A Guide to Juvenile Fiction Portraying the Handicapped* (New York, NY: R. R. Bowker, 1977), p. xvi.

[11]Ibid., p. 63.

[12]Lucretia M. Harrison, "Acquiring Foreign Children's Books," *School Library Journal* 25 (1978): 25.

Chapter 13 Bibliography

Baskin, Barbara H., and Harris, Karen H. *Notes from a Different Drummer: A Guide to Juvenile Fiction Portraying the Handicapped.* New York, NY: R. R. Bowker, 1977.

Coombs, Arthur W. *Educational Accountability: Beyond Behavioral Objectives.* Washington, DC: Association for Supervision and Curriculum Development, 1972.

Dreyer, Sharon Spredemann. *The Bookfinder: A Guide to Children's Literature about the Needs and Problems of Youth Aged 2-15.* Vol. 1. Circle Pines, MN: American Guidance Service, 1977.

Gardner, Richard K. *Library Collections: Their Origin, Selection, and Development.* New York, NY: McGraw-Hill, 1981.

Goldberger, Judith M. "Easy to Read: Hard to Review." *Booklist* 73 (1976): 480-81.

Good, Carter V., ed. *Dictionary of Education.* 3rd ed. New York, NY: McGraw-Hill, 1973.

Hains, Maryellen. "Beginning Readers: A Bridge to Literary Conventions." *Ripples: Newsletter of the Children's Literature Assembly* 5 (1980): 5-8.

Harrison, Lucretia M. "Acquiring Foreign Children's Books." *School Library Journal* 4 (1978): 22-25.

Helbig, Alethea K. "Instant Boredom: Easy-to-Reads." *Ripples: Newsletter of the Children's Literature Assembly* 5 (1980): 1-5.

Johnson, Ferne, ed. *Start Early for an Early Start: You and the Young Child.* Chicago, IL: American Library Association, 1976.

McDowell, Kyle, and Estes, Thelma J. "Preschoolers Become Part of the Learning Community." *Instructor* 85 (1975): 124.

Ollila, Lloyd O., ed. *The Kindergarten Child and Reading.* Newark, DE: International Reading Association, 1977.

Quisenberry, Nancy L.; Shepherd, Terry R.; and Williams-Burns, Winona. "Criteria for the Selection of Records, Filmstrips, and Films for Young Children." *Audiovisual Instruction* 18 (1973): 37-42.

Taylor, Barbara. *A Child Goes Forth.* Provo, UT: Brigham Young University, 1975.

Thompson, Frances A. "A Pre-school Program in the Elementary School." *Hoosier School Libraries* 14 (1974): 8-9.

Wehmeyer, Lillian W. "The Student-Centered Media Center." *California School Libraries* 45 (1974): 19-24.

14
MEETING THE SPECIAL NEEDS OF INDIVIDUALS

Although each person is unique, he or she may be part of a group that shares characteristics that may require special consideration in materials selection. This chapter examines:

1. The special needs of user groups.
2. Criteria for selecting materials to meet those needs.
3. Sources of information about materials to meet their needs.

As you read about these special group characteristics, consider the message of a poster, which reminds us to "label cans, not people." This chapter categorizes people by a single common attribute. Remember, however, that these people are individuals with many other needs. The groups discussed in this chapter include exceptional children (physically, mentally, emotionally, and visually disabled; deaf or hearing-impaired; gifted); poor and reluctant readers; and adults working with children.

Exceptional Children

The United Nation's proclamation that 1981 was the International Year of Disabled Persons was a response to the need for public awareness and education about disabilities. The theme "the full participation of disabled persons in the life of their society" serves as a reminder to those of us working with children that our responsibility is to help not only those considered disabled, but all children, to understand each other. The need for increased public awareness is evident when examining the mix of terminology used to describe disabled people. Baskin and Harris explain a significant difference between a disability and a handicap:

Technically, a *disability* is a reality, for example, the loss of vision. The restrictions and opportunities imposed by society determine whether or not the disability becomes a *handicap.*

That is, "handicap" actually should be understood to be situational and attitude bound.[1]

Attitudes affect how the subject is approached. Many of the writers who will be cited later in this chapter emphasize this point.

A variety of terms, such as handicapped, disabled, exceptional, dysfunctioning, impaired and special, are used in works and tools cited in this chapter to describe individuals and their needs. A positive approach is found in Baskin and Harris' use of the term "emotion dysfunction" for "mental illness" to bypass the connotation of sickness and to suggest a lack of permanence.[2] As the needs of children and the characteristics of the tools are examined, it should be noted that terminology is only one way in which to begin to address the needs of the disabled.

The Education for All Handicapped Children Act, PL 9-142, includes within its categories individuals who are mentally retarded, hard of hearing, deaf, orthopedically impaired, speech impaired, visually handicapped, seriously emotionally disturbed, and those with special learning disabilities. Both PL 94-142 and Section 504 of the Rehabilitation Act of 1973, which sets forth the civil rights of all handicapped Americans, have focused national attention on the educational needs of all children.[3]

A broader term used to refer to those identified earlier as disabled or handicapped is "exceptional children," an expression that also includes gifted children. The information resources for teachers and media specialists that deal with these categories often overlap. To address this problem, this section discusses the following groups of exceptional children: disabled children (physically, mentally, emotionally, and visually disabled; deaf or hearing-impaired) and gifted children.

Children with Disabilities

Children's interests, regardless of disabilities, usually relate to those held by peers. One can anticipate the interests of a particular age group, but one must also know a child's individual interests. A general knowledge of the characteristics of children and their interests is essential when working with all children. This knowledge helps media specialists anticipate the recreational and informational ways in which children will use materials. Children need to be provided with materials that will best meet individual needs. Information about the characteristics of disabilities, and the materials recommended to meet the needs of the disabled, can guide collection activities. The characteristics of a specific disability, however, may not apply to all individuals with that disability. Multiply disabled children will often have needs identified in more than one type of disability.

In order to meet the variety of needs of disabled children, the writers of "Selection Materials for Children with Special Needs" offer three principles to guide collection activities:

1. It is important to focus on the particular interests, abilities, and needs of the child and not to overemphasize the disability.

2. It is essential to look at existing collections in new ways. Adaptations or alternate uses of present library resources are frequently more appropriate and always less expensive than seeking new materials. There are times, however, when new materials must be selected.

3. It is necessary to consider all forms and formats of media.[4]

Not only do media specialists need to know the individuals and the materials appropriate for disabled children in the collection, but we have a responsibility to know the resources available to them in the community. These may include rehabilitation agencies, information agencies, and other educational or recreational programs. For example, this writer's community has a recreation area designed to accommodate wheelchairs. Trails provide easy access to picnic areas, a fishing pier, and nature paths. Along the trails, information stations use models, large charts, printed information, and recorded messages to point out items of interest. The sheltered eating areas provide spaces for wheelchairs interspersed with regular picnic benches. The park is now a beautiful spot that all people can enjoy. Information about such facilities should be included in the card catalog as possible field trip sites.

Physically Disabled

Manipulation of materials and equipment may pose difficulties for the physically disabled. "The weight of a book may be important to a child with a muscle development problem."[5] Special reading stands or automatic page turners may be needed by some individuals. An alternative is to provide materials in tape or other recorded format. Automated formats such as cassette tapes are easier to use than reel-to-reel tapes. Talking books, once available only to those considered legally blind, are now available to individuals who cannot read standard printed items. Other individuals will be able to handle paperbacks or books with large print or thick cardboard or laminated pages.

The impact of a visible physical disability may interfere in the media specialist's work with a disabled child. Attention may focus on the disability rather than on the child; the child's physical needs may cause the specialist to overlook the individual's need for intellectual stimulation, support, and motivation. "All physically handicapped children and their families," according to Dresang, "have to fight the pervacive [sic] notion that the disabled cannot learn and progress."[6]

Mentally Disabled

Mentally disabled people have difficulty understanding written and spoken language and abstract concepts. Their attention span is shorter than that of their peers. Visually explicit materials (large, uncluttered visuals) can aid in communication. Both illustrations and text should be clear and to the point. Large print with wide margins is desirable. Concepts should be logically developed. Each step should be complete and sequential. "Redundancy is very desirable. The children need the message told; they need it told again, and they need the message retold."[7] Folktales with their use of repetition and refrains encourage "the child ... to come into a story on the refrain and anticipate what is going to happen."[8] Content should be presented with easy vocabulary, simple structure, and uncomplicated sentences. Time manipulations, flashbacks, or change of narrators within a story can confuse a mentally disabled child. Harris also notes that, "Mentally retarded children tend to be very literal and devices such as irony tend to be inappropriate."[9] Formats that involve the use of the senses, such as puppets, toys, games, puzzles, relief maps, natural objects, and models, provide a means for the child to gather information through touch.

Recorded materials need to be aurally explicit; sound must be clear and direct. For some individuals, the speed may need to be slower than normal.

Magazines with numerous illustrations, simple sentences, short articles, and easy vocabularies are also helpful. This format is popular with people of all ages and does not carry the stigma of being easy or special. Contextual clues may help mentally retarded children comprehend technical terms, especially in subjects of special interest. "If mentally retarded children are going to develop a lifelong habit of reading," Harris claims that "it is going to grow out of reading popular magazines."[10]

Emotionally Disturbed

Emotionally disturbed children need certainty and success. Otherwise, their difficulties in coping with situations and their emotional problems can inferfere with academic performance. Materials should be minimally frustrating with easy vocabulary and uncomplicated sentences. These individuals have short attention spans and are easily distracted. When selecting materials for emotionally disturbed children, special consideration should be given to thematic content. Harris warns that topics such as abandonment, child abuse, alcoholism, death, and drug abuse may be useful for other children but

> librarians need to be cautious in using them with children or young adults who have emotional problems.... Books for the emotionally dysfunctional should provide nonthreatening situations showing models of acceptable, coping behavior; and books that show social problems, familial problems, and interpersonal relationships of all kinds are good choices, but the books should show a resolution of differences and disputes. Books that are open-ended and contain unresolved situations are not the kind of books that we need for children who like and need certainty and closure.[11]

Work with the child's teacher, therapist, or other professional worker to learn whether specific themes will help or harm the individual.

Visually Impaired

Children who have vision problems may require special types of materials. Some partially sighted individuals can use regular-print materials, while others need large-print materials. One cannot make the assumption that large-print materials are appropriate for all partially sighted children. Low vision aids, hand-held magnifiers, or closed circuit television can magnify standard-print materials. Braille books, games, and outline maps can be used by specially trained children. A totally blind person can read printed materials by using option machines that allow the user to feel sensation on his or her fingertips. For others, readers and taped materials may be most useful.

Visually disabled children can participate in all media center activities. Useful equipment include: rear-projection screens, which permit children to get close to the screen without blocking images; tape recorders; speech compressors, which eliminate pauses between words and thus reduce the time needed to access recorded materials; and talking calculators.[12]

Visually and physically disabled people can use talking books, tapes and records of books, textbooks, and magazines (available in English and other languages, including Spanish), a free service of the National Library Service for the Blind and Physically Handicapped, Library of Congress. Arrangements can be made through the local public library. Recordings for the Blind, Inc. is another organization that provides recorded books.

Titles available in large type can be identified in *Large Type Books in Print.* The 1980 edition lists more than 4,000 titles (adult, juvenile, and textbook) and indicates the type size and book size for each. *For Younger Readers: Braille and Talking Books* is a biennial catalog of Braille, disc, and cassette books announced in *Braille Book Review* and *Talking Book Topics* from the National Library Service for the Blind and Physically Handicapped. The latter three titles are available free to the blind or disabled. Another type of material provided by the service is called "twin-vision," a format in which printed text is interpaged with Braille text in one volume. The American Foundation for the Blind is another organization that publishes useful pamphlets, such as *Guidelines for Public School Programs Serving Visually Handicapped Children* and other sources of information including the *Journal of Visual Impairment and Blindness.*

Deaf or Hearing-Impaired

Hearing-impaired children have difficulty hearing spoken language and, as a result, often have difficulty understanding written and spoken language and abstract concepts. Metcalf reports:

Children with significant hearing losses learn primarily by sight. For this reason ideas and concepts must be presented in a visual format in order for the children to understand them.... Instructing with pictures alone may not suffice because hearing impaired children have some difficulty interpreting illustrations. Their language handicaps make it difficult for them to infer reactions, conversations, or events which are not specifically depicted in the illustrations. In order for hearing impaired children with significant hearing loses to understand a concept or story, librarians should use both pictures and total communication (using spoken and manual communication) simultaneously.[13]

Visuals should be large, presenting a single, distinct concept or idea. Illustrations and print should be immediately recognizable. Language patterns and sentence structures need to be simple.[14] The hearing-impaired also need materials that are repetitious and provide reinforcement.

Captioned films, filmstrips, and videotapes are also useful for the hearing-impaired child. Information about the captioned films program can be obtained from the Captioned Films and Telecommunications Branch, Division of Media Services, Bureau of Education for the Handicapped, United States Office of Education, Washington, DC 20202. Check with your local educational television station for information about captioned programming and the equipment necessary to receive it. Nonverbal 16mm films are listed in *Films Too Good for Words.*

Children who have learned sign language will want signed books, films, filmstrips, and videotapes. Sources of professional materials and books in sign language are available from Alexander Graham Bell Association for the Deaf, Inc., 3417 Volta Place, N.W., Washington, DC 20007; Gallaudet College Bookstore, Gallaudet College, Washington, DC 20002; and National Association of the Deaf, 814 Thayer Avenue, Silver Spring, MD 20910. Reviews of games, kits, and learning materials designed for use with hearing- or speech-impaired children are found in *ASHA: A Journal of the American Speech-Language-Hearing Association.*

Gifted Children

Gifted individuals have been identified as those who possess exceptional abilities in any one of six areas: 1) general intellectual ability; 2) specific academic aptitude; 3) creative or productive thinking; 4) leadership ability; 5) visual or performing arts; and 6) psychomotor ability. They share needs and interests, including the quest for understanding themselves and their interpersonal relationships, common to all students. In addition,

they need to learn the social skills of negotiating, of letting others discover things for themselves, and of not "hiding their light under a bushel." Finding the fine lines between confidence and arrogance, between pride and conceit, and between communication and condescension is very difficult.[15]

Media specialists' acceptance of their independence and quick grasp of a topic can lead us to send them off on their own when less able children are making demands on our time. Gifted children deserve full attention. These individuals need:

1. *Challenge* for the refinement of talents
2. *Outlets* for creative impulses
3. *Opportunity* for trial-and-error experimentation
4. *Interaction* with as varied a range of people as possible
5. *Provision of worthy adult models* in whom to place confidence
6. *Love and acceptance*[16]

To meet these needs, the media specialist must become acquainted with gifted students, learn about their interests, encourage them to consider many possibilities, and ensure that they are provided with additional materials.[17] The media specialist also needs to stimulate "new patterns of interest" in gifted students whose interests are not already wide-ranging."[18] To achieve these goals, the collection will need to have a wide range of materials in a variety of formats and on a wide range of subjects. Human resources from the community can provide an added dimension as students explore their interests.

The school, according to Hoback and Perry, must provide:

Tolerance for controversy. Especially at the secondary level, gifted students may explore and experiment in sensitive areas, creating public relations problems. Helping the gifted distinguish between freedom and license is often a difficult task.[19]

Gifted children can be so intense about their interests, or so persistent in their pursuit of special interests, that their requests require great patience on the part of media specialists. These children threaten an adult's sense of knowledge or control. However, gifted children are human beings. By talking with them and listening, the media specialist can also learn.

Sources of Information on Exceptional Children

Information about working with all types of exceptional children and about materials designed especially for these children can be obtained from a variety of sources. The National Center on Educational Media and Materials for the Handicapped (NCEMMH), located at the Ohio State University College of Education, has produced evaluation guidelines and forms for instructional materials. The department also produced *Guidelines for the Representation of Exceptional Persons in Educational Materials* in 1977. The intent of the latter guidelines is to assure a positive, fair, and balanced representation of exceptional persons in educational materials.

The National Information Center for Special Education Materials (NICSEM) at the University of Southern California provides a database for computerized retrieval of information on instructional materials. NICSEM's publications include NICEM *Index to Nonprint Special Education Materials—Multimedia Learner Volume* and *Professional Volume, Special Education Index to Learner Materials, NICSEM Special Education Thesaurus, Special Education Index to Parent Materials*, and *Special Education Index to Assessment Devices.* The Thesaurus lists the controlled search vocabulary NICSEM uses to index materials and is the primary tool for retrieving information from the database. Lockheed's DIALOG system markets this database as "Special Education Materials" (File 87). The database has three files: bibliographic, thesaurus for subject terms, and sources of the materials. Additional information about services is described in the following articles:

> Henry C. Dequin, "Selecting Materials for the Handicapped: A Guide to Sources," *Top of the News* 35 (1978): 57-66;

> Dequin, "Sources of Information about the Handicapped," *School Library Journal* 26 (1979): 38-41; and

> Edward John Kazlauskas and Georgia Sales, "NICSEM: Special Education Database," *Instructional Innovator* 25 (1980): 30-32.

How to Get Help for Kids, edited by Barbara Zang, is a directory of national agencies, groups, and organizations offering services to exceptional children for diagnosis, education, financial and legal assistance, respite care, parent support, and recreation.

The following journals are of interest for adults working with exceptional children: *Exceptional Children, The Exceptional Parent, Journal of Learning Disabilities, Journal of Special Education*, and *Teaching the Exceptional Child.*

The Council for Exceptional Children provides information to nonmembers about education for both disabled and gifted children. The ERIC Clearinghouse on Handicapped and Gifted Children located at the Council distributes bibliographies, conference papers, curriculum guides, and other documents.

Poor and Reluctant Readers

Those who encourage reading skills and literature appreciation have always been challenged by both poor readers and reluctant readers. The poor reader is "a child who is reading below his capacity to read; however, a child who is not necessarily retarded;"[20] a reluctant reader is "a child who is a capable learner and reader but who is not inclined to read."[21] Books with high appeal and appropriate reading levels can help these students. The phrases "High Interest/Low Vocabulary" or "High Interest/Low Reading Level" (HILRL) are used to describe these works. Bates,[22] an editor of such titles, offers the following criteria:

1. Design elements recommended—wide margins; extra leading (space) between lines; short chapters with breaks or space gaps dividing the text in sections; type style that looks easy to read; paper opaque to prevent "see-through."

2. Fiction—direct and simple narrative lines; dialogue and action used to develop story line; one-person point of view rather than multiple or shifting; limited and strongly identified characters; familiar situations; emotional appeal; a good opening sentence that plunges the reader into the text.

3. Nonfiction—carefully delineated subject; direct and progressive organization of material; lively writing; illustration throughout the text to supplement it; topics with appeal.

4. Style—simple vocabulary; sentences of varying lengths (not over two and a half printed lines); short paragraphs; simple concepts; sensory appeal; good rhythm and pace.

In "A Checklist for High/Low Books for Young Adults," Munat expands on Bates' criteria and presents a way to evaluate the physical characteristics, reading level (by use of the Fry formula), style, approach, and subject matter or content.[23] Although designed for use with materials for high school students, the checklist can also be applied to materials for younger students.

Three standard tools in this area are *Good Reading for Poor Readers* by Spache, *Gateways to Readable Books*, and *High Interest-Easy Reading for Junior and Senior High School Students.* Spache provides bibliographic and reading level information and brief annotations for trade books, text materials, magazines, newspapers, and programmed materials. Teachers and media specialists find the opening chapters especially useful in their work with these students. The revised Spache Readability Formula is provided in the appendix. As its subtitle proclaims, *Gateways to Readable Books* is "an annotated graded list of books in many fields for adolescents who are reluctant to read or find reading difficult." The annotations, directed to the student, cover more than 1,000 titles, including magazines, newspapers, dictionaries, and books. *High Interest-Easy Reading for Junior and Senior High School Students*, also designed for student use, lists titles with contemporary themes and issues of appeal to this age group. Examples of subject headings include "Love and Friendship," "Cars and Cycles," and "Science Fiction." The annotations are in the form of miniature book talks.

The High/Low Report: For Professionals Concerned with Literature for the Teenage Reluctant Reader has signed reviews and provides full bibliographic information, Fry readability level, an extensive evaluation of the item's qualities as an HILRL book, an evaluation of appeal, and a specific recommendation. A work that examines titles for grade one through eight vocabulary levels is the "High Interest-Low Vocabulary Reading Materials Supplement" issue of the *Journal of Education* published by Boston University School of Education. The 1978 supplement used annotations directed to the teacher. This special issue can be purchased separately and is usually announced in the literature.

Adults Working with Children

Adults involved in the school include those who have teaching responsibilities as well as those who work with children in other ways, including administrators, guidance counselors, social workers, nurses, speech therapists, aides, and parents. The portion of the collection that is designated to fulfill these people's needs is usually called the professional collection. As in the rest of the collection, a variety of formats should be available. If you recall the opening-day scene at the beginning of this book, the principal needed a discussion-starter to use with a civic group. He specifically requested a film or videotape on mainstreaming. If the collection did not include either, the media specialist would need to know where such material could be obtained.

Teachers have needs other than those identified in earlier sections of this book. They may want information about a subject, such as sociology or behavioral psychology. A kindergarten teacher may want ideas for activities for her class; the physical education teacher may ask for information about movement education. The new teacher may need information about writing lesson plans and how to present a unit; an eighth-grade English teacher may want to know about forthcoming television programs so her students can analyze them. Others, who perhaps have not completed all the continuing education credits required for this year, may ask you for the year's schedule of programs.

To meet these and other needs, the professional collection will need to include books, pamphlets, government documents, journals, films, filmstrips, videotapes, audiotapes, curriculum materials, bibliographic and selection tools, television and radio program guides, information about community resources, and program announcements of educational programs and teacher associations. You will need to know what is available in the district media collection. If there is a listing or catalog of these materials, obtain a copy. State education agencies and professional associations can provide a variety of information.

How do you keep up-to-date on all these sources of information? Professional journals in library science and education often publish articles or announcements. Additional sources of information about materials for the professional collection are listed in appendices 1 and 2. Materials identified include:

1. Journals that contain reviews for curricular and program areas.
2. Subject-oriented selection and bibliographic tools.

3. Articles that discuss criteria for evaluating materials on a particular subject.

4. Agencies and associations that provide publications or offer other information services, such as clearinghouses or information networks.

You can ask other media specialists in the district or teachers in your building about the sources of information that they find most useful. Rosenau offers this advice:

> First, identify the information resources and services that are intended to help you — those nearest you, those most responsive, those with the most capable personnel.
>
> Then determine your own information — seeking priorities. (For example, you simply can't afford to subscribe to every publication or phone every information center that might offer useful information.) For which topics and at what level of detail do you really need valid new information?
>
> Finally, think through with care, in advance, the questions you will pose. The art of asking focused, precise questions is well worth cultivating.
>
> In addition, keep in mind that learning opportunities are more likely to improve if you don't limit your information searches only to sources and ideas that confirm your long-held beliefs and preferences.[24]

Besides familiarity with outside sources of information, you will need tools to guide the selection of materials for your collection. *The Teacher's Library* offers suggestions about how to establish a professional collection and recommends specific titles of books, pamphlets, periodicals, and nonprint materials. Professional association publications include articles about materials for teachers, such as "A Minimal Professional Reference Library on the Language Arts for Elementary School Teachers," which appears in *Language Arts.* Other recommendations can be found in *Elementary School Library Collection.*

If parents use the professional collection in your school, be sure to share many of the titles identified earlier in this book, such as *Babies Need Books.* Journals such as *Horn Book Magazine* or *Teachers' Guide to Television* often carry information of interest to parents. Newsletters designed for this audience include "Why Children's Books?" from the Horn Book, Inc. and "News for Parents" from the International Reading Association.

Summary

This chapter points out, perhaps more than any other chapter in this book, that recommendations for the collection program cannot be carried out adequately unless the media specialist respects individuals.

Much of selection activity requires the analysis of group needs, but media specialists, must never forget the individuals who make up these groups. We can learn about the characteristics of groups and try to understand their needs. If, however, in the process of working with groups, we lose sight of the unique qualities of the individuals who must live with our decisions, then the collection will not be responsive to individual needs. In our efforts to help children understand each other, we, too, can grow in our own acceptance of others. Each individual has something to offer. Our mutual experience as human beings can always provide a common point of contact.

Notes to Chapter 14

[1]Barbara H. Baskin and Karen H. Harris, *Notes from a Different Drummer: A Guide to Juvenile Fiction Portraying the Handicapped* (New York, NY: R. R. Bowker, 1977), p. x.

[2]Ibid.

[3]For a fuller discussion see William Schipper, "Overview of the Legislation—P.L. 94-142," *School Media Quarterly* 8 (1979): 17-21; and Ruth A. Vellman, *Serving Physically Disabled People: An Information Handbook for All Libraries* (New York, NY: R. R. Bowker, 1979), pp. 258-63.

[4]Library Service to Children with Special Needs Committee, Association for Library Service to Children, a division of the American Library Association, *Selecting Materials for Children with Special Needs* (Chicago, IL: American Library Association, 1980), p. 1.

[5]Karen H. Harris, "Selecting Library Materials for Exceptional Children," *School Media Quarterly* 8 (1979): 23.

[6]Eliza T. Dresang, "There Are No *Other* Children: Special Children in Library Media Centers," *School Library Journal* 24 (1977): 23.

[7]Harris, "Selecting Library Materials," p. 24.

[8]Ibid., p. 25.

[9]Ibid., p. 24.

[10]Ibid., p. 25.

[11]Ibid., p. 26.

[12]John F. Henne, "Serving Visually Handicapped Children," *School Library Journal* 25 (1978): 36; and Bashir Masoodi and John R. Ban, "Teaching the Visually Handicapped in Regular Classes," *Educational Leadership* 37 (1980): 354.

[13]Mary Jane Metcalf, "Helping Hearing Impaired Students," *School Library Journal* 25 (1979): 27.

[14]Ibid., p. 29.

[15]John Hoback and Phyllis Perry, "Common Sense about Educating the Gifted and Talented," *Educational Leadership* 37 (1980): 347.

[16]Ibid.

[17]H. Thomas Walker, "Media Services for Gifted Learners," *School Media Quarterly* 6 (1978): 261.

[18]Ibid.

[19]Hoback and Perry, "Common Sense about Educating," p. 348.

[20]Carter V. Good, ed., *Dictionary of Education*, 3rd ed. (New York, NY: McGraw-Hill, 1973), p. 472.

[21]Ibid., p. 472.

[22]Barbara S. Bates, "Identifying High Interest/Low Reading Level Books," *School Library Journal* 24 (1977): 20-21.

[23]Florence Howe Munat, "A Checklist for High/Low Books for Young Adults," *School Library Journal* 27 (1981): 23-27.

[24]Fred S. Rosenau, "Knots in the Network of Information Sources about Education," *Educational Leadership* 37 (1980): 432.

Chapter 14 Bibliography

Baskin, Barbara H., and Harris, Karen H. *Notes from a Different Drummer: A Guide to Juvenile Fiction Portraying the Handicapped.* New York, NY: R. R. Bowker, 1977.

Bates, Barbara S. "Identifying High Interest/Low Reading Level Books." *School Library Journal* 24 (1977): 19-21.

Bush, Margaret. "Books for Children Who Cannot See the Printed Page." *School Library Journal* 26 (1980): 28-31.

Dresang, Eliza T. "There Are No *Other* Children: Special Children in Library Media Centers." *School Library Journal* 24 (1977): 19-23.

Good, Carter V., ed. *Dictionary of Education.* 3rd ed. New York, NY: McGraw-Hill, 1973.

Harris, Karen H. "Selecting Library Materials for Exceptional Children." *School Media Quarterly* 8 (1979): 22-28.

Henne, John F. "Serving Visually Handicapped Children." *School Library Journal* 25 (1978): 36-37.

Hoback, John, and Perry, Phyllis. "Common Sense about Educating the Gifted and Talented." *Educational Leadership* 37 (1980): 346-48, 350.

Hunsicker, Marya. "When the Blind Begin to Read; Selecting Reading List for Legally Blind Children." *School Library Journal* 19 (1972): 79-80.

Kamisar, Hylda, and Pollet, Dorothy. "Talking Books and the Local Library." *Library Journal* 99 (1974): 2123-25.

Kazlauskas, Edward John, and Sales, Georgia. "NICSEM: Special Education Database." *Instructional Innovator* 25 (1980): 30-32.

Lance, Wayne D. "Who Are *All* the Children?" *Exceptional Children* 43 (1976): 66-67.

Library Service to Children with Special Needs Committee, Association for Library Service to Children, a division of the American Library Association. *Selecting Materials for Children with Special Needs.* Chicago, IL: American Library Association, 1980.

Masoodi, Bashir, and Ban, John R. "Teaching the Visually Handicapped in Regular Classes." *Educational Leadership* 37 (1980): 351-55.

Metcalf, Mary Jane. "Helping Hearing Impaired Students." *School Library Journal* 25 (1979): 27-29.

Munat, Florence Howe. "A Checklist for High/Low Books for Young Adults." *School Library Journal* 27 (1981): 23-27.

National Center on Educational Media and Materials for the Handicapped. "Standard Criteria for the Selection and Evaluation of Instructional Material." *Illinois Libraries* 59 (1977): 531-40.

Pond, Patricia, and Liesener, James W., eds. "Networks, Data Bases, and Media Programs." Theme Issue. *School Media Quarterly* 6 (1977): 9-38, 51-59.

Putnam, Lee. "Information Needs of Hearing Impaired People." *HRLSD Journal* 2 (1976): 2-14.

Rosenau, Fred S. "Knots in the Network of Information Sources about Education." *Educational Leadership* 37 (1980): 426-28, 430-32.

Schipper, William. "Overview of the Legislation—P.L. 94-142." *School Media Quarterly* 8 (1979): 17-21.

Smith, Lotsee Patterson, and Watson, Bill, eds. "Special Education: A Continuum of Services." Theme Issue. *School Media Quarterly* 6 (1978): 230-54, 259-63.

Thomson, Peggy. "Closed Captions for TV: Opening a New World to the Hearing Impaired." *Today's Education* 70 (1981): 38-40.

Velleman, Ruth A. *Serving Physically Disabled People: An Information Handbook for All Libraries.* New York, NY: R. R. Bowker, 1979.

Weinthaler, Judith, and Rotberg, Jay M. "The Systematic Selection of Instructional Materials Based on an Inventory of Learning Abilities and Skills." *Exceptional Children* 36 (1970): 615-19.

Wires, Catherine B. "Books for Children Who Read by Touch or Sound." *Quarterly Journal of the Library of Congress* 30 (1973): 159-62.

Zang, Barbara, ed. *How to Get Help for Kids: A Reference Guide to Services for Handicapped Children.* Syracuse, NY: Gaylord Professional Publicatons in association with Neal-Schuman Publishers, 1980.

PART III

Administrative Concerns

Did you ever see a battered book in a media center? If you had a chance to glance at its title, you probably recognized it as a popular work that is rarely on the shelves. The media specialist has probably been trying for some time to rescue it to have it mended. Some books go from one student to the next with hardly a pause at the circulation desk.

Have you seen study print edges crumbling from too many pin holes, games with missing pieces, or torn filmstrips? Are the shelves of the media center overflowing in one section and bare in another? These situations happen in every collection. It is a challenge to ensure that they don't happen regularly.

You, as a media specialist, will be the administrator of the collection. If the word "administrator" conjures up images in your mind of pushing papers and filling out forms in triplicate, then you have overlooked important administrative roles. An administrator must be a planner, organizer, policy maker, business person, and evaluator. Through these roles, you can shape a collection that is dynamic and responsive to the demands and changes generated by the students, curriculum, and teachers. Making selection decisions and receiving new materials may be the more glamorous, exciting aspects of your work with the collection. Administrative decisions, however, can ensure that those new materials will get to students.

15
ACQUISITION PROCEDURES

When the selection process has been completed, it is time to obtain materials. Acquisition, the process of obtaining materials, includes confirming that materials are available, verifying ordering information, identifying and selecting the sources of the materials, arranging for order transmission and fulfillment, allocating budgetary funds, and record-keeping. Materials may be acquired through purchase, rental arrangements, solicitation of free materials, gifts, or exchanges. Many of these procedures are often handled by the district media center's processing center. This chapter focuses on the components of the acquisition process (shown in figure 22, page 228) most likely to directly involve the building-level person, and will:

1. Review the relationship of acquisition procedures to acquisition policy.

2. Describe the procedures for acquiring materials.

3. Describe bibliographic tools and other sources of information, indicating the availability of materials.

4. Identify sources of materials.

5. Discuss the relationship between media professionals and publishers/producers.

Bibliographic information for acquisition tools, including those cited in this chapter, can be found in Appendix 2. The bibliography for this chapter lists works on the acquisition process that provide information outside the scope of this discussion.

Relationship of Acquisition Procedures to Policies

As explained in chapter 6, policies state what will be done and why it will be done; procedures state how it will be done and who will do it. An acquisition policy may state that materials shall be purchased from the least expensive and most efficient source, e.g., a jobber. The policy may go on to state that if an item is needed immediately, it may be purchased

Figure 22. Components of the Acquisition Process

RESEARCH ITEM INFORMATION	SELECT SOURCE	PREPARE, SUBMIT & COMPLETE ORDER
• Check Holdings • Search Outstanding Order File • Determine Availability • Verify Bibliographic Information	• Publisher/ Producer • Wholesaler • Book Dealer	• Item Inspection • Record Keeping • Processing
USE: • Bibliographic Tools	• Media Program Policy • Directories • Catalogs	• Media Program Procedures

locally. A policy could also state that 16mm films are to be obtained from the district film collection, a film rental agency, or through a free distributor; that is, 16mm films are not to be purchased for the building-level collection.

Acquisition policies are likely to be uniform throughout the school district. Many procedures are also dictated by the school district or by an agency within the district. For example, the district purchasing agent may specify the order forms to be used. Procedures for accounting and record-keeping are also frequently established at the district level. Ask the director of the district media program for a listing of the policies and procedures. This information is often available in handbook form for all media specialists within the system.

Overview of Acquisition Activities

The first stage of preorder activities includes checking for the requested item in the present holdings and the file of outstanding orders, checking the availability of the item, and verifying the accuracy of bibliographic information. The second stage is selecting the best source for the material. The third stage includes preparing and submitting the order. When the materials are received, items are checked against the original order and the invoice, and the condition of the materials is assessed. Are pages missing? Are all the units of a kit enclosed? If the order is complete and in good condition, expenditure of funds and other records are completed.

Preorder Checking

The first step in the acquisition process is to determine whether the item is already part of the collection. The requested item may be a new edition of a book recently acquired or a filmstrip that is part of a currently held kit. If the item is in the collection, you may want to check with the requestor to determine if the existing item is sufficient. If the collection does not have the item, find out if it has been ordered or is being processed. In some libraries, a copy of the order skip is filed in the card catalog under title entry at the time the order is placed. This procedure facilitates the checking process. Other libraries maintain a separate on-order file.

If the media center has a standing order with a publisher, you will not need to initiate orders for titles that might be delivered under the conditions of the standing order. For example, the American Library Association has categories of standing orders for materials relating to children and school libraries. You may have a comprehensive membership in an association, such as the Association for Supervision and Curriculum Development, that includes an automatic shipment of all pamphlets and books issued by the association during the year of membership. Your media center may also belong to a book club. These agreements must be examined to determine whether requested items are included. Titles announced are ones you may not want to duplicate.

Tools on Availability of Materials

When checking whether materials are available, you will be using sources of information that can be categorized as current or forthcoming. Tools, such as the NICEM (National Information Center for Educational Media) indexes or *Children's Books in Print*, report what is available at the time they are prepared for publication. This information can be updated through the information found in subsequent reviewing journals, publishers' catalogs, and supplements. Announcements of forthcoming publications, informing media specialists of what materials may be published or produced, appear in journals, such as *School Library Journal*, and in flyers from producers and publishers.

To determine if an item is available, use a special type of bibliography called a "trade bibliography." These tools provide ordering information for materials that are currently "in print" or otherwise available. Bibliographic tools that indicate availability may also state:

1. Whether the item is available through purchase, rent, or loan, and the purchase or rental price.

2. Whether the item must be ordered directly from the publisher/producer or is available through a jobber or distributor.

3. Whether there are postage or delivery charges, the person(s) responsible for the pick up and return deliveries, the length of the loan, the notice to ensure delivery on a desired date and appropriate alternative arrangements.

The information included for each item may vary from one tool to another.

If the item is in printed format, the bibliographic entry may include author, title, edition, publisher, date of publication, series, title and number, available bindings, price, and International Standard Book (Serial) Number. If the item is in audiovisual format, the bibliographic entry may include title; available formats; production and prelease dates; producer and/or distributors; physical characteristics (such as color/black and white, captioned or sound, phonodisc or cassette, length [running time], special equipment needed); number of pieces included (such as 4 study prints, 1 teacher's guide); languages (such as English, Spanish, bilingual); price; and special conditions of availability. To locate information about the availability of the wide range of materials found in a media center, many bibliographies will be used.

A few examples will illustrate the situation. To determine the price of a particular juvenile book title, look in *Children's Books in Print*, using the title or author as the point of access to the information. To find out whether the same title is available in audiovisual format, you could turn to the appropriate NICEM (National Information Center for Educational Media) index. Thus, you might check the *Index to 16mm Educational Films, Educational Records, Educational Video Tapes*, etc. These examples do not include all the NICEM series, nor do they include tools needed for information about viewing equipment or realia. Be sure to use the latest edition for the most recent information about price and availability.

The funds necessary for ready access to these tools will strain even the strongest budgets. For example, individual NICEM indexes range in price from $34.00 to $126.00. The tools may be available in other larger collections or in special libraries, such as the district media center, the local public library, or a nearby college.

Other Information Sources

If your school is not receiving advertisements from various publishers/producers, you can write for their free catalogs. However, this approach has hidden costs, including clerical time, postage, and filing and storage of the materials. Even though bibliographic tools provide quicker access, especially to materials on a given subject, catalogs do provide full ordering information and often provide other useful information—a suggested grade level, a possible reading level, and curriculum application.

"Catalogs are important to school librarians and often represent the only contact a publisher makes with them," according to Hatfield, who notes, "Librarians must be aware, however, that a promotional catalog is not a reviewing tool and should be used mainly to check prices and availability of materials."[1]

Catalogs frequently quote parts of reviews, but full citations to the reviews are usually not given. Fast notes:

> Even though we can never expect producers and publishers to list unfavorable reviews, full information about the ones they do mention would enable the user to locate the complete review more readily.[2]

Sometimes the bibliographies and catalogs provide information that facilitates the processing of materials prior to arrival at the media center. Information, such as the LC (Library of Congress) card number, the availability of CIP (Cataloging in Publication), suggested Dewey Decimal or LC classification numbers, and suggested subject headings, can facilitate ordering and cataloging.

Catalogs are not the only form of advertising that media specialists find useful. Publishers, producers, wholesalers, or distributors may offer a subject catalog to draw attention to the uses of their materials within curriculum areas. New materials are often advertised through flyers and forthcoming announcements. Sales representatives may visit a school to present information about their publications/products.

Listings for publications and products can be found in catalogs from governmental agencies, manufacturers, professional associations, museums, and extension services. These listings may include "free and inexpensive" materials used to promote or advertise the products and services of the sponsoring producer.

Publications about your community may be found through announcements in the local newspapers or through local civic and social organizations. The local chamber of commerce may have pamphlets about the community, economics, recreation, and geography. The local historical society may have pamphlets or slides about historical buildings or events.

Choosing the Appropriate Source

Tools that indicate what is available may indicate the original source (publisher or producer) but do not indicate the best source from which to obtain the material. The choice of a particular source is based on who offers the best price for the item; how soon can the item be delivered; and if other services, such as cataloging or processing, are provided.

Chief sources of materials include wholesalers, distributors, publishers, producers, subscription agencies, dealers, and local sources. Wholesalers buy materials from publishers or producers and sell them to bookstores and libraries. Subscription agencies function as wholesalers for magazines. The word "distributor" may refer to a wholesaler, but more frequently means a vendor of magazines, paperbacks, or audiovisual materials. The term "jobber" can be used interchangeably with the word "wholesaler." Wholesalers, distributors, and jobbers are middlemen between the publisher/producer and the buyer, the media center.

Children's Media Market Place, a directory of sources of materials for preschool children through eighth-graders, lists publishers, audiovisual producers and distributors, wholesalers, juvenile bookstores, juvenile book clubs, and TV program distributors. Personnel at the district level will probably decide which wholesaler to use. Whether you participate in that decision or not, Melcher's goals of library acquisition offer useful advice.

Find a way to buy service instead of discount. The great majority of libraries of all types have long since won their freedom from blind acceptance of the low bid. You can, too. You must.

Encumber only upon receipt. If necessary, have an agreement in writing with the supplier that all his shipments are "on approval" until paid for, although you do not expect to take advantage of this.

Pay on the supplier's invoice; ask no special billing.

Pay promptly. Pay for partial shipments. Pay invoices as rendered; spot-check their accuracy later. If you are dealing with a reputable supplier, you can be sure he won't hesitate to rectify errors found later.

Order often. Don't keep your readers waiting. An order of 50 to 100 books is not too small.

Simplify your paperwork. Make one writing meet all needs. Order by slip, not list. Have no more than five parts to your form set.

Get what you order. Enforce your contracts. Spot-check performance.

Know your inside costs. Let your supplier do anything he can do cheaper.[3]

Libraries can expect wholesalers to have a large inventory of titles, to fill orders promptly and accurately at a reasonable cost, and to report on items not in stock.

There are many advantages of ordering materials through wholesalers:

1. The cost and paperwork of ordering through many publishers is avoided.
2. There is only one source to contact for follow-up on orders.
3. Libraries receive substantially better discounts from wholesalers than from publishers.
4. Some publishers refuse to deal directly with libraries or give poor service to small orders.
5. Many wholesalers provide full processing, catalog cards, pockets, and plastic jackets for materials.
6. Preselection plans—"approval plans" in which the library examines new titles at the usual discount rate with full return privileges—are frequently available.

There are also disadvantages of using wholesalers:

1. It usually takes one month for the majority of an order to be filled, whereas publishers can deliver in one week to two weeks.

2. The availability of older titles is dependent upon the inventory of the wholesaler.

3. No wholesaler can supply every available title. Some titles, such as materials produced by professional organizations, can only be purchased through direct order.

4. Policies on return of defective or damaged copies may state that credit or replacement isn't granted until the returns have been received by the wholesaler, a stipulation that can result in monies encumbered for as long as a year.

Many schools have a policy that funds not spent within a specific time period must be reverted back to the school's general fund. As Eaglen observes

school librarians get a bit angry when they see their book money being used to resurface the school parking lot![4]

Changes occurring in the book industry continually affect media programs. Recent legislation has resulted in shorter runs of books per printing, a decrease in the warehousing of back titles, and delays in reprinting a title until there is a proven market. These changes especially affect retrospective purchases. Book titles only five years old may now be difficult to obtain.

Relationship between Media Specialists and the Media Industry

As purchasers of materials, media specialists have expectations of the quality and types of materials we want to provide for our users. If materials or services received are not of acceptable quality, they should be returned with an explanation. When questioning the quality of a book's binding, Jacobs recommends writing the wholesaler and sending a copy of the letter to the Association of American Publishers, who will transmit the letter to the appropriate publishing personnel.[5]

Communication with publishers and producers need not be limited to complaints. If the children in your school become excited about a particular work, why not share that information with the publisher or producer? If you need information about authors, extra book jackets, or other promotional materials, write a letter to people responsible for library service or library promotion at publishing houses. Addresses of the companies and the names of their personnel can be found in *Literary Market Place* or *Children's Media Market Place.* Media specialists share a common bond with individuals responsible for promoting the use of materials, a bond that can only be strengthened by two-way communication. Marketing departments have services to share, such as posters; media specialists can share how students respond to materials and make suggestions for materials we need, suggestions that can result in future products.

Summary

Acquisition activities can be time- and energy-consuming. Searching for accurate information may require travel to gain access to needed tools. Detailed record-keeping and correspondence demand patience. Many routines cannot be slighted or handled in haste. A media specialist's organizational abilities, mathematical skills, and business sense frequently come into play. Errors or misjudgments can be costly. Delays or inaccurate fulfillment of orders can try one's patience. It can all be worthwhile, however, when a student or teacher declares that the materials they have found are precisely what they wanted.

Notes to Chapter 15

[1]Frances S. Hatfield, "How to Promote Your Books to School Libraries," *Publishers Weekly* 207 (1975): 48.

[2]Betty Fast, "Publishers' Catalogs: Puffery or Resource?" *Wilson Library Bulletin* 51 (1976): 179.

[3]Daniel Melcher, *Melcher on Acquisition* (Chicago, IL: American Library Association, 1971), p. 3.

[4]Audrey B. Eaglen, "Book Wholesalers: Pros and Cons," *School Library Journal* 25 (1978): 118.

[5]Peter J. Jacobs, "Book Publishing Today: Its Problems and How School Librarians Can Cope," *Catholic Library World* 49 (1977): 60.

Chapter 15 Bibliography

Belland, John. "Factors Influencing Selection of Materials." *School Media Quarterly* 6 (1978): 112-19.

Cantor, Phyllis. "School Library Book Market: Supply or Demand?" *School Media Quarterly* 6 (1978): 197-201.

Duke, Judith W. *Children's Books and Magazines: A Market Study.* White Plains, NY: Knowledge Industry Publications, 1979.

Eaglen, Audrey B. "Book Distribution: Present Conditions and Implications for the Future." *School Library Journal* 26 (1979): 55-59.

Eaglen, Audrey B. "Book Wholesalers: Pros and Cons," *School Library Journal* 25 (1978): 116-19.

Eaglen, Audrey B. "More about the Discount Mess." *School Library Journal* 26 (1979): 105-108.

Eaglen, Audrey B. "Out of Patience—Indefinitely." *School Library Journal* 24 (1978): 23-26.

Eaglen, Audrey B. "Short Discount Shuffles—What It's All About." *School Library Journal* 25 (1979): 30-33.

Fast, Betty. "Publishers' Catalogs: Puffery or Resource?" *Wilson Library Bulletin* 51 (1976): 178-79.

Ford, Stephen. *The Acquisition of Library Materials.* Rev. ed. Chicago, IL: American Library Association, 1978.

Gerhardt, Lillian. "Out of Control—Indefinitely." *School Library Journal* 24 (1977): 63.

Harrison, Lucretia M. "Acquiring Foreign Children's Books." *School Library Journal* 25 (1978): 22-25.

Hatfield, Frances S. "How to Promote Your Books to School Libraries." *Publishers Weekly* 207 (1975): 48-49.

Hensel, Evelyn, and Veillette, Peter D. *Purchasing Library Materials in Public and School Libraries: A Study of Purchasing Procedures and the Relationships between Libraries and Purchasing Agents and Dealers.* Chicago, IL: American Library Association, 1969.

Hill, Janet. *Children Are People: The Librarian in the Community.* New York, NY: Crowell, 1973.

Jacobs, Peter J. "Book Publishing Today: Its Problems and How School Librarians Can Cope." *Catholic Library World* 49 (1977): 58-62.

Kaiser, Lillian S. "Searching for Out-of-Print Books." *School Library Journal* 26 (1980): 45.

Kline, Carol. "142,000 Paperback Titles and How to Get Them." *Top of the News* 34 (1977): 79-83.

Melcher, Daniel. *Melcher on Acquisition.* Chicago, IL: American Library Association, 1971.

Nemeyer, Carol A., and Paul, Sandra K. "Book Publishers and the School Library Market." *School Media Quarterly* 6 (1978): 173-78.

Philos, Daphne. "Selection and Acquisition of Nonprint Media." *School Media Quarterly* 6 (1978): 179-87.

Roth, Harold. "An Analysis and Survey of Commercial Supply Houses." *Library Trends* (1976): entire issue.

Topolski, Sandra. "Serving Libraries' Paperback Needs: The Educational Paperback Association." *Top of the News* 34 (1977): 59-62.

Turow, Joseph. *Getting Books to Children: An Exploration of Publisher-Market Relations.* ALA Studies in Librarianship, No. 7. Chicago, IL: American Library Association, 1978.

Van Orden, Phyllis. "Librarians and Publishers: An Idea Exchange through Library Promotion." *School Library Journal* 24 (1977): 24-26.

Van Orden, Phyllis. "Promotion, Review, and Examination of Materials." *School Media Quarterly* 6 (1978): 120-22, 127-32.

Verrone, Robert J. "Why Books Cost So Much." *School Library Journal* 25 (1979): 20-22.

Walch, David B. "Price Index for Nonprint Media." *Library Journal* 106 (1981): 432-33.

Walker, Nancy C. "Automation and Acquisitions." *Drexel Library Quarterly* 5 (1969): 80-83.

16
MAINTAINING THE COLLECTION

An effective collection maintenance program serves two purposes. First, materials and equipment are available in usable condition. Second, policies and procedures for preventive maintenance lead to economical and efficient management of the collection. Maintenance activities include keeping a record of what is in the collection (an inventory), inspecting materials, and repairing, replacing or removing items.

This chapter focuses on the following elements of the maintenance program:

1. Policies
2. Procedures
3. Reevaluation processes

Information about forms for record-keeping and suggestions for specific ways to repair materials can be found in the titles listed in the bibliography for this chapter.

Policies of Maintenance

Maintenance policies are usually adopted at the district level. Policies related to equipment maintenance address:

1. When and why equipment will be traded in or discarded.
2. The level of repairs that will be handled at the building level, the district level, and through repair contracts.
3. The records to be kept on equipment usage, repair, and maintenance.

Responsibility for repairs should be assigned with regard to the degree of difficulty, time, type of supplies and equipment needed to do the repair, and the availability of trained personnel. For example, simple repairs and cleaning are best done where the equipment is used.

Data collected through equipment records can be used to analyze the cost-effectiveness of a given item. This information can be used to determine when repair costs are excessive and when the item should be replaced.

Policies relating to the maintenance of materials have already been identified in chapter 6 in the "Evaluation of the Collection" section of the collection program policy. That section of the policy describes criteria by which materials will be evaluated for replacement, repair, or removal from the collection.

Establishing Procedures

Working within parameters of the district policies, the media specialist at the building level is responsible for establishing collection maintenance procedures that should provide for systematic inspection of all materials and equipment. While technicians or aides are responsible for repairing and cleaning materials and equipment, the media specialist is responsible for identifying maintenance problems, diagnosing causes, establishing corrective measures, and monitoring the quality of the work completed, whether it is done within the media center or through an outside contract.

The procedures can provide for continual checking of materials as a part of the circulation system and/or for the instruction of users in the care and handling of materials. Users should always be encouraged to report damaged and malfunctioning equipment.

Routine maintenance procedures include:

1. Books and printed materials: placing protective jackets, repairing torn pages, mounting pictures.
2. Audio materials: splicing tapes, cleaning records.
3. Equipment: cleaning areas of heavy use—film gates, playback heads, lenses.

Other maintenance procedures relate to the identification and listing of holdings. If the district has an inventory control and maintenance form for equipment, establish a procedure for keeping those records up-to-date. If this type of inventory has not been required by the district office, begin one. For materials, the shelf list serves this record, noting where an item should be stored and how many copies are owned. Often a similar list does not exist for equipment. A system needs to be devised that will list what equipment is owned, where it is assigned or stored, and when it is maintained, cleaned, and repaired. Procedures should state how record-keeping activities and systematic inspection of materials will be accomplished.

Another concern addressed in *Audiovisual Equipment Security* states:

Accessibility is an extremely important word to all instructional media professionals. Much effort is given to making audiovisual equipment as accessible as possible to teachers and students alike. But with this ease of access comes the problem of assuring that the equipment is neither lost nor stolen. Therefore, developing adequate security procedures becomes extremely important to insure that the equipment is readily available when needed throughout its normal life expectancy.[1]

As a security precaution, permanently affix the school identification number, assigned by the National Center for Educational Statistics (NCES) in Washington, DC, to all equipment. This number can be obtained from your state Department of Public Instruction (Education). The first two digits in the number identify the state; the next five digits identify the school. With this number, your ownership of recovered stolen equipment can be easily ascertained.

Reevaluation Process

The reevaluation process, an evaluation technique for the collection as a whole, will be discussed in the following chapter. The current discussion focuses on inventory and on criteria for repairing, replacing, or removing items.

Inventory is the process by which items and information listed in the holdings record are verified, and the physical condition of each item is assessed. The record should indicate the number of copies currently owned. The physical condition of the item and its container, its circulation records (card and pocket), and its cataloging information should be checked. A filmstrip container may need a new label; a circulation card may be in the wrong book; teacher's guides for a set of study prints may be missing. A detailed examination of materials can uncover problems overlooked during the routine check of items as they are returned from circulation.

Some schools close collections for inventory purposes. This frees the staff from other duties so they can do an in-depth review of the collection. Closing the collection in this manner is in direct conflict with efforts to integrate the media program with the school's activities during that period of time. Some school districts recognize this conflict and hire media staff for an inventory period when the schools are not in session. Others rotate sections of the collection for inventory over a three-year period. Inventory can take place, however, when items are in circulation. By tabbing the shelf list card, one can check periodically to see if unexamined materials have been returned to the shelves. Circulation cards can also be tabbed. The size of the staff and collection, the amount of time available, and the demands of users often determine whether the whole collection can be examined or whether sections should be examined on a rotating basis.

One must take steps to ensure that patrons have access to information and that the information is available in a usable form. Having a collection whose materials are out-of-date and in poor condition can create a misleading view of the worth of the collection. Jefferson Elementary School's collection was started in 1938 and for many years was touted as a model for other schools. The librarian and principal prided themselves on the size of the collection in comparison to others. In 1978 when Anne, the new media specialist arrived, she found a collection of over 30,000 titles crowded onto the shelves — many books in unattractive bindings, records piled on tables, study prints leaning against the card catalog, and a deteriorating realia collection. Throughout the school year, Anne attempted to create some order. Fortunately, the district hired the media center staff to do a badly needed inventory the week after the close of school.

First, the collection was arranged according to the shelf list, and a penciled check was put on the shelf list for the items at hand. When an item was missing, an identifying clip was put on the shelf list card. Equipment was checked against the inventory sheet, and the date noted. Second, Anne and the clerk began to check each fiction title against the shelf list. As each item was examined, a note was made on a job slip if the book was to be mended, rebound, discarded, or recataloged or if it needed a new circulation card. While examining each item, Anne found books with small print, unattractive bindings, and missing pages. In many cases, there were unnecessary duplicate copies, which made for easy withdrawal decisions. Of the 19 copies of *Twenty Thousand Leagues under the Sea*, the three copies Anne kept were effectively illustrated and in good condition.

The inventory and weeding of this collection could not be accomplished in one week. However, the removal of several hundred unattractive and out-of-date titles made an impression. The principal was upset over the decreased quantity of items in the collection. Some teachers missed their favorite titles that were at the bindery or being replaced; however, supporters spoke of the improved atmosphere created by less-crowded shelves and the removal of worn and unattractive books. This story could continue, as it did for Anne. But for this writer's purposes, it exemplifies the time involved and the attitudes encountered when one properly inventories and weeds a collection. You may face similar situations: your conviction about the value of removing materials will be tested by others. You may have to overcome your own reluctance to discard materials. Avoiding this responsibility is usually more comfortable than facing it. The reasons and excuses that people give for avoiding weeding are numerous.[2] Typical attitudes include:

1. Books are sacred objects: only vandals destroy books.

2. Someone may need this in the future.

3. I don't have enough time to examine the whole collection.

4. There may be a "scene" if a teacher wants this.

5. We don't have time to remove an item from the shelf list.

6. There isn't any policy to justify the removal of materials bought with public funds.

7. I cannot decide when a book is "out-of-date," especially a fiction story.

8. This filmstrip is scratched but the students like the story.

9. Films are expensive to replace.

10. These study prints are no longer available (even when the corners are torn and the explanatory text is missing).

11. Someone may want to compare these editions.

12. A class could probably use this 10-year-old set of encyclopedias.

13. I remember when Johnny made that model.

One should be able to justify the removal of works as readily as one is prepared to justify adding or retaining matrials. Criteria used when adding materials to the collection can also be used when deciding whether to remove them. In addition, criteria relating to the condition of materials can serve as a basis for judging when an item should be removed. These criteria should be recorded in the same manner as were the criteria for selection.

Criteria for removal of materials can include:

1. Appearance and condition: unattractive covers or packaging, small print, dull or faded illustrations, missing pages or parts, garbled sound tracks, warped sound recordings.

2. Superfluous or duplicate volumes: unneeded titles, unillustrated editions, subjects no longer of interest, and works with information available in newer materials.

3. Language: works in languages not called for by the users.

4. Age of materials (exceptions are often noted with this criteria): materials 10 years old and not listed in standard catalogs, excluding materials about the state and local community; out-of-date materials (e.g., photographs in filmstrips that show automobiles or fashions from 10 years ago).

5. Classes of books and materials: almanacs and yearbooks that have been superseded, encyclopedias five or more years old, materials on pure sciences and technology that are five or more years old, travel and geography information over 10 or more years old, periodicals five or more years old and not indexed.

6. Use patterns: materials not circulated for five years and not listed in a standard catalog or index; reference materials not used in the media center during the past five years.

Removing materials from one collection for some of the above reasons may not mean that the items have no value. An item should be removed if it does not meet the needs of that particular collection.

When there is a change in the grade levels served, then the collection must also change. The Grape Arbor School District had three elementary schools serving kindergarten through eighth grade. They decided to make Concord Elementary School into a middle school serving fifth through eighth grade. The remaining schools were to serve kindergarten through fourth grade. The media specialist at Concord was notified of this decision in late May. She negotiated with the media staff of the other schools to exchange materials so each collection could meet their new demands by September.

Some large school districts establish exchange centers to provide temporary storage for materials no longer needed by schools. Check the school district policy about withdrawing and discarding materials. Practices vary; some schools must burn discarded materials, while others may sell them or give them away to other agencies. Schools that have been vandalized or suffered loss of materials from a fire or tornado may need materials no longer useful to your collection. Before deciding to share your unwanted materials, consider a recent conversation with a visitor from a third-world country. He appreciated the generosity of Americans who had sent their discarded books. However, he wondered about the books they sent, which were inaccurate and out-of-date. He asked, "Do they think my people don't know what is going on in the world?"

Summary

Broken pieces of equipment, projectors that eat up film, speakers that distort sound, missing pieces of a puzzle, and books with missing pages are common occurrences in school collections. If this is the impression an individual has of a collection, he or she may become a potential nonuser. Collection maintenance is easy to delay. There is always someone who needs the media specialist's attention. Materials can wait, as they did at Jefferson School, until the task is overwhelming. The chore of straightening out records can be boring. The disposal level of materials can become excessive, resulting in emotional responses and negative reactions.

Maintaining materials and keeping records on a regular basis can help avoid many of these problems. There will always be surprises, circumstances outside of your control. A brief story reveals how one's talent at smelling may be needed to locate the source of a maintenance problem. An odor pervaded the media center. It didn't seem to come from the air ducts and, at first, it filled the entire room. As the sniffing investigators toured the room, they detected the strongest smell at the beginning of the fiction section. Books were removed; shelves were checked and moved. Nothing was found on or behind them. However, as the books were replaced, one of them felt slightly damp. A recent bookmark was found—a juicy dill pickle.

Notes to Chapter 16

[1]Ralph Whiting, Joseph Hagaman, and Dale Mallory, *Audiovisual Equipment Security* (Menomonie, WI: Instructional Technology Services, University of Wisconsin-Stout, 1979), p. 1.

[2]Howard F. McGaw, "Policies and Practices in Discarding," *Library Trends* 4 (1956): 271-76.

Chapter 16 Bibliography

American Association of School Librarians, American Library Association, and Association for Educational Communications and Technology. *Media Programs: District and School.* Chicago, IL: American Library Association; Washington, DC: Association for Educational Communications and Technology, 1975.

Brown, James W.; Norberg, Kenneth D.; and Srygley, Sara K. *Administering Educational Media: Instructional Technology and Library Services.* New York, NY: McGraw-Hill, 1972.

Chisholm, Margaret E., and Ely, Donald P. *Media Personnel in Education: A Competency Approach.* Englewood Cliffs, NJ: Prentice-Hall, 1976.

Erickson, Carlton W. H. *Administering Instructional Media Programs.* New York, NY: Macmillan, 1968.

Jerome, Frank A. "Inventory and Maintenance Management of Audiovisual Aid Equipment." *Audiovisual Instruction* 20 (1975): 98-99.

McGaw, Howard R. "Policies and Practices in Discarding." *Library Trends* 4 (1956): 269-82.

Martin, Betty, and Carson, Ben. *The Principal's Handbook on the School Library Media Center.* Syracuse, NY: Gaylord Professional Publications, 1978.

Nickel, Mildred. *Steps to Service: A Handbook of Procedures for the School Library Media Center.* Chicago, IL: American Library Association, 1975.

Perkins, David L., ed. *Guidelines for Collection Development.* Chicago, IL: American Library Association, 1979.

Prostano, Emanuel T., and Prostano, Joyce S. *The School Library Media Center.* 2nd ed. Littleton, CO: Libraries Unlimited, 1977.

Rush, Betsy, "Weeding vs. Censorship: Treading a Fine Line." *Library Journal* 99 (1974): 3032-33.

Slote, Stanley J. *Weeding Library Collections—II.* 2nd rev. ed. Littleton, CO: Libraries Unlimited, 1982.

Topper, Louis. "Back to Basics: Some Problems and Pointers for Those Introducing AV Materials into the Library." *Wilson Library Bulletin* 47 (1972): 42-45.

Weeding the Small Library Collection. Lansing, MI: Michigan State Library, 1965.

Weisburg, Hilda K., and Toor, Ruth. *Elementary School Librarian's Almanac: A Complete Media Program for Every Month of the School Year.* West Nyack, NY: Center for Applied Research in Education, 1979.

Whiting, Ralph; Hagaman, Joseph; and Mallory, Dale. *Audiovisual Equipment Security.* Menomonie, WI: Instructional Technology Services, University of Wisconsin-Stout, 1979. Distributed by Wisconsin Audiovisual Association, c/o Don Jorgensen, McKinley I.S.C., 1010 Huron Street, Manitowoc, WI 54220.

17
EVALUATING THE COLLECTION

How can the worth of a collection be determined? Several types of value can be derived from the concepts of collection discussed in chapter 2. You will recall that a collection can be described as:

1. Being a physical entity.
2. Being composed of materials in a variety of formats.
3. Fulfilling purposes — meeting the needs of the school's goals and programs; meeting the informational, instructional, and personal needs of users.
4. Providing access to human and material resources of the community.
5. Providing access to information and material from other library/information agencies.
6. Functioning as an element within the media program.

Each of these concepts of collection identifies something that can be measured or evaluated. Evaluation is the process of 1) identifying a problem; 2) establishing methodology; 3) collecting, analyzing, and interpreting data; and 4) reporting the information. This process, often a continual assessment of the collection, provides a basis for decision-making. One can measure how well the collection meets the definition and how effectively the concept is being addressed at any given time.

This chapter opens with an exploration of the question, "Why evaluate?," followed by a discussion of evaluation and measurement, and selection of measurement techniques and instruments. Techniques for measuring a collection described in this chapter include:

1. Checking lists, catalogs, bibliographies
2. Examining the collection directly
3. Compiling statistics
4. Checking citations from papers of library users
5. Obtaining user opinions

6. Comparing the collection to standards

Each technique is described with a discussion of its advantages and disadvantages and its application in the school setting.

Why Evaluate?

As managers, media specialists need information on which to base decisions. The evaluation process, as seen in figure 23, reveals information that helps answer questions such as the following:

1. Is the collection responsive to changes in the school's program?
2. Does the collection support curricular and instructional needs?
3. Is the collection meeting the needs of users?
4. Does the collection provide access to materials from outside the school?
5. Does the collection include formats preferred by users?
6. Does the collection hinder or facilitate the media program?

Figure 23.   The Use of the Evaluation Process in the Collection Program

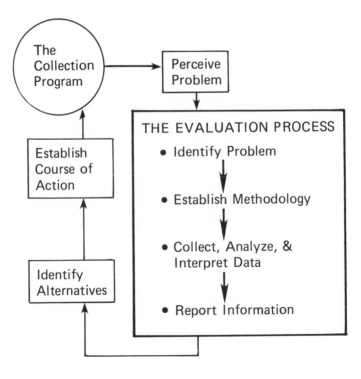

The preceding questions identify general areas of investigation that are broad and complex. One cannot examine all these questions at the same time; this would be an overwhelming task for many reasons — time being only one factor. Smaller issues, components of the larger questions, can be evaluated more readily.

Before beginning an evaluation project, one must identify what information will be collected, how it will be recorded, how it will be analyzed, how it will be used, and with whom it will be shared.

Evaluation and Measurement

Evaluation is the process of determining worth or value; measurement, a component of the evaluation process, is the process of identifying extent or quantity. We can count the number of items circulated in any given period of time, but that information does not constitute an evaluation; counting provides quantitative data. Quantitative data give an objective measure, lacking the element of judgment found in qualitative data.

A count of the number of items circulated in any given period of time does not indicate how the materials were used, who used them, whether similar materials were borrowed from other libraries, or what materials were used within the facility. A mere number count of the circulated science titles cannot indicate how adequately the collection supports the science curriculum. And yet, without a qualitative analysis, there is no objective basis for changing a collection policy.

Measurement, however, can lead to meaningful evaluation. Daniel offers five principles for the effective use of measurement:

1. *Measurement is a process, not a product.* It is an ongoing activity involving analyzing, planning, implementing, and evaluating in a continuous cycle.

2. *Measurement requires value judgments.* Not everything of worth can be measured. The selection of what to measure and the interpretation of the results of measurement require professional and personal value judgments.

3. *Measure only where it makes a difference.* If there is no possibility of correcting, changing, or reinforcing a particular aspect being measured, it probably is a waste of time to measure it.

4. *The most important resource of the librarian is time.* Financial resources are important, but the school library is a labor-intensive activity. The choice of where and how the librarian spends his time will affect the overall direction of the program more than anything else. Time spent on planning will ultimately have a bigger impact than time spent on repetitive clerical tasks.

5. *The most useful tool for the librarian is knowledge.* This means knowledge of the range of alternatives and their

anticipated consequences, the experiences and considerations of others faced with similar problems, the operational effectiveness of the particular library in question, and the managerial perspectives and techniques to administer that library. In the face of continuing change, media specialists realize that education is a lifelong process in all fields of endeavor and that yesterday's knowledge is only the base of tomorrow's knowledge requirements.[1]

The purpose for collecting information can indicate whether to use quantitative or qualitative techniques, or a combination of both.

The collection of quantitative data is only a small part of the total process of measurement and evaluation. Before the data are collected, the criteria against which meaning will be extracted from the results must be carefully thought through and specified. The inferences of quality from measures of quantity must be based on prior specification of whether more or less is better or in what combination of quantities does goodness lie. Further, the inferences of quality deduced from the collected data must be used as an integral part of the management process of continually changing, shaping, building, and creating a dynamic school media center program. Performance measurement goes hand in hand with performance goals, performance specifications, and the planning process.[2]

Information produced by evaluation can be judged by four criteria: validity, reliability, timeliness, and credibility. If the information is essential to a decision, it has validity. If the information can be reproduced when repeating the same techniques, the evaluation has reliability. If the information reaches the decision-maker when needed, it has timeliness. If decision-makers trust the information, it has credibility. These criteria should be considered when planning how and when evaluation is to take place.

Techniques for Measuring a Collection

There are many ways to measure the value of a collection. The most effective and most commonly used techniques for measuring collection value are described in the following section. Several instruments designed to measure and evaluate collections will be identified. As you consider the instruments, ask yourself:

What type of data will be collected?

What effort is required to collect the data? How many people are needed? What costs are involved? How much time will it take?

What will the instrument measure?

What will it not measure?

Once the information is obtained, how should it be organized?

With whom can the information be shared?

How can the information be used to communicate with others?

The answers to these questions will become evident when it is decided what is to be evaluated and why. This provides the basis for deciding which techniques and instruments to use.

1. Checking Lists, Catalogs, and Bibliographies

Description: In this procedure, the shelf list, catalog, or other holdings list is compared against a bibliography, list, or catalog of titles recommended for a certain purpose or type of collection. During the procedure, you record the numbers of titles owned and not owned. The percent of recommended titles that the collection contains can be obtained from this data.

Lists that can be used in this technique include 1) standard catalogs; 2) specialized bibliographies; 3) basic subject lists; 4) current lists; 5) reference works; 6) periodicals; 7) lists designed to meet a specific objective; 8) citations in textbooks or curriculum guides; or 9) catalogs from jobbers, publishers, and producers. Examples of current lists include the Association of Library Service to Children's Notable " ... Books," " ... Films," " ... Filmstrips." Current lists of this nature identify highly recommended titles, but you must judge whether those titles are needed in your collection.

The purpose of an evaluation will indicate which list is appropriate. If your purpose is to measure the general coverage of titles appropriate for the audience you serve, standard catalogs, such as *Children's Catalog, Junior High School Library Catalog,* or *Canadian Books for Young People*, would be useful. If your comparison reveals that the collection had a high percentage of the recommended titles, then, presumably, you have a successful collection. The closer the purpose of the tool matches the objectives of your program, the more beneficial this information will be. The collection development policy can provide a basis for judging the appropriateness of a list.

Advantages

1. A wide range of lists are available.
2. Many of the lists are selective and include informative annotations.
3. Lists of this nature are frequently updated.
4. Lists can be compiled to meet the needs of your collection.
5. The procedure of searching lists is a comparatively easy way to evaluate a collection.

6. Most lists are compiled by competent professional librarians or subject specialists.

Disadvantages

1. The only available lists may be the ones you have used as purchasing guides.

2. The lists may recommend titles that are out of print.

3. The cost of the list may be high compared to the benefit of its use.

4. Not every subject or need can be covered by a single list.

5. Bibliographies cover mateirals for all ages and may have limited usefulness for evaluating a collection established to serve a specific age group.

6. Lists are arbitrary compilations; they are not necessarily standards of quality.

7. This approach does not give credit to titles in the collection that may be equal to or better than those recommended in the list.

Application

This approach is especially helpful for identifying titles on a specific subject or checking certain sections of the collection. When Fermi Middle School adopted a new science curriculum, the media specialists used general tools, such as *Junior High School Library Catalog*, and subject-oriented tools, such as *Science Books and Films.*

Several teachers at Jefferson Elementary School were so successful in motivating children to read poetry that shelves for these works were often empty. The media specialist compared the holdings with selection tools and indexes to poetry. In addition to identifying titles not in the collection, she recorded two items of information. First, on the pages of the index that listed the works indexed, she recorded the call number of titles in the collection. This information helped children locate anthologies that contained specific poems. Second, on the shelf list card for each poetry work, she recorded the name of the tool which indexed that particular work. This information was useful later when she was deciding which poetry anthologies should be retained.

In schools where teachers use textbooks or curriculum guides, which include bibliographies of recommended materials, the collection can be measured against those lists. Teachers appreciate having a list of available titles with their call numbers. Creating such a list for the teachers can also alert you to gaps in the collection and, at the same time, provide an opportunity to suggest alternate materials.

2. Directly Examining the Collection

Description: This technique, a physical examination of the materials on the shelf, can reveal the size, scope, and depth of a collection. An assessment of the recency of materials and their physical conditions can help identify which materials need to be mended, repaired, bound, replaced, or discarded.

The examiner can be a member of the media center staff or from an outside source. The latter is usually someone knowledgeable about materials on a specific subject or school collections. Fermi Middle School had a science consultant examine the collection and recommend additional materials. The school library consultant in your state can help with this. State consultants usually have a broad base of experience and will visit your school on request.

The collection can be examined by the media center staff at two levels. The more cursory approach is to examine only the shelves. Are there shelves that are consistently empty? Is that a sign of the popularity of the subject or just improper distribution? Are teachers giving assignments that call for those materials? Does the collection program policy provide for adequate coverage in this area? Do duplicate copies and superseded editions inflate the collection?

A more in-depth approach is a systematic review of the collection. The materials are examined in light of the collection program policy, and the priorities established in the policy statement provide the basis for examining the materials. If users' needs have changed, a policy change is imperative. In sections which have low priority in a collection, infrequently used materials are probably not needed. Knowledge of the collection program policy and the growth rate of the collection can be used to set goals for the review program.

Criteria must be established to guide in making decisions about each item. Should it be kept, repaired, replaced, discarded, or relegated to storage or another collection? Decisions can be based on:

1. Proven use: circulation data, time on the shelf, in-house use, interlibrary loan circulations, and patron recommendation.

2. Estimated use: subject field; publication date, acquisition date, language of work.

3. Value/quality criteria method: comparison with standard lists, faculty review, application of selection criteria, assessment of physical condition.

4. Shelf reading and book slip method: dated slips in books indicate those being considered for withdrawal; when a patron uses the book or requests it be kept, the slip is removed—books with slips remaining after a fixed period of time are removed.

5. Undesirable duplication monitored through shelf reading.

Ideally, such a review is an ongoing process. It is easy to check the physical condition of books and periodicals when they are returned by users. More time, however, is required to check the condition of a filmstrip or to listen for distortion or scratches on a sound recording. Other aspects of this process were described in chapter 16 in the discussion on reevaluation.

Advantages

1. A cursory examination can be accomplished quickly.

2. Libraries considering cooperative sharing can readily identify the weaknesses and strengths of a collection.

3. Reviewing a collection on a systematic and ongoing basis ensures that both the collection development policy and the collection are responsive to school goals and user needs.

4. Establishing criteria for decisions about relegating, repairing, binding, replacing, and discarding materials facilitates those processes.

Disadvantages

1. Materials being circulated must be checked on the shelf list.

2. The process is time-consuming and requires trained staff.

3. If the collection program policy and the rate of growth are not considered, individual items will be evaluated rather than the collection as a whole.

4. Resources accessible through cooperative efforts are not considered.

5. Outside people who are knowledgeable about the school program as well as a subject area may be difficult to locate.

Application

When Anne found materials at Jefferson Elementary School had not circulated in three years and were not recommended in standard catalogs, she placed the materials in the teacher's lounge. A big sign invited teachers to indicate on a slip in the material any item they wanted to be kept. Using this approach, Anne had an opportunity to learn the interests of individual teachers and to suggest newer materials that would suit the same purpose as the item being considered for withdrawal.

3. Compiling Statistics

Description: Although the limitations of quantitative methods have been discussed earlier in this chapter, there are reasons for collecting this type of data.

Quantitative measures are important for measuring many aspects of program [sic] in order to make sound decisions for program improvement. While they do not reveal quality, quality will be nonexistent if quantitative measures are not present and meaningful: children can't read widely without books at their disposal; reading skill will not increase if progressively difficult books are not available; children won't read unless they are given time and encouragement to do so; teachers won't use 16mm projectors if there are never enough to go around or if they constantly break down.[3]

Statistics can be collected about:

1. Size: total number of volumes or titles, number of titles in various formats, subjects, or classifications, or measurement of the shelf list.

2. Volumes added within a given period of time: number of volumes by format, subject, or classification, cataloging statistics, or compared to circulation statistics.

3. Expenditures for materials: by format, classification, or genre, percentage of total budget, or amount per user or category of user.

4. Circulation statistics and use: by format or classification, by categories or users, or by imprint date of material, as compared to acquisition statistics by subject or genre, or number of reference works removed from the shelves or reference questions answered within a given period.

5. Unfilled requests and filled requests: by format or subject.

6. Interlibrary loan requests: by format, subject, or user.

7. Rate of growth: percentage of increase in total size of collection. However, Lancaster warns that:

   when considering the degree to which a library satisfies the demands placed upon it, both absolute size and rate of growth must be taken into account. Percentage rate of growth alone could present a somewhat distorted picture of the quality of a collection. A library may show a high percentage rate of growth if it fails to discard obsolete items while collecting new ones. Such a library, however, is performing a great disservice to its users. In addition to creating chronic storage problems, such a policy is likely to lead to diminution in the quality of a collection. Percentage rate of growth as an indicator of the utility of a collection penalizes the library that pursues an active policy of weeding.[4]

Advantages

1. Easy to compile if records have been kept.

2. If application is clearly defined, easy to understand and compare.

3. Relate directly to the users in the case of requests filled or not filled.

Disadvantages

1. Lack of standard definitions of the content or quantity of a unit.

2. Difficulty in counting nonprint items and sets of materials.

3. Significance may be difficult to interpret.

4. Possible inaccuracy or inconsistency in data collection and recording.

5. Statistics are usually inapplicable to a library's goals and objectives.

Application

The gathering of statistics is commonly used to compare one collection with another, rate a collection against similar collections for accreditation purposes, examine subject balance within a collection, or decide if resources should be shared.

If the collections in your district are being compared, data must be gathered in the same way. Check for the district's guidelines. Are you to do a volume or title count? If each volume of an encyclopedia set or each record in an album is counted, the total size of the collection may be distorted. Some districts with centralized processing may count an item as it appears in its main entry. For example, since each school may have a separate main entry, a school owning a kit containing two filmstrips, five books, and a teacher's guide might record one kit, while another school with only one of the filmstrips and one of the books might record two items, a book, and a filmstrip. An encyclopedia set cataloged as one item would count as one title. A multivolume set in which each volume is separately cataloged would be recorded as the number of individual titles.

When information is to be used for allocating funds, there is an advantage to having uniform data about the amount of materials accessible to each student. One could argue that more than one child can use the encyclopedia set; however, circulating materials such as kits are usually checked out to one individual at a time. Data that include both a title and a volume count reveal more about the accessibility of materials than a volume count alone. This procedure accounts for duplicate titles that can serve more people for a specific item but limits the total range of resources available.

Silver, a junior high school media specialist, writes of her concern that daily circulation counts are not important and states that:

> what *is* important is: approximately how many students and faculty members used the services of the center and approximately how many different kinds of media did they use?[5]

She reports that on one day only 50 items were checked out because the eighth-grade English classes were working on reports about the influence of television and radio on the average American family. These students had been told not to check materials out since their classes would be meeting in the media center for the next three days. Silver estimated that the 105 students used approximately two items each, a total of 210 items in Reference, the 500s, 300s, and 600s. By adding estimates for the other classes in a similar manner, she estimated the total circulation for that day as 1,690, with a total attendance of 295. The result is dramatic when compared with the figure of the original 50 items circulated.

Keeping statistics about unfilled requests and materials borrowed from other agencies can be used to determine what materials should be added to a collection. When students or teachers ask for information or specific items not in the collection, make a note and keep track of materials that must be borrowed from other agencies. When the same request occurs frequently, consider the item for purchase.

4. Checking Citations from Papers of Library Users

Description: This method can be used in situations where the users of the collection also use other libraries. In schools where students write term papers or do independent projects, one can carry out this procedure of checking the bibliographies to identify titles cited that are not holdings of the school collection.

Advantages

1. Lists are easily obtained.
2. The method relates directly to the user.
3. The procedure is easy to apply.
4. Information identifies works not in the collection.

Disadvantages

1. The value is limited if students use only the collection being evaluated.
2. Citations are limited to the subject of the paper, a small portion of the total collection.
3. The method is limited by number of students who engage in writing papers.

Application

One example of how this technique can be used in the school comes from Fermi Middle School's program for students gifted in the area of science. These students demonstrated an exceptional interest and ability in science. Their projects were among the ones judged outstanding at the district science fair. One of their assignments was to do term papers on a recent advance in science. They were encouraged to use resources of other libraries, such as the nearby university and industrial libraries. When the students completed their projects, the media specialist checked their citations to see which titles were used in other collections. A title cited by several students was considered for addition to the school's collection.

5. Obtaining User Opinions

Description: This method requires a survey of users or user groups, soliciting verbal or written responses through interviews, questionnaires, or a combination of methods. User opinions can be gathered informally, leading the media specialist to believe that users needs have been identified. A formal survey provides a more systematic and thorough way to obtain information.

Through carefully worded questions, one can identify the strengths and weaknesses of the collection as perceived by the users. The questions should be directed to specific goals, which may or may not be of significance to the user. If policy does not reflect a requested service or type of materials, it may need to be changed.

Advantages

1. The survey can be developed to relate directly to the needs of users and to the goals and objectives of the collection.

2. The information collected may reflect current interests.

3. A survey can be used for most types of users.

Disadvantages

1. The method requires aggressive opinion-seeking.

2. Those polled may be passive about participating or lack a point of comparison.

3. Users' interests may be narrower than the collection program policies.

Application

Users' needs can be assessed formally and informally. At one level a student may ask for a specific title that his cousin recommended, while another may ask for the latest recording by her favorite singer. These requests reveal students' interests. A busy media specialist may forget to write down the request or be unable to obtain sufficient information on which to initiate an order. Individual requests may not reflect priorities established in the collection program policy. Through a more formal approach, one can obtain a consensus of opinion and direct the inquiry more closely to the goals of the school.

A number of survey instruments that include questions directly related to the collection are available to examine services and provide program evaluation. The instruments identified at the end of this chapter range from simple checklists or inventories to complex instruments involving mathematical or statistical techniques. Gaver's *Services of Secondary School Media Center* illustrates the type of checklist where respondents indicate their perceptions of the availability of a service. Liesener's *A Systematic Process for Planning School Media Programs* presents a way to get respondents to record their perceptions of what exists and what should exist, to suggest priorities and to provide data for cost estimates of resources and time. Liesener's plan provides a way to gather both quantitative and qualitative data.

Before people can indicate priorities, they need to decide on potential alternatives as well as the conditions necessary to make them available. Liesener's "Inventory of School Library/Media Center Services," a self-administered questionnaire for library staff, teachers, administrators, and students (excluding elementary students), is an effective tool for making participants aware of the range of services that can be provided. This step is crucial to obtain meaningful assessment of user needs.[6]

Loertscher and Land agree.[7] They used the Purdue Self Evaluation System for School Media Centers (PSES) with second-, fourth-, and fifth-graders. Their report in *School Media Quarterly* offers practical advice about the wording and administration of the instrument. The bibliography for this chapter identifies a number of sources that provide further information and that should be consulted before conducting a survey or using any of the identified instruments.

6. Application of Standards

Description: In this procedure, the collection is compared to quantitative and qualitative recommendations listed in standards, guidelines, or similar publications. The issuing body may be a professional association, such as in the case of *Media Programs: District and School* published by the American Association of School Librarians and the Association for Educational Communications and Technology. An example from a state agency is *Florida School Media Programs: A Guide for Excellence.* Accreditation agencies are another source, for example, the Southern Association of Colleges and Schools' Commission on Elementary Schools, *Guide to Evaluation and Accreditation of Schools.*

Advantages

1. The guidelines will generally be relevant to media center and school goals and objectives.
2. Standards or guidelines are usually widely accepted and considered authoritative.
3. They can be used in persuasive ways to solicit support.

Disadvantages

1. The recommendations may be so generally stated that a high degree of professional knowledge and judgment may be needed to interpret the statements.
2. Knowledgeable people may disagree about the application of the statements.
3. Minimum standards may be perceived as maximum standards.

Application

Questions that one can raise about standards or guidelines include:

Who (people, associations, agencies) created the document?

How and by whom were the standards approved, accepted, or endorsed?

Are the recommendations rigid, or are alternative approaches suggested?

Do the guidelines represent the long-range goals of your program, or has it developed beyond the recommendations?

Is the philosophy and rationale of the guidelines acceptable to you and to those with whom you work?

On what basis would you recommend these guidelines to others?

These questions imply some of the uses of standards. First, the recommendations serve as a basis for comparison of your collection against accepted standards so that weaknesses in the collection can be identified. However, standards are just an opinion of the level of collection needed to support a program, and accreditation agencies use them in this way.

Be familiar with the recommendations of the state and national guidelines. These documents can be used with administrators, teachers, and others to interpret the concept of the media program, articulate needs, and formulate goals and objectives. Some media specialists obtain copies of such documents for their administrators, underlining sections applicable to the media program.

Summary

Techniques for measuring and evaluating collections are not limited to those described in this chapter. References in the bibliography can serve as a starting point for learning more about the techniques described here and about other techniques.

The techniques described in this chapter included qualitative and quantitative measures. Often two or more techniques are used together to obtain more meaningful results. The final example illustrates a combination of 1) examining the collection, 2) identifying unfilled requests, and 3) checking lists.

Three years after the introduction of the new science curriculum at Fermi Middle School, the media staff became increasingly aware that the collection was weak in other curricular areas. Since no additional funds had been provided to accommodate the new curriculum, monies had been spent predominantly for that one subject. Teachers expressed concerns about the datedness of the social science materials. They complained that geography titles gave inaccurate information. Students asked for biographies not in the collection.

This situation was prevalent throughout the school district. Following an organized evaluation process, media specialists analyzed the shelf list in their schools for holdings represented by classification numbers for the social sciences. The analysis included number of titles, number of volumes, number of formats, and date of publication. This analysis created a profile of the nonfiction works in each collection. To analyze the fiction holdings, a list of appropriate subject headings was created. The card catalog was checked for the number of titles, types of formats, and date of publications for works under the subject headings. After collecting these profiles, each media specialist met with teachers at the individual schools to compare and discuss the profiles and areas of needs identified by the teachers. Using this information, the media specialists checked subject-oriented selection tools for titles not found in most collections. The district sponsored a two-week exhibit of the recommended titles, where teachers and students examined the materials and indicated their selections. A side benefit of this evaluation was the increased teacher awareness of the ways fiction titles could be used to teach social studies.

The evaluation process provides an opportunity to work with students, teachers, and administrators to ensure that the collection meets their needs.

Notes to Chapter 17

[1]Evelyn H. Daniel, "Performance Measures for School Librarians: Complexities and Potential," in *Advances in Librarianship*, vol. 6, edited by Melvin J. Voight and Michael H. Harris (New York, NY: Academic Press, 1976), p. 37.

[2]Ibid., p. 5.

[3]Blanche Woolls, David Loertscher, and Donald Shirey, *Evaluation Techniques for School Library/Media Programs: A Workshop Outline* (Pittsburgh, PA: Graduate School of Library and Information Sciences, University of Pittsburgh, 1977), p. 12.

[4]F. W. Lancaster, *The Measurement and Evaluation of Library Services* (Washington, DC: Information Resources Press, 1977), p. 168.

[5]Carole K. Silver, "On Counting Statistics: Isn't It Time We Re-educated Ourselves?" *Wilson Library Bulletin* 47 (1973): 876.

[6]James W. Liesener, *A Systematic Process for Planning Media Programs* (Chicago, IL: American Library Association, 1976), p. 30.

[7]David V. Loertscher and Phyllis Land, "An Empirical Study of Media Services in Indiana Elementary Schools," *School Media Quarterly* 4 (1975): 17.

Selected Standards and Guidelines

American Association of School Librarians, American Library Association, and Association for Educational Communications and Technology. *Media Programs: District and School.* Chicago, IL: American Library Association; Washington, DC: Association for Educational Communications and Technology, 1975.

Florida Department of Education, School Library Media Services Section. *Florida School Library Media Programs: A Guide to Excellence.* Tallahassee, FL: Department of Education, n.d.

Kansas Association of School Librarians. *Guidelines for School Library Media Programs in Kansas.* n.p.: Kansas Association of School Librarians, 1980.

Maryland State Department of Education. *Criteria for Modern School Media Programs.* Baltimore, MD: Maryland State Department of Education, 1975.

Southern Association of Colleges and Schools. Commission on Elementary Schools. *Guide to Evaluation and Accreditation of Schools.* Atlanta, GA: Southern Association of Colleges and Schools, 1979.

Evaluation Instruments

Association for Educational Communications and Technology, Committee on Evaluation of Media Programs. *Evaluating Media Programs: District and School.* Washington, DC: Association for Educational Communications and Technology, 1980.

Gaver, Mary Virginia. *Services of Secondary School Media Centers: Evaluation and Development.* ALA Studies in Librarianship, No. 2. Chicago, IL: American Library Association, 1971.

Kentucky Department of Education, Division of Instructional Media. *Guidelines for Merit Media Programs.* Frankfort, KY: Kentucky Department of Education, 1979.

Liesener, James W. *Instruments for Planning and Evaluating Library Media Programs.* Rev. ed. 1980. Available from Student Supply Store, University of Maryland, College Park, MD 20742.

Liesener, James W. *A Systematic Process for Planning Media Programs.* Chicago, IL: American Library Association, 1976.

Loertscher, David, and Stroud, Janet G. *PSES: Purdue Self-Evaluation System for School Media Centers: Elementary Catalog.* Idaho Falls, ID: Hi Willow Research and Publishing, 1976.

Loertscher, David, and Stroud, Janet G. *PSES: Purdue Self-Evaluation System for School Media Centers: Junior, Senior High School Catalog.* Idaho Falls, ID: Hi Willow Research and Publishing, 1976.

Martin, Betty, and Carson, Ben. *The Principal's Handbook on the School Library Media Center.* New York, NY: Gaylord Professional Publications, 1978.

Michigan Department of Education, State Library Service. *Performance Criteria for Evaluating the Library/Media Program in Michigan Schools.* Lansing, MI: Michigan Department of Education, 1975. Designed to be used with *Guidelines for Media Programs in Michigan Schools*, 1975.

National Study of School Evaluation. *Elementary School Evaluative Criteria H: Learning Media Services.* Arlington, VA: National Study of School Evaluation, 1973.

National Study of School Evaluation. *Middle School/Junior High School Evaluative Criteria, Section X: Learning Media Services.* Arlington, VA: National Study of School Evaluation, 1979.

Palmour, Vernon E.; Bellassai, Marcia C.; and De Wath, Nancy V. *A Planning Process for Public Libraries.* Chicago, IL: American Library Association, 1980.

Woolls, Blanche; Loertscher, David; and Shirey, Donald. *Evaluation Techniques for School Library/Media Programs: A Workshop Outline.* Pittsburgh, PA: Graduate School of Library and Information Sciences, University of Pittsburgh, 1977.

Chapter 17 Bibliography

American Association of School Librarians, American Library Association, and Association for Educational Communications and Technology. *Media Programs: District and School.* Chicago, IL: American Library Association; Washington, DC: Association for Educational Communications and Technology, 1975.

Barber, Raymond W., and Mancall, Jacqueline C. "The Application of Bibliometric Techniques to the Analysis of Materials for Young Adults." *Collection Management* 2 (1978): 229-41.

Bonn, George S. "Evaluation of the Collection." *Library Trends* 22 (1974): 265-304.

Daniel, Evelyn H. "Performance Measures for School Librarians: Complexities and Potential." In *Advances in Librarianship*, edited by Melvin J. Voight and Michael H. Harris, pp. 1-51. Vol. 6. New York, NY: Academic Press, 1976.

Lancaster, F. W. *The Measurement and Evaluation of Library Services.* Washington, DC: Information Resources Press, 1977.

Liesener, James W. "The Development of a Planning Process for Media Programs." *School Media Quarterly* 1 (1973): 278-97.

Liesener, James W. *A Systematic Process for Planning Media Programs.* Chicago, IL: American Library Association, 1976.

Loertscher, David, and Land, Phyllis. "An Empirical Study of Media Services in Indiana Elementary Schools." *School Media Quarterly* 4 (1975): 8-18.

McGaw, Howard R. "Policies and Practices in Discarding." *Library Trends* 4 (1956): 269-82.

Perkins, David L., ed. *Guidelines for Collection Development.* Chicago, IL: American Library Association, 1979.

Rush, Betsy. "Weeding vs. Censorship: Treading a Fine Line." *Library Journal* 99 (1974): 3032-33.

Silver, Carole K. "On Counting Statistics: Isn't It Time We Re-educated Ourselves?" *Wilson Library Bulletin* 47 (1973): 876.

Slote, Stanley J. *Weeding Library Collections—II.* 2nd rev. ed. Littleton, CO: Libraries Unlimited, 1982.

Stroud, Janet G., and Loertscher, David V. "User Needs and School Library Service." *Catholic Library World* 49 (1977): 162-65.

Weeding the Small Library Collection. Lansing, MI: Michigan State Library, 1965.

Woolls, Blanche; Loertscher, David; and Shirey, Donald. *Evaluation Techniques for School Library/Media Programs: A Workshop Outline.* Pittsburgh, PA: Graduate School of Library and Information Sciences, University of Pittsburgh, 1977.

18
CREATING AN INITIAL COLLECTION
AND CLOSING A COLLECTION

This chapter might be entitled "Challenging Situations in Dealing with Collections." It is unlikely that you will face these challenges in your first year as a media specialist. However, more frequently than ever, student populations shift as birth rates decline. And as schools face financial problems, media specialists are being called on to create an initial collection or to close a collection.

Each situation makes different demands upon media specialists' knowledge and skill as we carry out the activities of the collection program. Both creating or closing a collection can be stimulating experiences that may call for tact. Emotions may become involved as we make decisions about closing a collection or losing a favorite group of students.

The Initial Collection

The need to create an initial collection usually occurs either when a new school building is to be opened or when a school has had classroom collections and decides to centralize the resources physically and/or bibliographically. Each of these situations places special demands upon the media specialist.

New Building

When a new building is being planned, various patterns of preparation can occur. As soon as the building contract has been awarded, it is time to plan for acquiring, and to begin to acquire, the new collection. This may mean that the media specialist and faculty will be hired to plan during the year preceding the opening of the building. This procedure has definite advantages. As the faculty work together identifying philosophy and goals, creating the curriculum, and developing plans, the media specialist benefits from participating in many activities. The media specialist's major responsibility during the year is to ensure that the desired types of learning environments will be ready on opening day. Orders must be placed early enough to allow for delivery and processing time and any necessary substitutions. Admittedly, school districts rarely have the financial resources or educational foresight to provide this year of planning.

Whether or not all the faculty are engaged in planning during the year prior to opening the school, the collection needs to be ready on opening day. If the school's staff has not been appointed, the responsibility often rests with district-level staff. Those planning the new facility need to be knowledgeable about the long-range goals and objectives of the total educational program as well as the materials needed for a base collection. Equipment should be appropriate to the goals and objectives of the school and the media program, should support the use of all formats within the collection, and should meet the criteria identified in chapter 10. Planners must also consider that teaching strategies may change within a school, and therefore design flexibility into the plans.

District-level staff from Montgomery County (Maryland) Schools, Division of Evaluation and Selection, serve in the planning stage. Their goal for the initial collection has been met

> if, in the opening days of a new school, the members of the media staff are able to cope effectively with 90 percent of users' needs and questions by direct referral to the collection.[1]

How does Montgomery County prepare for this goal? Staff recognize both the ideal that "none of the budget ... be encumbered until the professional media staff of the new facility can be involved"[2] and the reality of deadlines. Materials selection must begin a year prior to a September opening, but often the media specialist may not be appointed until July. To accommodate this situation, a three-phase plan for creating a collection was developed for the district. According to the plan, the Division of Evaluation and Selection uses one-third of the initial collection budget to acquire basic materials. This takes place prior to the appointment of the school staff. Another third of the budget is spent on materials recommended by the principal and the professional staff responsible for opening the school. The final third is reserved for the media specialist who works with teachers and students to make selections. In phase one dealing with the initial collection budget, staff use standard reviewing sources to try to cover a broad range of information on different levels in appropriate formats, keeping in mind the needs and interests of the students.[3] This practice can apply equally well for the individual media specialist responsible for creating an initial collection.

There are guidelines for basic collections in works such as *Media Programs: District and School* and in state publications such as the State of Maryland's *Criteria for Modern School Library Media Programs*, the Kansas Association of School Librarian's *Guidelines for School Library Media Programs in Kansas*, or *Florida School Library Media Programs: A Guide for Excellence.* This information provides guidance on the range of formats and number of items on which a collection can be built.

Specific titles for the collection can be identified through selection tools. Particularly useful books include:

Canadian Books for Young People

Children's Catalog

Core Media Collection for Elementary Schools

Elementary School Library Collection

Junior High School Library Catalog

The broad scope and coverage of these tools can help in identifying titles that will meet the wide range of informational needs that can be anticipated during the opening days of the collection.

Centralizing Classroom Collections

Although the concept of centralized collections is not new, Ladd reports the National Center for Education Statistics survey of a nationally representative sample of public schools in 1974 indicates that

> 14,000 schools serving more than one million children did not have library/media centers. The primary reason in most of those cases is the small size of the schools (on the average, fewer than 75 children per school). However, in some instances, a policy of providing classroom-level collections of specialized materials is followed.[4]

The transition from classroom collections to a centralized collection needs to be planned as carefully as creation of a new collection. Like any other change, this consolidation of materials is likely to meet with resistance. Teachers, accustomed to having specific titles in their rooms, may be reluctant to share the materials and slow to appreciate the benefits gained from the centralized collection. Teachers may reflect so possessive an attitude that it is even difficult to obtain bibliographic information.

As materials are consolidated, the media specialist may have to explain why an item is not up to the standards of the collection. Diplomacy and tact are called for regularly. Remember that the item may have been used regularly in the classroom. The teacher may not know about better materials in the collection and may only want to use what is familiar. Extended loan periods can reassure teachers that materials are not being taken from them. As you work with teachers on the plans for the collection and learn of their individual preferences, make suggestions of materials they may find useful.

Usually, there is pressure to process materials quickly in this situation. Anxieties about unavailable materials can be alleviated when materials can be readily located. The transition also goes much smoother when processing is completed during the summer.

As you demonstrate the benefits of the centralized collection, teacher support will increase. If there are an excessive number of duplicate titles, see if other media centers are willing to exchange materials. During the transition, you may want to borrow materials from the district center or another library to help demonstrate how teacher and student needs can be met better through a wider range of materials. Such borrowing is a stop-gap measure, however, and could lead to further problems unless the necessary funding is provided to fill in the gaps in the collection.

As you attempt to create a collection during the transition, you will primarily be identifying what is in the building. Until the basic bibliographic record is established, it is difficult to check for gaps in the collection and to identify areas for purchase. Personnel at the district level can be very supportive throughout this process. The district may have a "floating" collection and provide processing services and in-service programs for teachers.

Closing Collections

When schools are closed or consolidated, the full impact may not be felt until the formal announcement is made. An individual should be assigned the responsibility for determining procedures for removing materials. Plans must be made for distributing materials.

Teachers who are being moved to other schools can help by indicating titles they would like to have available. These items should be the first materials reallocated so they can be processed into those collections. Damaged and out-of-date materials should be discarded. Old magazines, especially ones on travel and natural science, can be clipped for picture and information files.

A list of the remaining materials can be distributed throughout the system so other media specialists can indicate titles desired. Unclaimed items must be stored, distributed, or discarded. Distribution possibilities include storing materials at an exchange center where they can be examined, adding duplicate titles to classroom collections, or donating the materials to other agencies serving children, such as hospitals or institutions. The materials might also be advertised for sale to beginning collections. Policies within the district will govern how materials can be dispersed and may grant approval for sale to individuals for fund-raising.

Consolidation may be a "hot" issue that calls for sensitivity on the part of the media specialist. One's sense of standards, diplomacy, and tact, along with a sensitivity to the politics of the situation, will be demanded. Hopefully, the loss can be turned into a gain for other schools in the district.

Notes to Chapter 18

[1]Frances Dean, "Design of Initial Media Collections for New Facilities," *School Media Quarterly* 2 (1974): 234.

[2]Ibid., p. 235.

[3]Ibid., p. 236.

[4]Boyd Ladd, *National Inventory of Library Needs, 1975: Resources Needed for Public and Academic Libraries and Public School Library/ Media Centers* (Washington, DC: U.S. Government Printing Office, 1977), p. 107.

Chapter 18 Bibliography

American Association of School Librarians, American Library Association, and Association for Educational Communications and Technology. *Media Programs: District and School.* Chicago, IL: American Library Association; Washington, DC: Association for Educational Communications and Technology, 1975.

Criteria for Modern School Media Programs. Baltimore, MD: Maryland State Department of Education, 1975.

Dean, Frances. "Design of Initial Media Collections for New Facilities." *School Media Quarterly* 2 (1974): 234-36.

Florida School Library Media Programs: A Guide to Excellence. Tallahassee, FL: State of Florida Department of Education, n.d.

Guidelines for School Library Media Programs in Kansas. n.p.: Kansas Association of School Librarians, 1980.

Hoberman, Judith Sloan. "Coping with School Library Consolidations," *School Library Journal* 26 (1979): 55.

Ladd, Boyd. *National Inventory of Library Needs, 1975: Resources Needed for Public and Academic Libraries and Public School Library/Media Centers.* Washington, DC: U.S. Government Printing Office, 1977.

Shaver, Johnny M. "Selecting Initial Media Equipment for New Facilities." *School Media Quarterly* 2 (1974): 227-33.

Von Ancken, Eva Elisabeth. "A Personal Account of Closing a School Library." *School Library Journal* 27 (1980): 38-40.

POSTSCRIPT

There may be days when you feel you are operating in a vacuum, isolated from anyone who shares your enthusiasm for what a media program can be. This is not unusual, particularly for the media specialist who works alone at the building level. Remember that through a telephone call or a letter, you can establish contact with someone who understands your concerns. These individuals may be nearby media specialists who you met through the county or state associations, personnel at the district or state level, association staff members, or former professors. Like the media program, you are part of a larger circle of people who share common interests.

Information and dialogue are available, if only you will initiate the action.

Appendix 1
ASSOCIATIONS AND AGENCIES

Alexander Graham Bell Association for the Deaf   Chapter 14
3417 Volta Place, NW, Washington, DC 20007
    Publishes *Volta Review* (seven issues per year); includes reviews of books for parents and teachers of deaf children. Also publishes books and audiovisual materials.

American Alliance for Health, Physical Education,   Chapter 12
  Recreation, and Dance
1900 Association Drive, Reston, VA 22091
    Journals include *Health Education* (formerly *School Health Review*) (bimonthly) and *Journal of Physical Education and Recreation* (monthly except July and August); have information about professional resources and occasionally have reviews or features on materials for children.

American Annals of the Deaf   Chapter 14
5034 Wisconsin Avenue, NW, Washington, DC 20016
    Publishes *American Annals of the Deaf* (seven issues per year); reviews books for teachers and parents.

American Association for the Advancement of Science   Chapter 14
1515 Massachusetts Avenue, NW, Washington, DC 20005
    Science Books and Films (sometimes listed as *AAAS Science Books and Films*) (five issues per year); includes review of books, films and filmstrips on mathematics and the sciences (social, physical, and life). The *AAAS Science Film Catalog* reviews films for audiences from primary school children through adult.

American Association of School Administrators   Chapters 7 and 14
1801 North Moore, Arlington, VA 22209
    Publishes *School Administrator* (11 issues per year), pamphlets, filmstrips, and books; sponsors conferences, conventions, and other information services.

American Association of School Librarians
  See American Library Association

American Federation of Teachers   Chapter 14
11 Dupont Circle, NW, Washington, DC 20036
    Publications include the periodicals *American Teacher* and *American Educator* (quarterly), newsletters, pamphlets, books, films, and videotapes.

American Foundation for the Blind   Chapter 14
15 West Sixteenth Street, New York, NY 10011
    Publishes *Journal of Visual Impairment and Blindness* (monthly except July and August); includes reviews of books, films, etc. The Foundation's publications

include books, films, pamphlets, such as Susan Jay Spungen's *Guidelines for Public School Programs Serving Visually Handicapped Children*, and bibliographies.

American Industrial Arts Association, Inc.   Chapter 12
National Education Association Headquarters Building
1201 Sixteenth Street, NW, Washington, DC 20036
    Man/Society/Technology (formerly *Journal of Industrial Arts Education*) (eight issues per year); has a column that reviews professional materials and media for students.

American Library Association   Chapter 4
50 East Huron Street, Chicago, IL 60611
    Publications, such as books or journals (e.g., *Booklist*), can be purchased through the Order Department. Inexpensive and specialized materials can be ordered directly from the issuing division at the above address.

    American Association of School Librarians   Chapters 2, 4, 7
        Publishes *School Library Media Quarterly*, bibliographies, and other materials.

    Association for Library Service to Children
        With the Young Adult Services Division publishes *Top of the News*.

    Office for Intellectual Freedom   Chapter 4
        Publishes policy statements, such as the "Library Bill of Rights."

    Young Adult Services Division
        Joint sponsors of *Top of the News*.

American Speech-Language-Hearing Association   Chapter 14
10801 Rockville Pike, Rockville, MD 20852
    Publishes *ASHA: A Journal of the American Speech-Language-Hearing Association* (12 issues per year); reviews games, kits, learning materials designed for use with hearing- or speech-impaired children.

American Vocational Association, Inc.   Chapter 12
2020 North Fourteenth Street, Arlington, VA 22201
    VOC ED (monthly September-June); includes announcements and reviews for professional materials and media for students.

Association for Educational Communications   Chapters 2, 4, 7
    and Technology
1126 Sixteenth Street, NW, Washington, DC 20036
    Publishes *Instructional Innovator* (nine issues per year), books, pamphlets, audiovisual materials of interest to media specialists.

Association for Supervision and Curriculum Development   Chapter 14
225 North Washington Street, Alexandria, VA 22314
    Publishes *Educational Leadership* (monthly October-May); contains reviews of professional books. ASCD publishes books, pamphlets, videotapes, and audiocassettes.

Association of American Publishers   Chapter 15
One Park Avenue, New York, NY 10016

Canadian Library Association   Chapter 7
151 Sparks Street, Ottawa, Ontario K1P 5E3
    Publishes *Canadian Materials*, a quarterly annotated critical bibliography.

The Children's Book Centre   Chapter 8
229 College Street, 5th Floor, Toronto, Ontario M5T 1R4
    Provides an examination center and information about new Canadian titles
for children.

Children's Book Council, Inc.   Chapter 8
67 Irving Place, New York, NY 10003
    Publishes "The Calendar" and other informational packets about children's
books.

Comics Magazine Association of America, Inc.   Chapter 4
60 East Forty-second Street, New York, NY 10017
    Publishes "The Code of the Association."

Consumer Education Resource Network (CERN)   Chapter 14
1500 Wilson Boulevard, Suite 800, Rosslyn, VA 22209
    A resource and service network in the consumer education field.

Council for Exceptional Children   Chapter 14
1920 Association Drive, Reston, VA 22091
    Teaching the Exceptional Child (quarterly); includes articles on instructional
methods and materials. Other publications include newsletters, books, and
media.

EDMARC (Educational Materials Review Center of the   Chapter 8
    Office of Education)
400 Maryland Avenue, SW, Washington, DC 20202
    A national examination center for children's books and learning materials;
open to the public.

Educational Film Library Association   Chapters 4 and 10
43 West Sixty-first Street, New York, NY 10023
    Numerous publications, such as *Film Library Quarterly* and *Manual on Film
Evaluation*, and the statement "Freedom to View."

ERIC (Educational Resources Information Center)
ERIC Document Reproduction Services (EDRS)
P.O. Box 190, Arlington, VA 22210
    Operated by the National Institute of Education (NIE) and the U.S.
Department of Education; ERIC has 16 clearinghouses to collect and
disseminate educational materials in specified areas. Abstracts of materials are
published monthly in *Resources in Education* (RIE).
    Clearinghouses dealing with information of particular interest for those
working in elementary and middle schools include:

    ERIC Clearinghouse for Science, Mathematics,   Chapter 12
        and Environmental Education
    Ohio State University
    1200 Chambers Road, 3rd Floor, Columbus, OH 43212

    ERIC Clearinghouse for Social Studies/   Chapter 12
        Social Science Education
    855 Broadway, Boulder, CO 80302

    ERIC Clearinghouse on Career Education   Chapter 12
    Center for Vocational Education, The Ohio State University
    1960 Kenny Road, Columbus, OH 43210

    ERIC Clearinghouse on Handicapped and Gifted Children   Chapter 14
    The Council for Exceptional Children
    1920 Association Drive, Reston, VA 22091

ERIC Clearinghouse on Information Resources   Chapter 10
School of Education, Syracuse, NY 13210

ERIC Clearinghouse on Languages and Linguistics   Chapter 12
Center for Applied Linguistics
1611 North Kent Street, Arlington, VA 22209

ERIC Clearinghouse on Reading and Communication Skills   Chapter 12
National Council of Teachers of English
1111 Kenyon Road, Urbana, IL 61801

ERIC Clearinghouse on Rural Education and Small Schools   Chapter 14
New Mexico State University
Box 3AP, Las Cruces, NM 88003
    Provides information analysis products relating to education of Indian
Americans, Mexican Americans, Spanish Americans, and children of
migratory farm workers.

ERIC Clearinghouse on Urban Education   Chapter 14
Columbia University, Teachers College
Box 40, 525 West 120th Street, New York, NY 10027

Friends of IBBY, Inc.   Chapter 13
    For membership information, contact
John Donovan
Friends of IBBY (International Board on Books for Young People), Secretary
P.O. Box 1137
Madison Square Station, New York, NY 10159
    Encourages interest in international children's literature through the
"Friends of IBBY Newsletter" and meetings.

Gallaudet College   Chapter 14
    Write the Gallaudet College Bookstore, Washington, DC 20002, for the
catalog of their materials for the deaf.

Information Center on Children's Cultures   Chapter 13
U.S. Committee for UNICEF
331 East Thirty-eighth Street, New York, NY 10016
    Source of list of names and addresses of domestic and foreign book dealers,
as well as publications about different countries.

International Reading Association   Chapter 12
800 Barksdale Road, P.O. Box 8139, Newark, DE 19711
    Publishes *Reading Teacher* on reading instruction at the elementary school
level and *Journal of Reading* on teaching reading at the high school level through
adult. Both journals are issued eight times a year and include reviews and
articles of interest. The association also publishes books, bibliographies, and
audio recordings.

Music Educators National Conference   Chapter 12
1201 Sixteenth Street, NW, Washington, DC 22091
    Publications include *Music Books for the Elementary School Library* by
Peggy Flanagan Baird, a selected annotated bibliography.

National Assessment and Dissemination Center (NADC)   Chapter 12
49 Washington Avenue, Cambridge, MA 02140
    Publishes *Bilingual Journal* (quarterly) and has a catalog of publications
developed for bilingual users.

National Association of Elementary School Principals   Chapters 7 and 14
1801 North Moore Street, Arlington, VA 22209
   Publishes *National Elementary Principal* (four times per year), books, pamphlets, and films.

National Association of Independent Schools   Chapter 14
18 Tremont Street, Boston, MA 02108
   Publishes *Independent School* (quarterly), books, reports, and curricular materials.

National Association of Secondary School Principals   Chapters 7 and 14
1904 Association Drive, Reston, VA 22091
   Publications include *Bulletin* (nine issues per year), *Curriculum Report* (bimonthly), and *The Practitioner* (quarterly).

National Catholic Educational Association   Chapter 14
One Dupont Circle, NW, Suite 350, Washington, DC 20036
   Publications include journals, books, pamphlets, audiocassettes. The association offers workshops, seminars, and consulting services.

National Center for Health Education   Chapter 14
901 Sneath Lane, Suite 215, San Bruno, CA 94066
   Provides information to schools interested in developing or redesigning health curriculums. Will direct individuals to programs and contacts within the Center's School Health Education Project (SHEP).

National Clearinghouse for Bilingual Education   Chapter 14
1300 Wilson Boulevard, Suite B2-11, Rosslyn, VA 22209
   Offers information about organizatons involved in bilingual education, publishes information analysis products, offers a computerized information database with limited on-line search services, and provides field representatives.

National Congress of Parents and Teachers   Chapter 14
700 North Rush Street, Chicago, IL 60611
   Publications include *PTA Today* (seven issues per year) and pamphlets on issues such as television's effect on children.

National Council for the Social Studies   Chapter 12
3615 Wisconsin Avenue, NW, Washington, DC 20016
   Their "Revision of the NCSS Social Studies Curriculum Guidelines" offers a set of standards for social studies programs including "Strategies of Instruction and Learning Activities Should Rely on a Broad Range of Learning Resources." Specifically mentioned within this section are printed materials for a wide range of reading abilities and interests; primary and secondary sources; a variety of media for learning through seeing, hearing, touching, and acting, and calling for thought and feeling; resource people; organizations; and the community (*Social Education* 43 [1979]: 270). The journal *Social Education* offers reviews of films, textbooks, children's trade books, and professional books. Articles in the journal frequently deal with selection and use of materials, as evidenced in "Sources and Resources in Consumer Education," by Steward Lee (October 1974), pages 519-23. Other publications include books and pamphlets such as *The Censorship Game and How to Play It* by C. Benjamin Cox.

National Council of Teachers of English   Chapters 3, 7, 12, 13
1111 Kenyon Road, Urbana, IL 61801
   Publications include *Language Arts* (elementary school, eight issues per year) and *English Journal* (middle school, junior and senior high school, nine issues per year) plus a wide range of materials: professional topics, literary maps, cassettes, and booklists. Two of their selection tools that are revised on a

periodic basis are *Adventuring with Books, A Booklist for Preschool-Grade 6* and *Your Reading: A Booklist for Junior High Students.*

NCTE has a Committee on Censorship and offers resources, aid, and support. *The Student's Right to Read* is currently being revised. Reprints on the topic of censorship available include: "Censorship: Don't Let It Become an Issue in Your Schools" by the NCTE Committee from *Language Arts*, February 1978, and "Organized Censors Rarely Rest: A Special Issue on Censorship" by Edward B. Jenkinson, from *Indiana English* theme issue in 1977.

Within the NCTE structure, two assemblies publish items of interest. The *ALAN Review* of the Assembly on Literature for Adolescents reviews hardbacks and paperbacks. *The Bulletin of the Children's Literature Assembly* (formerly *Ripples*) provides in-depth discussion on specific topics within this subject.

Also at NCTE is the ERIC Clearinghouse on Reading and Communication Skills, which provides information analysis products (interpretative summaries, research reviews, and bibliographies) in the areas of reading, writing, speaking, and listening.

National Council of Teachers of Mathematics   Chapter 12
1906 Association Drive, Reston, VA 22091

Arithmetic Teacher (elementary, nine issues per year) and *Mathematics Teacher* (junior high school through teacher education, nine issues per year); include reviews and articles of interest, such as "Guidelines for Evaluation of Published Metric Materials" by Cecil Trueblood and Michael Szabo (*Arithmetic Teacher*, February 1978, pages 46-50). NCTM's selected bibliography *Mathematics Library-Elementary and Junior High School* is revised approximately every five years. *Instructional Aids in Mathematics*, the 34th yearbook, discusses the selection and use of print mateirals, teaching machines, models, manipulative devices, and games.

National Education Association   Chapter 14
1201 Sixteenth Street, NW, Washington, DC 20036

Publishes *Today's Education* (every other month during the school year), books, pamphlets, curricular resource materials, and audiovisual materials. An example of a recent publication is "Selected and Annotated Bibliography on Teaching Refugee Children (Indochinese, Haitian, Cuban)," which identifies materials to use with children, sources of information on their cultural backgrounds, and agencies that provide services and information to those involved in teaching refugee children. This publication is available free to members.

National Library Service for the Blind and Physically Handicapped   Chapter 14
Library of Congress, 1291 Taylor Street, NW, Washington, DC 20540

Publications include *For Younger Readers: Braille and Talking Books* (biennial catalog); *Talking Books Topics* and *Braille Book Review* (bi-monthly magazines which announce books and magazines available in these formats). The agency also provides information about equipment, bibliographies, and information about blindness and physical handicaps.

National Science Teachers Association   Chapter 14
1742 Connecticut Avenue, NW, Washington, DC 20009

Science and Children (elementary and middle schools, eight issues per year); has two monthly columns of reviews, one on curriculum materials and the other on resources (books and audiovisual materials). Articles often discuss the use of materials, such as "Using Fiction to Teach Environmental Education" by Joyce Powers (October 1974), pages 16-17. Other publications include books, kits, audiotapes, posters, and pamphlets.

National Study of School Evaluation   Chapter 17
5201 Leesburg Pike, Falls Church, VA 22041
    Publishes evaluation instruments.

Recordings for the Blind, Inc.   Chapter 14
215 East Fifty-eighth Street, New York, NY 10022
    Provides recordings requested by blind people, who must furnish two copies of the book.

Southern Association of Colleges and Schools   Chapter 17
Commission on Elementary Schools
795 Peachtree Street, NE, 5th Floor, Atlanta, GA 30309
    Publishes *Guide to Evaluation and Accreditation of Schools.*

Speech Communication Association   Chapter 14
5105 Backlick Road, Annandale, VA 22003
    Communication Education (quarterly); includes reviews of books and nonbook materials useful to teachers of speech. The association publishes books, pamphlets, and audiocasettes. It also distributes publications from the ERIC/RCS Speech Communication Module, such as "Censorship of Sexual Materials: A Selected, Annotated Basic Bibliography" by Thomas L. Tedford.

Appendix 2
BIBLIOGRAPHIC AND SELECTION TOOLS

Numbers at the end of the entry indicate the chapter where the title is specifically mentioned or where the tools that are useful to carry out the activities are discussed. Use the index to find exact page numbers. Addresses are provided for journals; see Appendix 1 for associations.

AAAS Science Film Catalog. Ann Seltz-Petrash, compiler. Washington, DC: American Association for the Advancement of Science, 1975. Published by AAAS and R. R. Bowker. Chapters 12, 15.

Identifies currently available 16mm films for viewers from primary grades through adult.

Abridged Readers' Guide to Periodical Literature. Monthly (September-May). Annual cumulations. Bronx, NY: H. W. Wilson. Chapter 10.

Indexes periodicals found in upper elementary and middle school collections.

Adventuring with Books: A Booklist for Preschool—Grade 6. Mary Lou White, editorial chair. Urbana, IL: National Council of Teachers of English, 1981. Chapter 13.

Provides annotations for 2,500 titles published between 1977 and 1980.

The ALAN Review. Assembly on Literature for Adolescents, National Council of Teachers of English. Order from Mary Sucher, ALAN Membership Chair, Dundalk Senior High, 1901 Delvale Avenue, Baltimore, MD 21222. Subscribers do not need to belong to NCTE. Chapter 12.

Reviews new hardback and paperback titles for adolescents and occasionally has in-depth reviews of professional books.

Appraisal: Children's Science Books. Children's Science Book Review Committee, Longfellow Hall, 13 Appian Way, Cambridge, MA 02138. Three times a year. Chapters 8, 12.

Reviews by children's librarians and science specialists for each of the 50 to 70 titles per issue.

Arithmetic Teacher. National Council of Teachers of Mathematics, 1906 Association Drive, Reston, VA 22091. Monthly (September-April). Chapter 12.

The column "Reviewing and Viewing" covers films and filmstrips.

Audio-Visual Equipment Directory, 1980-81. National Audio-Visual Association, Dept. 80EQ, 3150 Spring Street, Fairfax, VA 22031. Every two years. Available in hardback or microfiche. Chapters 9, 15.

Photographs and text describe the type of products available.

AVMP 1981. Audiovisual Market Place 1981: A Multimedia Guide. New York, NY: R. R. Bowker, 1981. Chapter 15.

Addresses and personnel for producers, distributors, production services, manufacturers, and equipment dealers.

Babies Need Books. By Dorothy Butler. New York, NY: Atheneum, 1980. Chapter 13.

Presents the "why" and "how" of using specific titles with children from infancy to six years of age.

Best Books for Children, Preschool through the Middle Grades. By John T. Gillespie and Christine B. Gilbert. 2nd ed. New York, NY: R. R. Bowker, 1981. Chapter 13.

Brief annotations for more than 13,000 fiction and nonfiction titles recommended by at least three review sources.

The Best in Children's Books: The University of Chicago Guide to Children's Literature. Zena Sutherland, editor. Chicago, IL: University of Chicago Press, 1980. Chapter 13.

Several indexes enhance the usefulness of this tool to identify recommended titles on development values for specific curricular subjects, types of literature, and specific grades or reading levels.

Bilingual Journal. National Assessment and Dissemination Center. Quarterly. NACD, 49 Washington Avenue, Cambridge, MA 02140. Chapter 12.

Includes articles and news announcements of interest to adults working with bilingual students.

The Black Experience in Children's Audio-Visual Materials. Diane DeVeaux, Marilyn Berg Iarusso, and Viola Jones Clark, compilers. New York, NY: New York Public Library, 1973. Chapter 13.

Supplement to *The Black Experience in Children's Books.* Barbara Rollock, selector. New York: New York Public Library, 1977. Chapter 13.

Black World in Literature for Children. By Joyce White Mills. Atlanta, GA: Atlanta University School of Library Science, 1974. Chapter 13.

Subtitle: A Bibliography of Print and Non-Print Materials.

Bookbird. Subscription through Hermann Schaffstein Verlag, Deutsche Bank AG, D-4600 Dortmund 1, Federal Republic of Germany. Quarterly. Chapter 13.

Published by the International Board on Books for Young People, this magazine features articles about books of international interest and reviews selection tools.

The Bookfinder: A Guide to Children's Literature about the Needs and Problems of Youth Aged 2-15. By Sharon Spredemann Dreyer. Vols. 1-2. Circle Pines, MN: American Guidance Service, 1977, 1981. Chapter 13.

Provides a synopsis and evaluation of titles on topics relating to the child's psychological and behavioral development.

Booklist. American Library Association, 50 East Huron Street, Chicago, IL 60611. Twice a month (1st and 15th); September to July, once in August. Chapters 8, 10, 11, 13.

Reviews current books, 16mm films, filmstrips, videocassettes, U.S. Government publications, and reference works.

Books and the Teenage Reader: A Guide for Teachers, Librarians, and Parents. By G. Robert Carlsen. 2nd rev. ed. New York, NY: Harper and Row, 1980. Chapter 14.
Includes annotated lists of recommended books.

Books in Other Languages: A Guide to Selection Aids and Suppliers, 1979. By Leonard Wertheimer. 4th ed. New York, NY: K. G. Saur Publishing, Inc., 1979. Chapters 13, 15.
Lists selection tools for non-English titles and identifies suppliers in Canada, United States, Africa, and Europe.

Books on American Indians and Eskimos. Mary Jo Lass-Woodfin, editor. Chicago, IL: American Library Association, 1977. Chapters 6, 13.
Subtitle: A Selection Guide for Children and Young Adults. Includes Poor, adequate, or good ratings.

Books to Help Children Cope with Separation and Loss. By Joanne E. Bernstein. New York, NY: R. R. Bowker, 1977. Chapter 13.

Building Ethnic Collections: An Annotated Guide for School Media Centers and Public Libraries. By Lois Buttlar and Lubomyr R. Wynar. Littleton, CO: Libraries Unlimited, 1977. Chapter 13.
Annotated 2,300 titles dealing with over 40 distinct groups.

Bulletin of Proyecto Leer. Books for the People, Inc., 1736 Columbia Road, NW, Suite 107, Washington, DC 20009. Chapter 13.
Annotates recommended titles.

Bulletin of the Center for Children's Books. University of Chicago Press, 5801 Ellis Avenue, Chicago, IL 60637. Monthly, except August. Chapters 8.
Clearly identifies which titles are marginal or not recommended.

Canadian Books for Young People/Livres Canadiens pour la Jeunesse. Irma McDonough, editor. Toronto: University of Toronto Press, 1980. Chapters 8, 17, 18.
Briefly annotates Canadian books and magazines in English and French for preschool through ninth-grade level.

Canadian Children's Literature. Canadian Children's Literature Association, Box 335, Guelph, Ontario N1H 6K5. Quarterly. Chapter 8.
Subtitle: A Journal of Criticism and Review.

Canadian Materials. Canadian Library Association, 151 Sparks Street, Ottawa, Ontario K1P 5E3. Quarterly. Chapter 8.
Subtitle: An Annotated Critical Bibliography for Canadian Schools and Libraries. Includes reviews of books and films.

A Child Goes Forth. By Barbara Taylor. Provo, UT: Brigham Young University, 1975. Chapter 13.
Describes criteria for selecting materials for young children.

Children and Books. By Zena Sutherland, Dianne L. Monson, and May Hill Arbuthnot. 6th ed. Glenview, IL: Scott, Foresman, 1981. Chapter 12.
A standard work on children's literature, including sources of information for teachers and media specialists.

Children's Book Review Service. Children's Book Review Service, Inc., 220 Berkeley Place #1D, Brooklyn, NY 11217. Monthly with two special supplements in fall and spring. Chapter 8.
Published in a looseleaf format, this journal reviews approximately 50 juvenile titles per issue.

Children's Books in Print, 1981-82. 13th ed. New York, NY: R. R. Bowker, 1981. Revised annually in December. Companion work: *Subject Guide to Children's Books in Print, 1980-81.* 11th ed. New York, NY: R. R. Bowker, 1980. Revised annually. Chapters 8, 10, 15.

    Lists juvenile titles available in hardback and paperback.

Children's Catalog. Richard H. Issacson and Gary L. Bogrant, editors. 14th ed. New York, NY: H. W. Wilson, 1981. Four annual supplements, 1982-1985. Standard Catalog Series. Chapters 8, 17, 18.

    Recommends juvenile titles. Includes author, title, subject, and analytical indexes.

Children's Literature: An Issues Approach. By Masha Kabakow Rudman. Lexington, MA: D. C. Heath, 1976. Chapter 13.

    Meant as a critical guide to children's literature. Includes professional sources on issues. Annotates and discusses books on siblings, divorce, death, aging, war, sex, blacks, and Native Americans.

Children's Literature in the Elementary School. By Charlotte S. Huck. 3rd ed. updated. New York, NY: Holt, Rinehart, and Winston, 1979. Chapter 12.

    Another standard work useful for teachers and media specialists.

Children's Magazine Guide. 2223 Chamberlain Avenue, Madison, WI 53705. Monthly (semiannual cumulations in February and August). Chapters 10, 13.

    Indexes magazines commonly found in juvenile collections.

Children's Mathematics Books: A Critical Bibliography. By Margaret Matthias and Diane Thiessen. Chicago, IL: American Library Association, 1979. Chapter 12.

    Annotations for works that are evaluated as not recommended, acceptable, recommended, or highly recommended.

Children's Media Market Place. Carol Emmens, editor. 2nd ed. Syracuse, NY: Gaylord Professional Publishers in association with Neal-Schuman Publishers, Inc., 1981. Chapters 8, 10, 15.

    Directory of publishers, producers, and distributors for juvenile books, audiovisual materials, television programs, etc.

The Chinese in Children's Books. New York, NY: New York Public Library, 1973. Chapter 13.

    Includes books in English and Chinese with settings in both the United States and China.

"Classical Music for Children and Young Adults: A Discography." *School Library Journal* 20 (1974): 3016-3023. Chapter 12.

    Recommends specific titles and explains the general criteria used.

Compute. Institute of Electrical and Electronics Engineers, Inc., Computer Society, 5855 Naples Plaza, Suite 301, Long Beach, CA 90803. Monthly. Chapter 11.

    Review column entitled "New Products."

Consumer Reports. Consumers Union of U.S., Inc., 256 Washington Street, Mt. Vernon, NY 10550. Monthly. Chapter 9.

    Evaluates products and includes reviews of sound recordings and movies.

Core Media Collection for Elementary Schools. By Lucy Gregor Brown, assisted by Betty McDavid. 2nd ed. New York, NY: R. R. Bowker, 1978. Chapters 4, 8, 18.

Creative Computing. 51 Dumont Place, Box 789-M, Morristown, NJ 07960. Bimonthly. Chapter 11.

    Subtitle: Magazine of computer applications and software.

Curriculum Review. Curriculum Advisory Service, 500 South Clinton Street, Chicago, IL 60607. Five issues a year. Chapters 8, 11.
  Reviews text materials, supplementary instructional materials, and multimedia kits.

EFLA Evaluations. Educational Film Library Association, Inc., 43 West Sixty-first Street, New York, NY 10023. Five times a year (bimonthly except July/August). Chapter 10.
  Uses looseleaf format and reviews approximately 500 films a year.

Educational Film Locator. Consortium of University Film Centers and R. R. Bowker Company, compilers and editors. 2nd ed. New York, NY: R. R. Bowker, 1980. Chapter 10.
  Lists the availability of films from lending libraries.

Educational Media Yearbook 1982. James W. Brown, editor. Littleton, CO: Libraries Unlimited, 1982. Chapter 15.
  Reports on audiovisual media sales, educational programs, associations, and recent developments.

Educator's Guide to ... series. Educational Progress Corp., Division of Educational Development Corporation.
  Lists availability of free and inexpensive materials by format or by subject noted in title.

  Educators Grade Guide to Free Teaching Aids. Chapter 15.
  Educators Guide to Free Audio and Video Materials. Chapters 11, 15.
  Educators Guide to Free Films. Chapters 10, 15.
  Educators Guide to Free Filmstrips. Chapters 10, 15.
  Educators Guide to Free Guidance Material. Chapters 12, 15.
  Educators Guide to Free Health, Physical Education, and Recreation Materials. Chapters 12, 15.
  Educators Guide to Free Science Materials. Chapters 12, 15.
  Educators Guide to Free Social Studies Materials. Chapters 8, 12, 15.
  Educators Index to Free Materials. Chapter 15.

Elementary School Library Collection. Lois Winkel, editor. 12th ed. Newark, NJ: Bro-Dart, 1979. Chapters 4, 8, 10, 13, 14, 18.
  Subtitle: A Guide to Books and Other Media, Phases 1, 2, 3. Uses phase designation to indicate priorities to consider in purchasing the recommended materials.

Eliminating Ethnic Bias in Instructional Materials: Comment and Bibliography. By Maxine Dunfee. Washington, DC: Association for Supervision and Curriculum Development, 1974. Chapter 11.

El-Hi Textbooks in Print 1982. New York, NY: R. R. Bowker, 1982. Published annually in the spring. Chapter 11.

EPIE Report. EPIE Institute, Box 620, Stony Brook, NY 11790. Bimonthly. Chapters 9, 10.
  Official publication of EPIE (Educational Products Information Exchange) Institute. Each issue is a consumer's report on a particular type of product.

Ethnic Film and Filmstrip Guide for Libraries and Media Centers: A Selective Filmography. By Lubomyr R. Wynar and Lois Buttlar. Littleton, CO: Libraries Unlimited, 1981. Chapter 13.
  Annotates over 1,400 film items related to 46 American ethnic groups.

Exceptional Children. The Council for Exceptional Children, 1920 Association Drive, Reston, VA 20091. Eight times a year. Chapter 14.

The Exceptional Parent. Box 101, BackBay Annex, Boston, MA 02117. Six times a year. Chapter 14.
Focuses on care of disabled children.

Film Library Quarterly. Film Library Information Council, Box 348, Radio City Station, New York, NY 10019. Quarterly. Chapter 10.
Includes book reviews, film reviews, and video reviews. Regular column, "Projections," reports current happenings.

Films Too Good for Words. By Salvatore J. Parlato. New York, NY: R. R. Bowker, 1972. Chapter 14.
Subtitle: A Directory of nonverbal 16mm films.

"The Filmstrip Industry — A Guide to the Production, Distribution, and Selection of Educational Filmstrips." By Angie Le Clercq. *Library Technology Reports* 12 (1976): 257-269. Chapter 10.

Fine Art Reproductions of Old and Modern Masters. Greenwich, CT: New York Graphic Society, Ltd., 1978. Chapter 10.
Illustrated catalog of photography reproductions, graphics, and museum replicas.

Folklore: An Annotated Bibliography and Index to Single Editions. By Elsie B. Ziegler. Westwood, MA: F. W. Faxon, 1973. Chapter 13.
Indexes by subject, motif, country, type of folklore, and illustrator.

For Younger Readers: Braille and Talking Books. National Library Service for the Blind and Physically Handicapped. Washington, DC: Library of Congress, Chapter 14.
Annotates braille, disc, and cassette books announced in *Braille Book Review* and *Talking Book Topics.*

Free and Inexpensive Learning Materials. Nashville, TN: George Peabody College for Teachers, 1981. Distributed by Incentive Publications, Inc. Biennial. Chapters 8, 10, 15.
Provides information for more than 3,000 instructional aids.

Gateways to Readable Books. By Dorothy E. Withrow, Helen B. Carey, and Bertha M. Hirzel. 5th ed. New York, NY: H. W. Wilson, 1975. Chapter 14.
An annotated, graded list of books in many fields for adolescents who are reluctant to read or who find reading difficult.

"Globes: A Librarian's Guide to Selection and Purchase." By James Coombs. *Wilson Library Bulletin* 55 (1981): 503-508. Chapter 11.
Describes types of globes and offers criteria for selection.

Good Reading for Poor Readers. By George D. Spache. 10th ed. Champaign, IL: Garrard, 1978. Chapter 14.
Annotates trade books, textbooks, workbooks, games, magazines, newspapers, and series books.

Guide to Microcomputers. By Franz J. Frederick. Washington, DC: Association for Educational Communications and Technology, 1980. Chapter 11.
Covers uses and criteria for microcomputers.

Guide to Microforms in Print: Author-Title 1980. Weston, CT: Microform Review. Annual. Chapters 10, 15. Companion work: *Guide to Microforms in Print: Subject 1980.* Chapters 10, 15.

Guide to Reference Books for School Media Centers. By Christine Gehrt Wynar. 2nd ed. Littleton, CO: Libraries Unlimited, 1981. Chapter 13.

Annotates titles recommended for kindergarten through 12th-grade users.

"Guidelines for Evaluation of Published Metric Materials." By Cecil Trueblood and Michael Szabo. *Arithmetic Teacher* 25 (1978): 46-50. Chapter 12.

Proposes a ranking system for assessing instructional and library materials dealing with the metric system.

Guidelines for the Representation of Exceptional Persons in Educational Material. Published by the National Center on Educational Media and Materials for the Handicapped, 1977. Available from Council on Exceptional Children. Chapter 14.

Offers guidelines for selection of materials.

High Interest-Easy Reading for Junior and Senior High School Students. Marian E. White, editor. 3rd ed. Urbana, IL: National Council of Teachers of English, 1979. Chapter 14.

Presents mini book talks aimed at the students.

"High Interest — Low Vocabulary Reading Materials 1978 Supplement." *Journal of Education* 160 (1978): 1-71. Chapter 14.

Annotates for the teacher, noting vocabulary and interest level.

The High/Low Report. Riverhouse Publications, 20 Waterside Plaza, New York, NY 10010. Monthly, 10 times a year (excluding July and August). Chapter 14.

Subtitle: For Professionals Concerned with Literature for the Teenage Reluctant Reader.

Horn Book Magazine: About Books for Children and Young Adults. The Horn Book, Inc., Park Square Building, 31 Saint James Avenue, Boston, MA 02116. Six times a year. Chapter 8.

Reviews approximately 50 titles per issue and has timely articles. The Horn Book, Inc., also publishes "Why Children's Books? A Newsletter for Parents."

How to Get Help for Kids. Barbara Zang, editor. Syracuse, NY: Gaylord Professional Publications, 1980. Chapter 14.

Subtitle: A Reference Guide to Services for Handicapped Children.

"Identifying High Interest/Low Reading Level Books." By Barbara S. Bates. *School Library Journal* 24 (1977): 19-21. Also available in *Young Adult Literature: Background and Criticism.* Millicent Lenz and Ramona M. Mahood, compilers. Chicago, IL: American Library Association, 1980. Chapter 14.

In Review: Canadian Books for Children. Ministry of Culture and Recreation, Provincial Library Service, Parliament Buildings, Toronto, Ontario M7A 2R9, Canada. Bimonthly. Chapter 8.

Index to Children's Songs. Carolyn Sue Peterson and Ann D. Fenton, compilers. Bronx, NY: H. W. Wilson, 1979. Chapter 13.

Indexes more than 5,000 songs in 298 children's song books published between 1909 and 1977.

Index to Collective Biographies for Young Readers. Judith Silverman, compiler. 3rd ed. New York, NY: R. R. Bowker, 1979. Chapter 13.

Subtitle: Elementary and Junior High School Level.

Index to Fairy Tales, 1949-1972, Including Folklore, Legends, and Myths in Collections. By Norma Olin Ireland. Westwood, MA: F. W. Faxon, 1973. Chapter 13.

Index to Poetry for Children and Young People, 1964-1969, Supplement: 1970-1975. John E. Brewton et al., editors. Bronx, NY: H. W. Wilson, 1972, 1978. Chapter 13.

Subtitle: A Title, Subject, Author, and First Line Index to Poetry in Collections for Children and Young People.

Instructor and Teacher. Monthly (except June and July). Instructor Publications, Inc., 7 Bank Street, Dansville, NY 14437. Chapter 14.

"New for Your Classroom" column reviews books and other materials for children.

Interracial Books for Children Bulletin. Council on Interracial Books for Children, Inc., Racism and Sexism Resource Center for Educators, 1841 Broadway, New York, NY 10023. Eight times a year. Chapter 8.

Includes reviews and articles about racism, sexism, and ageism in materials for children.

Junior High School Library Catalog. 4th ed. Standard Catalog Series. Bronx, NY: H. W. Wilson, 1980. Four annual supplements 1981-1984. Chapters 8, 17, 18.

Companion work to *Children's Catalog.*

Kirkus Reviews. Kirkus Service, Inc., 200 Park Avenue, South, New York, NY 10003. Twice a month. Chapter 8.

Reviews approximately 1,200 juvenile titles per year.

Kliatt Paperback Book Guide. 425 Watertown Street, Newton, MA 92158. Three issues a year with five interim supplements. Chapter 13.

Reviews paperbacks for the 12 through 19 year old.

Landers Film Reviews. Landers Associates, Box 69760, Los Angeles, CA 90069. Five times a year. Chapter 10.

Large Type Books in Print, 1980. New York, NY: R. R. Bowker, 1980. Chapters 14, 15.

Lists books for all ages.

Let's Read Together. 4th ed. Chicago, IL: American Library Association, 1981. Chapter 14.

Subtitle: Books for Family Enjoyment.

Libraries and Young Adults: Media, Services, and Librarianship. By JoAnn V. Rogers. Littleton, CO: Libraries Unlimited, 1979. Chapter 14.

Collection of informative essays.

Library Technology Reports. American Library Association, 50 East Huron Street, Chicago, IL 60611. Bimonthly. Chapters 9, 10.

Each issue concentrates on one particular type of equipment and supplies.

Libros en Español. New York, NY: New York Public Library, 1977. Chapter 13.

Subtitle: An Annotated List of Children's Books in Spanish.

Literary Market Place with Names and Numbers. New York, NY: R. R. Bowker, 1981. Chapter 15.

Directory of companies, people, and associations in the book world.

Literature by and about the American Indian: An Annotated Bibliography. By Anna Lee Stensland. 2nd ed. Urbana, IL: National Council of Teachers of English, 1979. Chapters 6, 13.

Includes comments by American Indian critics. Covers more than 775 books published since 1973.

Literature for Today's Young Adults. By Kenneth L. Donelson and Alleen Pace Nilsen. Glenview, IL: Scott, Foresman, and Company, 1980. Chapter 12.

Manual on Film Evaluation. By Emily S. Jones. Rev. ed. New York, NY: Educational Film Library Association, 1974. Chapter 10.

Media and Methods: Exploration in Education. North American Publishing Co., 401 North Broad Street, Philadelphia, PA 19108. Nine times a year. Chapters 8, 11.
   Articles and reviews on timely topics.

Media Equipment: A Guide and Dictionary. By Kenyon C. Rosenberg and John S. Doskey. Littleton, CO: Libraries Unlimited, 1976. Chapter 9.
   Provides basic information.

Media Review Digest. Pierian Press, 500 Washtenaw Avenue, Ann Arbor, MI 48104. Quarterly with annual cumulation. Chapter 8.
   Subtitle: The Only Complete Guide to Reviews of Non-Book Media. Successor to *Multimedia Review Index.*

"Microcomputers in Education." *Educational Technology* 19 (1979): 7-67. Chapter 11.
   Entire issue on microcomputers.

Microform Review. Microform Review, Inc., Box 405, Saugatuck Station, Westport, CT 06880. Quarterly. Chapter 10.
   Includes articles and reviews of microform titles.

"A Minimal Professional Reference Library on the Language Arts for Elementary School Teachers." *Language Arts* 58 (1981): 225-248.
   Annotations for journals and resources on all aspects of language arts.

More Films Kids Like. Maureen Gaffney, editor. Chicago, IL: American Library Association, 1977. Chapter 10.
   Describes 16mm films based on reactions of children under 13 years old. Includes titles from its predecessor, *Films Kids Like.*

A Multimedia Approach to Children's Literature. Ellin Greene and Madalynne Schoenfeld, compilers. 2nd ed. Chicago, IL: American Library Association, 1977. Chapter 14.
   Subtitle: A selective list of films, filmstrips, and recordings based on children's books.

NICEM Indexes. National Information Center for Educational Media. University of Southern California, University Park, Los Angeles, CA 90007.
   Lists available titles for formats and subjects mentioned in the name of the index.
   Index to Educational Audio Tapes. 5th ed. Chapters 11, 15.
   Index to Educational Overhead Transparencies. 6th ed. Chapters 10, 15.
   Index to Educational Records. 5th ed. Chapters 11, 15.
   Index to Educational Slides. 4th ed. Chapters 10, 15.
   Index to Educational Video Tapes. 5th ed. Chapters 8, 10, 15.
   Index to 8mm Motion Cartridges. 6th ed. Chapters 10, 15.
   Index to Producers and Distributors. 5th ed. Chapter 15.
   Index to 16mm Educational Films. 7th ed. Chapters 10, 15.
   Index to 35mm Filmstrips. 7th ed. Chapters 10, 15.
   NICSEM Special Education Thesaurus. Chapters 14, 15.
   Special Education Index to Assessment Devices. Chapters 14, 15.

Special Education Index to In-Service Training Materials. Chapters 14, 15.

Special Education Index to Learner Materials. Chapter 15.

Special Education Index to Parent Materials. Chapters 14, 15.

NCCT Forum: Quarterly Journal of the National Council for Children and Television. 20 Nassau Street, Suite 215, Princeton, NJ 08540. Chapter 10.

Subtitle: A forum for information, research, and opinion published by the National Council for Children and Television.

Newsletter on Intellectual Freedom. Office for Intellectual Freedom, American Library Association, 50 East Huron Street, Chicago, IL 60611. Bimonthly. Chapter 4.

Provides information on current events, timely articles, and reviews.

Notes from a Different Drummer. By Barbara H. Baskin and Karen H. Harris. New York, NY: R. R. Bowker, 1977. Chapter 13.

Subtitle: A Guide to Juvenile Fiction Portraying the Handicapped.

Paperback Books for Young People. By John T. Gillespie. 2nd ed. Chicago, IL: American Library Association, 1977. Chapter 10.

Subtitle: An Annotated Guide to Publishers and Distributors.

Paperbound Books for Young People. 2nd ed. New York, NY: R. R. Bowker, 1980. Chapter 10.

Subtitle: From Preschool through Grade 12.

Periodicals for School Media Programs. By Selma K. Richardson. Chicago, IL: American Library Association, 1978. Chapter 10.

Provides evaluative annotations for approximately 500 titles for kindergarten through 12th-grade level.

Picture Books for Children. By Patricia Jean Cianciolo. 2nd ed., revised and enlarged. Chicago, IL: American Library Association, 1981. Chapter 12.

Discusses criteria and titles of this genre.

The Picture File: A Manual and a Curriculum-Related Subject Heading List. By Donna Hill. 2nd ed. Hamden, CT: Shoe String Press, 1978. Chapter 10.

Describes the creation of a picture file and uses of pictures.

"The Planning for a Print and Poster Collection in Children's Libraries." By ALSC Print and Poster Evaluation Committee. *Top of the News* 37 (1981): 283-87. Chapter 10.

Includes criteria for selection.

Popular Reading for Children. Chicago, IL: American Library Association, 1981. Chapter 13.

Subtitle: A Collection of the *Booklist* Columns.

Reading for Young People series. Chicago, IL: American Library Association. Chapter 12.

The Midwest. By Dorothy Hinman and Ruth Zimmerman, 1979.

The Northwest. By Mary Meacham, 1980.

The Middle Atlantic. By Arabelle Pennypacker, 1980.

The Southeast. By Dorothy Heald, 1980.

The Rocky Mountains. By Mildred Laughlin, 1980.

The Great Plains. By Mildred Laughlin, 1979.

Each work annotates titles of books about the respective region.

Reading Ladders for Human Relations. Eileen Tway, editor. 6th ed. Washington, DC: American Council on Education, 1981. Also available from the National Council of Teachers of English. Chapter 13.
   Annotates recommended titles for preschool through mature readers.

Reference Books for Children. By Carolyn Sue Peterson and Ann D. Fenton. Metuchen, NJ: Scarecrow Press, 1981. Chapter 13.
   Supersedes *Reference Books for Elementary and Junior High School Libraries.* Includes approximately 900 annotations on reference works and selection tools.

Reviewing Librarian. Ontario School Library Association, 2397 A Bloor Street, West, Toronto, Ontario M6S 1P6. Four times a year. Chapter 8.

School Library Journal. R. R. Bowker, Subscription Service Department, P.O. Box 67, Whitinsville, MA 01588. Monthly (September through May). Chapters 8, 10, 13.
   Provides timely articles; news of events; new products and reviews: books, 16mm films, videocassettes, filmstrips, slides, prints, multimedia kits, sound recordings. The "SLJ Checklist" column often announces specialized and inexpensive bibliographies.

Selected U.S. Government Publications. Superintendent of Documents, U.S. Government Printing Office, Washington, DC 20402. Monthly. Chapter 10.
   Ask to be placed on the mailing list for this announcement of pamphlets, charts, maps, and photographs from government agencies.

Selecting Materials for Children and Young Adults. Association for Library Service to Children and Young Adult Services Division. Chicago, IL: American Library Association, 1980. Chapter 13.
   Subtitle: A Bibliography of Bibliographies and Review Sources.

Selecting Materials for Children with Special Needs. Library Service to Children with Special Needs Committee, Association for Library Service to Children. Chicago, IL: American Library Association, 1980. Chapter 14.
   Offers general and useful advice.

"Selecting Materials for the Handicapped: A Guide to Sources." By Henry C. Dequin. *Top of the News* 35 (1978): 57-66. Chapter 14.
   Coverage includes data base.

Selecting Materials for Instruction: Media and the Curriculum. By Marda Woodbury. Littleton, CO: Libraries Unlimited, 1980. Chapter 12.
   Includes examples of evaluation forms. Companion works: *Selecting Materials for Instruction: Issues and Policies* and *Selecting Materials for Instruction: Subject Areas and Implementation.*

Serving Physically Disabled People. By Ruth A. Velleman. New York, NY: R. R. Bowker, 1979. Chapter 14.
   Subtitle: An Information Handbook for All Libraries.

Sightlines. Quarterly. Educational Film Library Association, Inc., 43 West Sixty-first Street, New York, NY 10023. Chapter 11.
   Provides reviews on books about films and television. "Recent film/video release" column provides an annotated listing.

"Sources of Information about the Handicapped." By Henry C. Dequin. *School Library Journal* 26 (1979): 38-41. Chapter 14.
   Complements his "Selecting Materials for the Handicapped: A Guide to Sources."

The Special Child in the Library. Barbara H. Baskin and Karen H. Harris, editors. Chicago, IL: American Library Association, 1976. Chapter 14.
  Includes essays on criteria for selecting and using materials.

"Standard Criteria for the Selection and Evaluation of Instructional Material." By the National Center on Educational Media and Materials for the Handicapped. *Illinois Libraries* 59 (1977): 531-540. Chapter 14.
  Includes the Center's evaluation forms for use by teachers.

Subject Guide to Children's Books in Print. Chapters 10, 15.
  Companion to *Children's Books in Print.*

Subject Index to Poetry for Children and Young People 1957-1975. Dorothy B. Frizzell Smith and Eva L. Andrews, compilers. Chicago, IL: American Library Association, 1977. Chapter 13.
  Indexes 263 anthologies using over 2,000 subjects.

Teachers' Guide to Television. 699 Madison Avenue, New York, NY 10021. Twice annually. Chapter 10.
  Announces forthcoming television programs and provides bibliographies on materials related to selected programs.

The Teacher's Library. Phyllis M. Hill, editor. Washington, DC: National Education Association, 1977. Chapter 14.

Toys to Go. Faith H. Hektoen and Jeanne B. Rinehart, editors. Chicago, IL: American Library Association, 1976. Chapter 11.
  Subtitle: A Guide to the Use of Realia in Public Libraries. Offers criteria and practical advice on how to handle these materials in a collection.

U.S. Government Publications for the School Media Center. By Alice J. Wittig. Littleton, CO: Libraries Unlimited, 1979. Chapter 10.
  How to use the "Monthly Catalog" and annotations for 348 items published by the U.S. Government.

The Vertical File and Its Satellites. By Shirley Miller. 2nd ed. Littleton, CO: Libraries Unlimited, 1979. Chapter 10.
  Subtitle: A Handbook of Acquisition Processing and Organization.

Video Source Book. Maxine Reed, editor. 2nd ed. Syosset, NY: National Video Clearinghouse, Inc., 1980. Distributed by Gale Research Company, Book Tower, Detroit, MI 48226.
  Lists over 30,000 available prerecorded video programs. Arranged by program title, the book has a main category index, a subject category index, and a wholesaler/distributor index.
  A companion work, *The Video Tape/Disc Guide: Children's Programs*, lists over 2,000 programs.

Voice of Youth Advocates. Six issues per year. Box 6569, University, AL 35486. Chapter 12.
  Includes feature articles and reviews of pamphlets, books, audiovisual materials, and professional books.

What Books and Records Should I Get for My Preschooler? By Norma Rogers. Newark, DE: International Reading Association, n.d. Chapter 13.
  Recommends specific titles for this age group.

"When the Blind Begin to Read." By Marya Hunsicker. *School Library Journal* 19 (1972): 79-80. Chapter 14.
    Subtitle: Selected Reading List for Legally Blind Children.

Yellow Pages of Learning Resources. Richard S. Wurman, editor. Cambridge, MA: MIT Press, 1972. Chapter 5.
    Directs the reader's attention to a wide range of community resources.

Your Reading: A Booklist for Junior High Students. Jerry Walker, editor. Urbana, IL: National Council of Teachers of English, 1975. Chapter 13.
    Briefly annotates over 1,600 titles. A new edition is forthcoming.

Young Adult Literature: Background and Criticism. Millicent Lenz and Ramona M. Mahood, compilers. Chicago, IL: American Library Association, 1980. Chapter 12.
    Collection of essays, including several about censorship.

INDEX

Entries (names, titles, subjects) are arranged letter by letter; acronyms are interfiled. Page references are to the main text and appendixes. Illustrations are indexed when they include titles of selection tools, e.g., *Booklist*, fig. 17 (p. 127). Numbers in italics indicate the page on which a term is defined. Subject headings are in bold type. Recommended readings for chapter 4 are entered under the subject modified by the phrase "recommended readings," e.g., **Comics** — Recommended readings, 68. Entries have been chosen to avoid duplication of information provided in the Table of Contents and the List of Illustrations.